JEAN JAURÈS

A STUDY OF PATRIOTISM IN THE
FRENCH SOCIALIST MOVEMENT

JEAN JAURÈS

A STUDY OF PATRIOTISM IN THE
FRENCH SOCIALIST MOVEMENT

BY HAROLD R. WEINSTEIN

OCTAGON BOOKS

A DIVISION OF FARRAR, STRAUS AND GIROUX

New York   1973

Reprinted 1973
by special arrangement with Columbia University Press

OCTAGON BOOKS
A DIVISION OF FARRAR, STRAUS & GIROUX, INC.
19 Union Square West
New York, N. Y. 10003

Library of Congress Cataloging in Publication Data

Weinstein, Harold Richard, 1906-
    Jean Jaurès; a study of patriotism in the French socialist move-
ment.
    Originally presented as the author's thesis, Columbia University.
    Bibliography: p.
    1. Jaurès, Jean Léon, 1859-1914.   2. Socialism in France.
DC342.8.J4   1973   335'.0092'4   [B]   73-3079
ISBN 0-374-98336-4

Printed in USA by
Thomson-Shore, Inc.
Dexter, Michigan

To

MY PARENTS

ACKNOWLEDGMENTS

THIS study of Jean Jaurès and his contemporaries in the French socialist movement before the World War owes much to those who read and criticized it in manuscript. The author is deeply in debt to Professor Carlton J. H. Hayes, of the Department of History of Columbia University, for his encouragement and stimulation. The manuscript gained in innumerable ways from the critical reading of Professor Geroid Tanquary Robinson, Professor Robert Livingston Schuyler, and Dr. Shepard B. Clough, of the same institution. Dr. Joseph Dorfman, of the Department of Economics of Columbia University, Mr. Solomon F. Bloom, of the Department of History of Brooklyn College, and Mr. William E. Tracy gave invaluable criticism and editorial guidance. Dr. Samuel Bernstein, of De Witt Clinton High School, New York, made helpful bibliographical suggestions and also criticized the manuscript. The subject of the study is highly controversial, and it is only fair to these critics to make explicit the author's assumption of full responsibility for the interpretations and conclusions.

HAROLD R. WEINSTEIN

COLUMBIA UNIVERSITY
August 3, 1936

CONTENTS

JEAN JAURÈS

A STUDY OF PATRIOTISM IN THE
FRENCH SOCIALIST MOVEMENT

I

INTRODUCTION: EARLY MARXISM AND REFORMISM IN FRANCE

BEFORE the World War the international socialist movement appeared to be a powerful force for peace. Socialists of every country were vociferous opponents of imperialistic adventures, military and naval competition, and bellicose diplomacy. On many occasions, the socialist parties of Europe joined hands across frontiers and warned aggressive governments that the world proletariat would tolerate no military conflicts.

And yet, when in 1914 the nations of Europe resorted to arms in the settlement of their rivalries, the Socialists abandoned their striving for peace, joined with the bourgeoisie of their respective countries, and marched against one another. A small handful of Socialists continued to protest, but the vast majority fell patriotically into line. This was true in France as in other countries. For years, the French Socialists had feared the disastrous consequences of a war with Germany and had tried to prevent the coming of the tragedy. But in 1914, few were the voices of the French Socialists who protested against their leaders' support of the government in the war.

This surrender of the French Socialists was no mere reversion to primitive tribalism. Nor was it a sudden upsurge of the hatred of Frenchmen for Germans. On the contrary, the patriotic support given to the French government by the Socialists was the result of a conscious decision—almost unanimously accepted by 1914—to defend France if she were the victim of aggression. By 1914, the watchword of the French Socialists had become: We will strive for peace, but we will defend republican France against an attack by imperial Germany. Indeed, the French Socialists had come to believe that upon the successful defense of the French Republic depended the future of socialism itself. The socialist ideal—the social ownership of the instruments of production and distribution—had by almost imperceptible steps become bound to national patriotism.

It was a national patriotism which we must distinguish carefully from extreme nationalistic passion. The terms "patriotism" and "nationalism" are not far from synonymous in ordinary American usage; but most French Socialists drew a clear distinction between them, a distinction to which we will adhere in this study. They considered "patriotism" as devotion to one's nation unaccompanied by invidious comparisons with other nations, while "nationalism" had aggressive implications similar to those of chauvinism.[1] While most Socialists were not loath to support a moderate patriotism in the sense defined above, few of them failed to oppose extreme nationalism. It was their antagonism to extreme nationalism which evoked from conservative Frenchmen the epithet "traitors" and obscured to the rest of the world the firm belief of the Socialists that patriotic devotion to the French Republic was essential for the attainment of their socialist ideal.

The association of patriotism with socialism was but one reflection of that general tendency to attenuate the doctrine of the class struggle which characterized the pre-War generation of European Socialists. If the Socialists had adhered to that doctrine they could not have been patriotic, for patriotism is irreconcilable with the view that socialism will result from the struggle of the international proletariat against the international bourgeoisie. National patriotism implies that a nationality, or a group of people having the same language, the same culture, and a consciousness of being distinct from other na-

[1] For a discussion of nationalism and the phenomena associated with it, see Carlton J. H. Hayes, *Essays on Nationalism* (New York, 1925). For a discussion of French nationalism, see his *Historical Development of Modern Nationalism* (New York, 1931), chs. ii-iv; *France, a Nation of Patriots* (New York, 1931), in *Social and Economic Studies of Post-War France*, edited by Carlton J. H. Hayes, Vol. V.

tionalities, is the important social unit. Patriotism also implies that all classes in a nationality have certain interests in common and that all classes must coöperate to defend or further these interests. Usually, these interests are the prosperity of the area inhabited by the nationality, the extension of the prestige of the nationality, and above all, the defense of the national state.

The socialist class struggle, on the other hand, implies that the class is the important social unit; that the proletarian class and the bourgeois class within the nationality are enemies; and that there can be no true coöperation between them to further what patriots consider the general interests of the nationality. It also follows that the two opposing classes are bound by common interest to the members of the corresponding classes in other nations; the French proletariat and the German proletariat are at one in their struggle against the combined French and German bourgeoisie. In short, whereas patriotism implies vertical unity of social classes within the nationality, socialist class struggle implies the horizontal unity of social classes across linguistic, cultural, or political barriers. As long as the French nation was viewed as consisting of two antithetical classes, it was impossible to accept both the nation and the class as the important social units. Little by little, the French Socialists gave up the concept of the class struggle; and the emphasis shifted from internationalism to national patriotism.

The attenuation of the class struggle and the acceptance of patriotism by the French Socialists resulted from their views on the method by which socialism could be attained. The class struggle is the root idea of socialism only when it is the point of departure for revolutionary strategy and tactics. In France, class struggle had been accepted by the first followers of the doctrines of Karl Marx. Looking forward to revolution and a dictatorship of the proletariat, the Marxists rejected every form of collaboration between bourgeoisie and proletariat; they were unwilling to defend the national bourgeois state or to further national economic interests; and they strove for close union between the proletarians of France and those of other countries. Hence, the early Marxists in France, as elsewhere, rejected national patriotism.[2]

In the period preceding the World War, however, Marxian socialism was opposed by reformist socialism. The Reformists paid lip-service to the idea that socialism would result from the international struggle of the proletariat against the bourgeoisie, but the class struggle was absent from their concrete political and social policies. The Reformists, accepting the French liberal tradition that the Republic has a high revolutionary value, believed that socialism could best be attained by the peaceful action of parliamentary procedure. This implied collaboration between the bourgeoisie and proletariat to obtain reforms. It also necessitated national unity to defend the Republic from attacks by monarchical neighbors, and to further the national prosperity upon which successful reforms depended. The appearance of patriotism in the doctrines of reformist socialism coincided with the disappearance of strict adherence to the concept of the class struggle.

In the conflict between Marxism and reformism, Jean Jaurès (1859-1914) was outstanding both as a symbol and as a force. He was for many years the foremost spokesman of the Reformists in their struggles against the revolutionary method and socialist anti-patriotism. Moreover, as the pre-eminent leader of French socialism and the acknowledged authority among French Socialists on foreign affairs, Jaurès contributed to the development of that patriotism which turned the French workers toward the German frontier in August, 1914.

Jaurès, however, did not enter the socialist movement officially until 1893. Already for more than a decade—ever since the rebirth of socialism in France after the defeat of the Com-

---

[2] One small group of revolutionary Socialists, the Blanquists, remained true to patriotism in spite of their revolutionary procedure. See below, pp. 77-78, 157, 162.

mune—the French Marxists and Reformists had been disput-
ing the question of national patriotism as it affected revolutionary procedure. When Jaurès became a Socialist, the process
by which patriotism and socialism eventually became linked
was well advanced.

The first period of conflict between the Marxists and the
Reformists owed much of its intensity to the events of 1870
and 1871. The insurrection of September 4, 1870, following
disastrous defeats in the war with Prussia, replaced Napoleon
III with a Provisional Government—the first step in the establishment of the democratic Republic. The people of Paris, however, continued to suffer from the effects of the lingering war.
These effects, together with the Parisians' suspicion of the
conservative National Assembly that replaced the Provisional
Government, and the desire of the Socialists to bring about a
new social order, contributed to the revolt of Paris on March
18, 1871, and the establishment of the Paris Commune.

Among the leaders of the Commune, the Socialists were in
a minority; but the latter's manifestoes and plans for the social
ownership of industry and commerce made the Commune appear to the Socialists as a significant milestone in history. Two
months after the establishment of the Commune it was crushed
by the army of the National Assembly. The Commune's defenders were severely punished by exile or death.

After the suppression of the Commune, there began a struggle between the republicans under the leadership of Gambetta,
and the monarchists. The struggle ended in the triumph of the
former; and by 1879 the democratic Third Republic seemed
firmly established.

The destruction of the Commune paralyzed the socialist
movement for years. And when the movement was finally re-
vived after 1879, the experiences and tragedy of the Commune continued to haunt it. The failure of the most recent
attempt to seize power discouraged some Socialists from try-

ing to employ revolutionary methods, while the consolidation of a Republic with democratic forms seemed to them an argument in favor of evolutionary development. The Marxists, on the other hand, regarded the Commune as the first glorious attempt to achieve socialism, and looked upon it as a model for future efforts. Moreover, they regarded the ruthless suppression of the Commune as everlasting evidence of the class character of the new parliamentary régime in France. They therefore thought the achievement of socialism possible only through a violent revolution.

The division between the Socialists holding these divergent opinions began with the return of the refugees to France around 1876.[3] The Marxists, expressing themselves through the newspaper *L'Égalité*, were grouped around Jules Guesde and Paul Lafargue. Guesde (1845-1922), who had been exiled for his political radicalism, returned to France as a "devoted and thoroughgoing advocate of out-and-out revolutionary socialism," and he became the most popular of the revolutionary leaders. Lafargue (1842-1911), a son-in-law of Karl Marx, was less a party organizer than a defender and elaborator of the economic determinism and class struggle doctrines of Marx.

The Reformists, gravitating to the newspaper *Prolétaire*, were led by Paul Brousse, Jean Allemane, and Benoît Malon. Brousse and Allemane were largely concerned with party organization and the practical achievement of reforms. The accepted theorist for the whole reformist group was its "spiritual father," Benoît Malon (1841-1895), a former shepherd and day laborer, and a member of the Paris Commune.[4] Working with Malon were three intellectuals: Gustave Rouanet, Eugène Fournière, and Georges Renard. All three were journalists, while Fournière and Renard held academic chairs as well. They were the principal contributors to *La Revue socialiste*,

[3] For a background of the rebirth of socialism—the history of socialism after the Commune—see Samuel Bernstein, *The Beginnings of Marxian Socialism in France* (New York, 1933), chs. ii-iv.
[4] See Eugène Fournière, *La Crise socialiste* (Paris, 1908), p. 42.

founded by Malon in 1885 and edited by him until his death, when the editorship passed to Renard.

For several years after 1876 the Marxists and Reformists were outwardly cordial to each other; and in 1879, at the Congress of Marseilles, the two groups attempted to form a united socialist party. This unity was short-lived. At the Congress of Saint-Étienne in 1882 a vital clash over the issue of immediate reforms divided the party.[5] The Marxists formed the *Parti ouvrier français* (P.O.F.), often known as the "Guesdists." The other group, generally known as the Possibilists, organized the *Fédération des travailleurs socialistes.*[6]

The English socialist leader, William Hyndman, remarked that the Marxists and Possibilists "could not meet in one hall without certainty of bloodshed, or at any rate, of severe contusions following."[7] The Marxists called the Possibilists "opportunists," while the latter retaliated with the terms "doctrinaires," "impossibilists," and "Marxist Capuchins."[8] Allemane and Malon resented Guesde's declaration that his doctrines were the only true socialism. Moreover, the Possibilists regarded Guesde and Lafargue as "Marxist proconsuls" who were abetting Marx's "domination" of international socialism; and their patriotism was offended by this "socialist ultramontanism."

The ideas of the Marxists were received with particular favor in the North and Center of France—in the regions of the great cotton works and metallurgical establishments.[9] The Marxist

[5] See Paul Louis, *Histoire du socialisme en France, de la Révolution à nos jours* (Paris, 1925), pp. 259-60; Jean Allemane, *Le Socialisme en France* (Paris, 1900), pp. 10-12.

[6] Allemane and Brousse parted in 1890 over the question of whether emphasis should be placed on reforms by the state or on reforms won by the trade unions. Malon split with both Allemane and Brousse for personal reasons, and became an "Independent." See Louis, *op. cit.,* p. 268.

[7] William Hyndman, *The Record of an Adventurous Life* (New York, 1911), p. 404.

[8] A. Humbert, *Les Possibilistes* (Paris, 1911), pp. 6-10.

[9] Alexandre Zévaès, *Le Socialisme en France depuis 1871* (Paris, 1908), pp. 62-63.

Parti ouvrier français derived its membership from such cities as Lille, Roubaix, Tourcoing, and Lyons, while the Marxist *Fédération du Nord* was the most powerful socialist group in France.[10] The Possibilists, on the other hand, derived their strength partly from Paris, and partly from the West and South, the regions which were "less brutally divided by the collision of classes, for they possessed a still well-developed industrial and agricultural middle class, more susceptible to Possibilist propaganda, which was less bitter, less vehement than that of the Guesdists."[11]

The many divisions and controversies of these two groups were colored by their fundamental divergence on the question of class struggle and revolution, as against political coöperation with other classes in the democratic state. The Marxists, basing their ideas on dialectical materialism, were opposed to the bourgeois democratic state.[12] Guesde, for example, declared that "the state is and always has been the government of a class, of a privileged class, whatever it might be."[13] He maintained that the Third Republic, as well as the former monarchies, was controlled by the capitalist bourgeoisie to further its "commercial, industrial, and financial speculations"; to protect its wealth; and to insure "the economic and political subordina-

[10] At the Congress of Paris in 1899, all the socialist organizations were represented by 1,452 mandates. Of these the *Parti ouvrier français* held 650, the Broussists 100, the Allemanists 200, the Independents 250, and the Blanquists 300. The mandates of the P.O.F. included almost all of the representatives of the socialist groups in the industrial departments of Allier (39), Aube (43), Isère (58), Marne (15), Rhône (34), Pas-de-Calais (45), and Nord (178).—*Congrès général des organisations socialistes françaises, Paris, 1899* (Paris, 1900), pp. 417-77.

[11] Zévaès, *op. cit.*, p. 63.

[12] Lafargue, particularly, expounded the economic determinism and class struggle doctrines of Marx. See Lafargue, *Le Déterminisme économique, la méthode historique de Karl Marx* (Paris, 1907); *Idéalisme et matérialisme dans la conception de l'histoire, conférence, 1894* (Lille, 1904), pp. 23-45; *Le Communisme et l'évolution économique* (Paris, 1892); *Right to Be Lazy and Other Studies* (trans. by C. H. Kerr; Chicago, 1907), pp. 139-54.

[13] Guesde, *Socialisme au jour le jour* (Paris, 1899), p. 471.

tion" of the proletariat.[14] As proof, Guesde pointed to the crushing of the Commune and to the suppression of strikes by the state.[15]

The institution of universal suffrage, Guesde held, did not alter the class nature of the state, and universal suffrage could not be used to improve the condition of the workers.[16] On one occasion, Guesde declared that because universal suffrage tended to obscure the class struggle to the detriment of the proletariat, it was positively harmful.[17] In spite of this statement, however, the Marxists usually conceded to universal suffrage the merit of bringing the antagonistic classes face to face during electoral periods, of "organizing the robbed against the robbers."[18] During the Boulanger Affair, this supposed advantage led the Marxists to speak a good word in favor of the republican *form* of government.[19] But Guesde warned that the use of the ballot was but a prelude to the use of the gun; and it was the use of the gun that would "definitely win the field."[20]

[14] For example, Guesde, *État, politique et morale de classe* (Paris, 1901), pp. 32-34, 92-93, 167-79, 406-9; *Çà et là* (Paris, 1914), p. 99.

[15] *Socialisme au jour le jour*, pp. 117-18; *Çà et là*, p. 49.

[16] Guesde, *Essai du catéchisme socialiste* (Brussels, 1878), pp. 80-85; *La Loi des salaries et ses conséquences* (Paris, 1881), p. 24; *Çà et là*, p. 107.

[17] Guesde held that before universal suffrage was established, society was divided into classes on the basis of "one class having rights, the other having but duties; and therefore union between the victims of the same political and economic exploitation was naturally established on the basis of these exclusions from all participation in the administration of public affairs." Now, however, the peasants and proletariat were divided into "different, rival groups, serving simply as spare change. In a word, they have fallen—if they permit me to make the comparison—to the rank of those mercenaries of the Middle Ages who fought each other, under colors which were not and could not be theirs—for the greater good of the common enemy."—*Çà et là*, p. 151.

[18] *État, politique et morale de classe*, p. 142. Writing together, Guesde and Lafargue explained that periods of electoral action were valuable, not to win deputies, but to propagandize socialism; and that socialist deputies in Parliament were useful for spreading socialist ideas throughout the country, for standing the bourgeoisie against "their own parliamentary wall."—Guesde and Lafargue, *Programme du Parti ouvrier* (Paris, 1883), p. 53.

[19] See below, p. 17n.

[20] *État, politique et morale de classe*, p. 338.

The Marxists did not agree with the Possibilists that substantial social betterment could be attained by gaining the coöperation of the liberal bourgeoisie. They doubted the possibility of winning over the bourgeoisie to humanitarian idealism. Lafargue maintained that philosophical and religious ideas were reflections of economic relations, and could not possibly be independent historical forces; and that the function of abstract ideas (justice, progress, liberty, civilization, humanity, *la patrie*) was to rationalize the supremacy of the bourgeoisie and "to chloroform" the workers.[21] The Socialists would achieve a social transformation, "not by appealing to the bourgeoisie, to its sentiments of justice and humanity, but by fighting it . . ."[22]

Thus the Marxists bitterly opposed the Radical Party, particularly the left wing under the leadership of Clemenceau, which espoused a certain measure of reform.[23] Guesde insisted that the left wing of the Radicals continually betrayed the workers in order to deliver them to the capitalists, and that there was no tangible difference between the followers of Clemenceau and the other republican groups, "for these party tents have always covered the same bourgeois merchandise."[24]

As early as 1878 Guesde began his long conflict with the Possibilists on the value of "public services." He and Lafargue argued, first, that "public services" such as schools, post offices, and mines, had always been used for the exclusive benefit of the bourgeoisie; secondly, that "public services" increased the power of the bourgeois state to repress the workers; thirdly,

[21] For example, Lafargue, *Le Communisme et l'évolution économique*, p. 3; *Le Déterminisme économique* . . . , pp. 7 ff.; *Social and Philosophical Studies* (trans. by C. H. Kerr, Chicago, 1906), pp. 73-75, 92-134; "Enquête sur l'anticléricalisme et le socialisme," *Le Mouvement socialiste*, 1903, IX, 457-61.

[22] *Right to Be Lazy and Other Studies*, pp. 151-56.

[23] To gain the support of the workers, the Radicals of Clemenceau's type favored such reforms as income and inheritance taxes and government ownership of banks, railways, mines. See Bernstein, *op. cit.*, pp. 78-79, 180.

[24] *État, politique et morale de classe*, pp. 29, 135-37, 224.

that they would prevent strikes—a necessary part of the class struggle.[25] As for reforms of amelioration, Guesde pointed to the iron law of wages and contended that if the government attempted to improve the workers' standard of living by such reforms as municipal housing—which was highly improbable —wages would fall.[26] For propaganda purposes, however, Guesde favored agitation for a minimum program of reforms.[27] The workers, he explained, by demanding reforms and not obtaining them, would realize that they must seize the state and expropriate the bourgeoisie.[28] Guesde also favored trade unions and defended strikes because they laid bare the class struggle and showed the workers that they must seize the state; but he cautioned against the belief that trade-union activities would bring any real amelioration to the workers.[29]

The workers, Guesde concluded, could better their condition or bring a social transformation only by resorting to revolution: the forcible seizure of the state by the proletariat in time of general economic collapse or war; the establishment of a temporary dictatorship of the proletariat to suppress the capitalist class; and the socialization of the instruments of produc-

---

[25] Guesde and Lafargue, *Programme du Parti ouvrier*, pp. 100, 119; Guesde, *Essai du catéchisme socialiste*, pp. 84-85; *Services publics et socialisme* (Paris, 1883), pp. 2-30; *Çà et là*, p. 18.

[26] *La Loi des salaires et ses conséquences*, pp. 24-28; *Çà et là*, p. 242; *Programme du Parti ouvrier*, p. 126.

[27] At the Congress of Marseilles, the minimum program—the object of which was "to lead them [the proletarians] much more rapidly to the young *Parti ouvrier*"—included the suppression of the public debt and the religious budget; prohibition of child labor; eight-hour day and six-day week; minimum wage law; scientific and professional education for all; government support of school children.—*Programme du Parti ouvrier*, pp. 1-3.

[28] *État, politique et morale de classe*, p. 97. Thus, during the unemployment crisis of 1884, Guesde agitated for national and municipal credits to supply immediate relief; but at the same time, he declared that the bourgeoisie, feeling safe under the protection of its army, would do nothing to help the proletariat, and so the latter must seize the state.—*Ibid.*, pp. 18, 27, 43-46, 55, 63, 97.

[29] *Ibid.*, pp. 336-38.

tion.[30] In 1886 Guesde believed that "the revolution is near."[31] The strong *Fédération du Nord* made him "itch for revolutionary action." And he remarked that "if the South were only organized as is the North, I should not wait any longer . . . no, no, I should not wait . . ."[32] The Possibilists refused to share Guesde's expectation of revolution or his desire for it. Malon feared revolution's "irreparable sacrifice of human life"; the tendency of revolutionaries to neglect present amelioration; and the danger that revolution would produce a period of misery, followed by "moments of discouragement and doubt so favorable to inexorable reaction."[33] In Malon's opinion, the social movement was "necessarily revolutionary" as long as the masses possessed no political power; but since the establishment of universal suffrage, social and political problems could be solved peacefully.[34] If the state were further democratized by a series of political reforms, it could be used as the instrument for attaining socialism.[35]

[30] See *Services publics et socialisme*, pp. 28-30; *État, politique et morale de classe*, pp. 57, 337, 428; *Çà et là*, p. 242; *Socialisme au jour le jour*, pp. 437; Guesde, *Collectivisme et révolution* (written 1879, Paris, 1906), pp. 20-23; *Programme du Parti ouvrier*, pp. 49-52, 112, 119-22. Guesde explained that the revolutionary dictatorship of the proletariat would be temporary, because after the socialization of property was completed the state would lose its coercive functions and would then disappear. See Guesde, *Quatres Ans de lutte de classe* (Paris, 1901), pp. 29-30; *Essai du catéchisme socialiste*, pp. 83-85.   [31] *État, politique et morale de classe*, p. 342.
[32] This is reported by Marcel Sembat in his *Defeated Victory* (trans. by Flory Henri-Turot; London, 1926), pp. 87-88.
[33] Malon, *Le Socialisme intégral* (Paris, 1891), I, 201, 402; II, xvi-xx; *Précis de socialisme* (Paris, 1892), p. 167. The declaration of principles drawn up at the Possibilist Congress of Paris in 1883, stated that "fertile revolutions must not be confused with useless insurrections and impotent uprisings, for the latter permit the power of the bourgeois class to decimate the proletariat." See Humbert, *op. cit.*, pp. 16-18.
[34] *Le Socialisme intégral*, I, 374, 402.
[35] Malon declared that the state was still entangled with "militarism and parasitism"; but he held that these evils could be eliminated by such reforms as the initiative and referendum; the franchise for women; transformation of the Senate into an economic chamber elected by professional representation of both workers and employers; the universalization of education; and the assurance of free speech, free press, and free assemblage.—*Ibid.*, I, 36, 376-95; II, xiv.

In fact, the Possibilist procedure takes its point of departure from the democratic state. That procedure was summarized in the resolution of the Possibilist Congress of Paris in 1885 in favor of "determined intervention of the state in the different branches of private work, shops, companies, banks—agricultural, commercial, industrial enterprises, *at first* to impose on the employers changes guaranteeing the interests of the workers and the collective interest; *then* to transform progressively all the bourgeois industries into socialist public services, in which conditions are regulated by the workers themselves."[36] Malon included in this program many ameliorative reforms, such as the eight-hour day and a heavy inheritance tax.[37]

Malon admitted that success was contingent upon the coöperation of the humanitarian bourgeoisie.[38] He argued, however, that the movement for socialism was larger than an exclusive class struggle, and that the socialist army consisted not of the industrial proletariat alone but "of all the sufferers, all the militants, all the hopeful."[39] He addressed himself "above all . . . to the bourgeoisie whose historical mission could be so beneficent, still so glorious."[40]

Malon and his collaborators on *La Revue socialiste* finally rejected Marxian economic determinism. They were "unwilling to shut up all of social life in the shell of economic processes"; they believed that many ideas have a subjective origin

[36] Humbert, *op. cit.,* p. 23.

[37] Among the other reforms demanded by Malon were laws regulating the hours and occupations of women and children; suppression of night work; public works for the unemployed; reform of the penal code and penitentiary system; social insurance of all types; and liberal agricultural credit.—*Le Socialisme intégral,* I, 305-6, 393-96; II, 113-4, 168, 203, 243-53, 303. Most of these reforms were incorporated into the programs of the Possibilists. See Maurice Charnay, *Les Allemanists* (Paris, 1911), pp. 105-12; Humbert, *op. cit.,* p. 23. Malon, it must be noted, regarded trade unions and coöperative societies as useful to prepare the workers for reforms. See *Le Socialisme intégral,* II, 22, 58-70.

[38] *Le Socialisme intégral,* I, 402.

[39] *Ibid.,* I, 28.

[40] *Précis de socialisme,* pp. ii, xi.

and may act independently of economic and political factors.[41] Malon warned the Marxists that great enterprises need "the all-powerful impulsion of altruistic sentiments," of the ideals of liberty, social justice, and *la patrie*.[42] Especially in dealing with the bourgeoisie, the Socialists must go beyond class interests and class hatreds.[43] Malon pointed to bourgeois state socialism and "professorial socialism"; to the acceptance of "public services" by "progressive political economy"; and to the fact that bourgeois parliaments were passing many social reforms.[44]

The difference between the two groups on class collaboration for defense of the national state was revealed sharply during the Boulanger crisis. Between 1887 and 1889 the popular General Boulanger, with the aid of the reactionaries, threatened to replace the Republic with a "popular" dictatorship.[45]

The Possibilists rushed to the aid of the Republic. They composed republican songs, issued anti-Boulangist manifestoes, and ran candidates against the supporters of Boulanger. In a

[41] *Le Socialisme intégral*, I, 202-3; Gustave Rouanet, "Le Matérialisme de Marx et le socialisme français," *La Revue socialiste*, 1887, V, 401-6, 587; Eugène Fournière, "Le Socialisme intégral," *La Revue socialiste, 1890*, XI, 260-68.

[42] Malon, *Le Socialisme intégral*, I, 40-41; Rouanet, "Le Matérialisme de Marx et le socialisme français," pp. 397, 530-31; Georges Renard, *Socialisme intégral et Marxisme* (Paris, 1896), pp. 6, 13-15, 21.

[43] See *Le Socialisme intégral*, I, 26-28, 40-45. See also Rouanet, "Le Matérialisme de Marx et le socialisme français," p. 397. Malon and his collaborators, considering idealism so important and believing Marxism too narrow, attempted to "enlarge" socialism to include all the ideas and activities that have been directed toward the goal of human happiness. This enlarging was called "integral socialism." See Malon, *Le Socialisme intégral*, I, 17-20, 23-37, 43-45; Renard, *op. cit.*, p. 7.

[44] *Le Socialisme intégral*, I, 205-8; II, 269. Malon was so certain of the success of class collaboration between bourgeoisie and proletariat that he recommended the establishment of a Minister of Labor in a bourgeois cabinet, one of whose functions would be to act as "arbitrator in the differences between the workers and capitalists, and thus prevent most of the conflicts between them."—*Ibid.*, II, 180-81. The other Possibilists also favored class collaboration. Charnay, describing the Broussists, says that they "made common cause with the Radical Party—even to the point of merging with it in the search for seats."—Charnay, *op. cit.*, p. 4.

[45] For a discussion of the Boulanger Affair, see below, p. 36.

special election for a deputy from Paris in 1889 the Possibilists supported the republican candidate, M. Jacques. In the general election of 1889 the Possibilists put up their own candidates on the first balloting, but "on the second balloting they observed the most rigorous discipline in behalf of the most popular republican candidate, whoever he was, however moderate his political shade."[46] On the other hand, the Possibilists set up opposing candidates against the socialist deputies who were too moderate in their opposition to Boulanger. Such leading Possibilists as Brousse, Allemane, and Chabert, occupied positions on the executive committee of the "Society of the Rights of Man and of the Citizen," along with Clemenceau, Ranc, Pelletan, and other Radicals.[47]

The Marxists, however, refused to collaborate with the bourgeoisie to save the Republic. A party manifesto during the general election warned the workers not to vote for either the republicans or the dictator, for either Ferry or Boulanger.[48]

[46] Humbert, op. cit., pp. 42-46.

[47] Ibid., p. 41. The object of the Society was given as follows: "Although belonging to different fractions of the great republican family, we believe that an alliance between all those who remain faithful to the Republic is necessary in order to put an end to the Boulangist adventure that is so humiliating for our country. The alliance must last as long as the peril." Quoted in Humbert, op. cit., p. 41. Malon also took an active part, insisting that La Revue socialiste would always fight against dictatorial movements, such as Boulangism, which were "perilous to the Republic and to the future of France." See Orry, op. cit., p. 16; Zévaès, op. cit., pp. 99-100.

[48] Aux travailleurs; Conseil national du P.O.F. (Paris, 1902), Manifesto of August, 1889, pp. 3-5. This manifesto, it must be noted, declared that the Republic is "the necessary form of proletarian emancipation. It must be preserved at all costs." As this idea seldom appeared in the works of the Marxists during this period, and as the manifesto itself denied the "at all costs" phrase by its rejection of collaboration with the republican bourgeoisie, one may conclude that the statement appeared for one or both of two reasons. First, the Marxists were presenting themselves as good defenders of the Republic in order to keep those workingmen who were both socialist and republican from giving their votes to bourgeois anti-Boulangists. Secondly, the Marxists were thinking of the value of universal suffrage in placing capital and labor face to face and in spreading socialist propaganda. S. Bernstein, discussing the attitude of the Marxists toward universal suffrage and the Republic in the late seventies, is inclined to think that the second reason was the chief factor in the Marxists' declaration of republicanism. See S. Bernstein, op. cit., pp. 118-22.

And Guesde stated: "The shoulder-strapper Boulanger and the employer Jacques both belong to the same enemy class which for a century has kept you, proletarian France, under a régime of hunger and lead. If you have played the rôle of dupes long enough, then in keeping your votes for yourselves, you will glue the exploiter and the killer to the same electoral wall—while you wait for the other [wall]."[49]

The theoretical controversy between Marxists and Possibilists extended to the issue of international labor solidarity. Guesde asserted that in the contemporary era of railways and telegraphs, "the exploitation and oppression of the workers knows no frontiers"; and because international working-class interests extend across national boundaries, the workers of all nations must unite to overthrow the exploiters of all nations.[50] Hence, Guesde and Lafargue regarded the Socialist International as a "Holy Alliance of the dispossessed" in opposition to the "Holy Alliance of proprietors," and as a union of the international proletariat for "the necessary revolution."[51] The French Marxists greeted a German socialist congress in these words: "Today we are with you in spirit, just as tomorrow— when you judge that the hour has come to answer force with force—we shall be with you in person."[52]

The Possibilists, of course, also favored international solidarity. But the important function of international action, as Malon viewed it, was to promote simultaneous pressure on national parliaments for a specific reform. This action was necessary, he explained, because if a single nation initiated a reform, that nation would suffer a competitive disadvantage.[53] The Possibilists regarded international congresses as discussion groups for the purpose of facilitating reforms by

---

[49] Guesde, *En garde!* (Paris, 1911), p. 106.
[50] *Çà et là*, pp. 156, 204-6; Guesde and Lafargue, *Programme du Parti ouvrier*, p. 56.
[51] *Çà et là*, pp. 205-6; *Programme du Parti ouvrier*, pp. 8, 77.
[52] Article in *L'Égalité*, quoted in S. Bernstein, *op. cit.*, p. 123.
[53] Malon, *Le Socialisme intégral*, II, 117, 437-38.

national parliaments, and they prevented the international congresses from setting up patterns of revolutionary action.[54] Malon explained that "different degrees of historical development and different economic constitutions must be expressed in divergences which are but different adaptations of the same principle."[55] In short, the Possibilists were giving socialism a national rather than an international orientation.

It was to be expected, therefore, that the two groups would espouse divergent views on the character and importance of the nation, of *la patrie*. The Marxists, of course, deplored the romantic apotheosis of the nation. Guesde had nothing but ridicule for Ernest Renan's "purely metaphysical" definition of a national entity.[56] To the romantic Renan, the nation was "a soul, a spirit, a spiritual family, that is the outcome of past memories, sacrifices, glories, often of common sorrows and regrets; and that is the outcome of a desire, in the present, of continuing to live together. A nation is not made by the speaking of the same language or the belonging to the same ethnic group; it is made by the doing of great things together in the past and the will to do still more in the future."[57] Guesde remarked simply that Renan's "nation" "never existed and exists less today than ever."[58] There are, he said, no common memories (except perhaps those of common violence); and the state, far from being a will to do "great things together" is only a "stock company" formed to compete with other states commercially.

Classes, Guesde held, are more important than nationality,

---

[54] In 1883 and 1886, the Possibilists took part in international congresses, but these were devoted chiefly to discussing reforms and the removal of laws restricting international union of workers' organizations.—Humbert, *op. cit.*, pp. 55-56. Humbert points out that the Possibilists took a leading part in turning the International against international antiparliamentarian, revolutionary tactics.—*Ibid.*, p. 62.

[55] Malon, *Le Socialisme intégral*, I, 306.

[56] Guesde, *État, politique et morale de classe*, pp. 396-400.

[57] Ernest Renan, *Discours et conférences* (Paris, 1887), p. iv.

[58] See *État, politique et morale de classe*, pp. 396-98.

for they "correspond to the growing antagonism of interests upon which present society rests."[59] The unity which Renan attributed to nations is "mathematically exact when attributed to classes." The working class is united by "common sufferings in the present, by common sorrows in the past"; and the workers, to free themselves, must make the same "common effort" which Renan regarded as characteristic of the nation. This common effort, Guesde added, is indeed the soul of every collective organism; but, as opposite interests create opposite wills, this common effort cannot possibly be shared by proletarian France and bourgeois France; "for they are so separated by the cadavers of June 1848 and of May 1871." This effort can be shared by the French proletariat and the German proletariat, who have been oppressed by their capitalist-controlled governments and are therefore united by a common need for emancipation.

The Marxists went so far as to pronounce the doom of the nation as a unit of organization in the society of the future. Lafargue stated that "property will be held in common by all the members of the great human family, without distinction of nationality, race, or color. The workers, bowed under the capitalist yoke, have recognized that [having been] brothers in misery, brothers in revolt, they must remain brothers in victory."[60] Guesde rejected nations still more explicitly. He held that the growth of human knowledge has been marked by a widening of horizons and by a decrease of group autonomy; humanity moved from family and tribal autonomy to communal autonomy; then the development of the railway and telegraph brought national autonomy.[61] But, by the same token, the autonomy of the nation itself is condemned; "and if the nationalists have the present—a present which escapes them more and more—the future, for which

[59] Ibid., pp. 398-400.
[60] Lafargue, Evolution of Property (London, 1894), p. 173.
[61] État, politique et morale de classe, pp. 424-26.

tate to point out that to subject French agriculture and industry to foreign competition, would prove a stimulus to revolution.[74]

Several theories and practices which aimed at preserving the
unity of the nation were opposed by the Marxists as obstruc-
tions to revolution. One of these was anti-Semitism. Such
nationalists as Edouard Drumont and Adolf Stöcker had
adapted anti-Semitism to national conservative purposes, holding that, as the Jews possessed an international religion and an
international economic power, they were a cause of cultural
disintegration and economic oppression. The Marxists, however, believed that anti-Semitism was a capitalist maneuver
to divide the workers and distract them from the class struggle by turning their attention to a struggle between Jews and
Christians.[75] Guesde declared that exploitation was not mo-
nopolized by the Jews; that the social cause of the workers'
misery was "not Moses and Co., but Christ and Co."; and
that banking, whether Jewish or Christian, contributed toward the centralization of industry that hastened the revolution.[76] Guesde approved the resolution of the International
Congress of Brussels in 1891, which declared that there must
be "no antagonism or combat of race or of nationality, but
only the class struggle of the proletarians of every race against
the capitalists of every race."[77]

Similar to the problem of anti-Semitism was that of anticlericalism. Some patriots—particularly those of a radical republican tendency—regarded the Catholic Church as a menace
to the nationality, and they desired to transfer education from
the hands of the clergy to those of the state. To be sure, the
Marxists inveighed against religion on the ground that it distracted the workers from revolutionary ends; and they held
that the Catholic clergy, through their services in schools and

[74] *Socialisme au jour le jour*, pp. 355-57.
[75] See *État, politique et morale de classe*, pp. 401-2.
[76] *Ibid.*, pp. 402-5, 446.   [77] *Ibid.*, pp. 400-401.

24   EARLY MARXISM AND REFORMISM

factories, acted as the "lackeys of the capitalist class."[78] But in Guesde's opinion, the purpose of anticlericalism was "to turn upon the Church the mounting tide of the workers' wrath,", and thereby to leave capitalist exploitation undisturbed.[79] Likewise, Guesde regarded the movement for the secularization of schools as an attempt on the part of the bourgeoisie "to put the capitalist faith in place of the Christian faith—in order to insure the greater security and the greater profit of our economic and political exploiters."[80] Through education by the state, the bourgeoisie could instill in the young workers a respect for the proprietor, the tax, and the law; and thus would be "completed the lessons of servitude."[81]

National tradition—even the liberal tradition of the French Revolution—was disowned by the Marxists. Guesde interpreted the Revolution as the struggle of the bourgeoisie to seize the privileges of the nobility and to insure "liberty of commerce," which Guesde considered equivalent to "liberty of theft."[82] The Revolution, he explained, freed capitalist landowners, merchants, and financiers, from the restraints to exploitation of labor imposed by the state and the guilds.[83] Lafargue believed that the Revolution had really harmed rather than helped the

[78] See *Socialisme au jour le jour*, p. 466; *Services publics et socialisme*, p. 19; Lafargue, *Social and Philosophical Studies*, pp. 44-45.

[79] *État, politique et morale de classe*, p. 401. The destruction of the ecclesiastical budget and the return of church property to the nation were included in the minimum program of the Marxists in 1879. This, however, seems to have been largely for propaganda purposes, and the Marxists subsequently repudiated this anticlerical part of their program. For example, Guesde later denounced the attempt of the Radicals in 1881 to separate Church and state, calling it a "bourgeois counterfeit" of the socialist idea. He explained that what the Socialists desired was "the de-Christianization of France" and "the abolition of religion, of all religions"; and he declared that the separation of Church and state could only be obtained through the complete triumph of socialism.—*État, politique et morale de classe*, pp. 295, 418-21.

[80] *Ibid.*, p. 277.   [81] *Ibid.*, p. 278.

[82] *Çà et là*, p. 163; *Socialisme au jour le jour*, p. 56.

[83] *État, politique et morale de classe*, pp. 427-28. See also *Programme du Parti ouvrier*, p. 79.

peasants, by depriving them of their common land and their right to pasture in the fields, and to gather wood in the forest.[84] Lafargue denounced the revolutionary slogans "liberty," "equality," "fraternity," and "justice," as catchwords used by the bourgeoisie to justify their class actions.[85] In his opinion the Declaration of the Rights of Man—"concocted by the metaphysical lawyers of the bourgeois revolution"—had only one function as far as the workingman was concerned: "to rivet him more closely and more firmly to his economic tasks."[86] Guesde added that the *Champs de Mars* witnessed the first massacre of the workingmen by the bourgeoisie.[87]

Pre-Marxian French socialist tradition likewise received scant attention from the Marxists. Lafargue regarded socialism in France up to and including 1848 as Utopian; that is, as based on idealism and collaboration of classes rather than on class struggle.[88] The Marxists considered the Commune a movement based on the scientific principles of Marxism; they treated it, however, not as an incident of French history, but as an event in the life of the international proletariat.[89]

[84] Lafargue, *Programme agricole du Parti ouvrier français* (Lille, 1894), pp. 23-31.

[85] *Evolution of Property*, p. 3.

[86] *Right to Be Lazy and Other Studies*, pp. 20, 157. Guesde remarked that the bourgeoisie, in proclaiming these ideals, were merely playing at *sans-cullotisme.—État, politique et morale de classe*, pp. 431-32.

[87] *État, politique et morale de classe*, pp. 429-30. Lafargue declared that in modern civilization horses are accorded more real and substantial rights than men, for they are better cared for and less overworked. He concluded that the Rights of Man are "about as useful as a cautery on a wooden leg"; and he called upon the workingmen to arise and, "since the buffoons of Parliament unfurl the Rights of Man, to demand boldly for yourselves, your wives, and your children, the Rights of the Horse."—*Right to Be Lazy and Other Studies*, pp. 160-61, 164.

[88] *Right to Be Lazy and Other Studies*, p. 140.

[89] Guesde described the international character of the Commune as follows: "On the one side of the Commune were all those who—whatever the nationality to which they belong, whatever political liberty they enjoy—are the dupes or the victims of the present order, and seek to overthrow it. On the other side were all those who benefit from this order and wish to conserve it. Here, the capitalist universe; there, the proletarian universe."—*Çà et là*, p. 63.

This repudiation by the Marxists of national patriotism, national defense, national interests, and national traditions, was contrary to the conceptions of the Possibilists. While the former preached revolution, the latter emphasized reforms. The desire of the Possibilists to attain socialism by democratic means led necessarily to the resolution to defend the Republic against attack. Muting the class struggle, they espoused the idea that various classes should work together for the interests of the nation as a whole.

The Possibilists approached patriotism through a glorification of French liberal tradition. Malon and the other Possibilists regularly praised the French humanitarian movement of the eighteenth century—the *philosophes* Rousseau, Diderot, D'Alembert, Helvetius, Abbé de St. Pierre, and others—as the real forerunners of modern socialism.[90] Malon had limitless admiration for the French Revolution and for the Declaration of the Rights of Man.[91] Although the Revolution was only half finished, he said, it opened the future to "the progress of the human spirit," and it laid the groundwork for socialism.[92] Malon was also fond of recalling the French Utopians and the Socialists of 1848.[93]

This French socialist tradition—"rich with so much glory, with so many ideas and so many works"[94]—was merged with the glory and the mission of France. Malon declared that the eighteenth century marked "the incomparable triumph and eternal glory of the French mentality, then predominant and triumphant"; and that the early nineteenth-century Socialists, with the exception of Owen, were of "French inspiration and teaching," an expression of the still supreme "French intellectual hearth."[95] Moreover, this tradition was a fulfillment of France's mission to serve humanity. It was the glory of the Socialists of 1848 that they had fought "for all of progressive

---

[90] Malon, *Le Socialisme intégral,* I, 39, 41, 45.
[91] *Ibid.,* I, 373-75.   [93] *Ibid.,* I, 158, 169; II, 175-204.
[92] *Ibid.,* I, 71, 123, 126.   [94] *Ibid.,* I, 162.   [95] *Ibid.,* I, 165, 167.

humanity."[96] The events of the Commune demonstrated that since 1851 France had "guarded the front, always crowned with the laurel wreath of revolutionary struggles, the shining star that guided the world."[97] In short, "militant France was always at its perilous post in the revolutionary vanguard of the world."[98] Hence, Malon hoped that "there may always rest in us the consciousness of the pacific and emancipating mission of France, and may this sentiment be fortified by another; that such a *patrie* must be loved not only with passion but also with foresight."[99]

In the view of Gustave Rouanet, Malon's collaborator, Marxism appeared "essentially anti-French," for it represented the reaction of the German historico-fatalistic school against eighteenth-century French philosophy; and this philosophy contained "all the eminently French qualities: flexibility, absence of local prejudices, clarity and precision, and above all, an enthusiasm and a passion which knows no obstacles—all the qualities that have made of France the glorious leader of the world."[100] Rouanet warned the Marxists that if they depreciated French socialist tradition, they would "distract France from the glorious redeeming mission which her revolutionary traditions have bequeathed to her."[101]

The Republic, heir and executor of such a glorious universal mission, must of course be preserved. Malon drew a distinction between "the menaced republics, which must arm themselves in order to defend themselves, and belligerent monarchies; between the free peoples on guard, and the villainous chancelleries that conspire, or the chauvinists that incite to war . . ."[102] He therefore proposed a militia system to increase France's security; government ownership of railways to facilitate military operations; and curbs on the speculation in

[96] *Ibid.*, II, 172.   [97] *Ibid.*, I, 187.   [98] *Ibid.*, I, 169.
[99] Malon, "La Guerre et la paix," *La Revue socialiste,* 1887, VI, 121.
[100] Rouanet, "Le Matérialisme de Marx et le socialisme français," *La Revue socialiste,* 1887, VI, 396-98, 579-89.
[101] *Ibid.*, p. 582.   [102] Malon, *Précis de socialisme, op. cit.,* p. 207.

grain in order to insure adequate food supplies during time
of war.[103] And he vowed that "on the day when the existence
of France is menaced, they [the French Socialists] will not
be the last to climb the slopes of the Vosges."[104]

Malon, to be sure, hated war.[105] He did not, however, believe that patriotism would inevitably bring war. He explained
that international conflicts were largely caused by the building
of heavy armaments and by the militarism and "nationalism"
which he considered synonymous with chauvinism.[106] In his
opinion, these abominations could be suppressed before capitalism itself was ended. To secure peace, he proposed the establishment of an international council of arbitration, the creation
of a federation of nations, and the abolition of standing
armies.[107] But Malon warned the proletariat that it must not
follow the example of the eighteenth-century internationalists,
who "pushed the hope [for a European federation] so far as
to distrust patriotism—often excessively, at least in France."[108]

Malon's conception of patriotism was not clearly defined,
and he was rather vague on the duties of the citizen toward
the nation. In the 1890's, however, much more attention was
given by the Socialists to patriotism. The change resulted, to
a considerable extent, from the influx into the socialist movement of an important group of men who were more conscious
of national patriotism and its problems. Of these newcomers to
socialism, Jean Jaurès became the most outstanding.

[103] Malon, *Le Socialisme intégral*, I, 394; II, 295, 422-23. For the attitude
of the other Possibilists toward national defense, see Jean Allemane, *Nôtre
programme* (Paris, 1902), pp. 35-36; Paul Brousse, "Le Désarmement,"
Le Mouvement socialiste, 1889, I, 580-81.
[104] Malon, "La Guerre et la paix," *op. cit.*, p. 121.
[105] See *Le Socialisme intégral*, I, 37, 63-65, 69.
[106] *Ibid.*, I, 69-70; *Précis de socialisme*, pp. 213-14; "La Guerre et la paix,"
p. 115.
[107] *Le Socialisme intégral*, I, 62, 394. For his "amphictyonic Grand Council of Federated Nations," Malon suggested such functions as international
arbitration; international labor legislation; unification of weights, measures,
and money; "scientific, progressive, and civilizing colonization"; and
"meteorological observation with the aim of ameliorating climatic conditions."—*Ibid.*, I, 398.   [108] *Précis de socialisme*, p. 210.

II

JAURÈS THE JACOBIN

JEAN-LOUIS-MARIE JAURÈS, who at the time of his dramatic assassination by a fanatical patriot in the tense days of July, 1914, was the pre-eminent leader of French socialism, joined the movement in 1893. He was one of a group of French intellectuals who were turning to a radical solution of the social question at the end of the nineteenth century. Jaurès and other prominent men in this group—which included Millerand, Briand, and Viviani—were Jacobins. They were devoted to the stock of ideas which, stemming out of the eighteenth century and the French Revolution, had dominated the thought of large sections of the middle class for a century. These ideas were loyalty to the democratic Republic; devotion to the nationality, the people who collectively composed the state; and a humanitarianism designed to raise the welfare of the nation as a whole. The socialism of this group was but an afterthought, a means for destroying the powerful traditions of the Old Régime—the monarchy, the aristocracy, and the state Church; and for retaining the support of the newly risen industrial proletariat and the peasants to the Republic.

Jaurès grew up in the great tradition of republican democracy of the French Revolution. To the present day the memory of the First French Republic is potent among a large part of the middle classes of France. The Jacobin tradition was a force in the overthrow of Charles X in 1830, of Louis Philippe in 1848, of Napoleon III in 1870; and it inspired the struggle from 1871 to 1879 to save the Third Republic from the onslaught of the monarchists.

After the crisis of May 16, 1877, the Republic entered a period of relative security; but in 1885 the monarchists united their forces and renewed the battle against it. Jacobinism was again on the defensive, and at the very moment when a large part of the small and middle bourgeoisie looked to the Republic to save them from the effects of the growing concentration of industry and commerce, and the extreme centralization of credit facilities in the hands of a few Paris banking institutions. The political reaction itself seemed to have been strengthened by the rise of large-scale industry, for some members of the capitalist bourgeoisie had sided with the opponents of the democratic Republic,[1] while some members of the Bourbon and Bonapartist aristocracy had gained a considerable share in the industrial life of France.

Both the Jacobins and their opponents strove to win the support of the peasantry and industrial proletariat. The spread of Marxian socialism, with the refusal of its protagonists to support the Republic, appeared to the Jacobins a new and a serious danger. Moreover, in seeking the support of the proletariat against the bourgeois Jacobins, many of the opponents of the democratic Republic—Count de Mun and the Boulangists, for example—supported restrictions on capitalist exploitation of the workers. To retain the favor of the proletariat, therefore, was one of the most important problems facing the Jacobins. In order to solve the problem, they turned to the concept of *la République sociale*, the Republic as the protector of labor.

It was at this tense moment in the drama that Jaurès gave up an academic career and entered politics. The young member of the Chamber of Deputies was a typical representative of the Jacobin politicians from the south of France. He was born in 1859 at Castres, Department of Tarn, in the Midi—a region that was strongly republican in the second half of the nine-

[1] See Louis Assanis, *La Société française à travers les siècles* (Paris, 1913), pp. 414, 423. Assanis remarks: "Forgetting more and more its humble origin, the *haute bourgeoisie* associated with the titled aristocracy; and like the latter, disdained the democracy which provided its means of living in opulence." See also Charles Seignobos, *Histoire sincère de la nation française* (Paris, 1933), p. 479.

teenth century.[2] His father was engaged in a small wholesale business, but possessed little capital and no commercial ability; and during Jean's childhood the father sold his business to acquire a small farm.[3] Two of the father's cousins, it may be noted, were admirals in the French navy. One of these, the Admiral Benjamin-Constant Jaurès, named after a famous French liberal, served as a general in the Franco-Prussian War. After the War he served as ambassador to Russia and then to Spain; and in 1881 he became, under good republican auspices, Minister of the Marine.

The mother of Jaurès was a pious Catholic; his education began at a small local school conducted by a priest; and his study in Paris was subsidized by a wealthy Conservative, M. Félix Deltour, with whom Jaurès remained on intimate terms for many years.[4] However, these conservative influences were swept aside when Jaurès, after attending the *Collège* at Castres, the *Collège de Sainte Barbe*, and the *Lycée Louis-le-Grand* in Paris, reached the *École normale*, a hotbed of Jacobin ideas. At the age of twenty-two Jaurès was absorbing the teachings of David Friedrich Straus, one of the founders of the "higher criticism" of the Bible, and of Ernest Renan, for whom he always retained the fondest admiration.[5]

In temperament, Jaurès was akin to the eighteenth-century enthusiasts who became the Jacobins of the Revolution. Jaurès passionately loved nature; and nature, art, music, literature, and the company of his friends were his greatest pleasures. He was utterly indifferent to money, luxury, and the *haute monde*. Jaurès, moreover, possessed a broad streak of humanitarianism:

[2] See Seignobos, *op. cit.,* pp. 432, 434.
[3] Charles Rappoport, *Jean Jaurès* (Paris, 1915), p. 6; Paul Desanges and Luc Mériga, *Vie de Jaurès* (Paris, 1924), p. 1.
[4] Lucien Lévy-Bruhl, *Jean Jaurès: esquisse biographique* (Paris, 1924) pp. 17, 25.
[5] See the letter from Jaurès in Lévy-Bruhl, *op. cit.,* pp. 158-59; and the statement of Robert Cornilleau in *Types et silhouettes* (Paris, n. d.), pp. 18-20.

a belief in the innate goodness of men and a sensitivity to the sufferings of the under-privileged.

Of importance in directing Jaurès to Jacobin views were the political and economic conditions of the region in which he lived. The economic make-up of the Tarn resembled, for the most part, that of France taken as a whole during the latter half of the eighteenth century. As in prerevolutionary France, agriculture was the chief occupation.[6] During the latter half of the nineteenth century the peasants still suffered from the traditional obstacle of land concentration in the hands of the noble families. They also suffered from the competition of large-scale capitalist agriculture, both foreign and domestic. In addition, the wine growers were almost completely ruined by phylloxera, which descended upon the Midi in 1865 and did not abate their destructive vigor until 1892. Consequently, the peasants were burdened with taxes, rents, and interest on mortgages. Agricultural depression resulted in economic unrest.

As in prerevolutionary France, there existed in the Tarn much small industry and petty capitalism.[7] In the sheltered valleys of the mountainous portions, small wool factories abounded. There were also many tanneries and leather factories, employing only eighteen men on the average. In addition, there were small establishments for making hats, coaches, and furniture, as well as a large variety of small mercantile enterprises. The industries of the Tarn were primitive, the little machinery they possessed being of small horsepower.[8]

Two economic developments since the eighteenth century

[6] Louis Valatx, *Monographie sur le mouvement de la population dans le Département du Tarn de 1901 à 1911; thèse pour le doctorat* (Albi, 1917), pp. 20-21.

[7] See *ibid.*, pp. 27-33.

[8] Valatx points out that in 1900 there were 402 establishments operating 448 machines with a total of 6,824 h.p.—*Ibid.*, p. 37. This may be compared with the Department of Nord which, in 1908, possessed 7,049 machines with 481,678 h.p. See E. Théry, *La Fortune public de la France* (Paris, 1911), p. 120.

served to strengthen Jacobinism and to bring it nearer to socialism. The first was the growth of a centralized banking system. In the towns of the Tarn were branch offices of all the big Parisian banks—such as the *Banque de France, Comptoir d'escompte, Crédit lyonnais,* and *Société générale.*[9] This meant that the mortgages burdening the peasants were held in the grip of the "financial oligarchy." As the financial wing of the *haute bourgeoisie* often appeared to be reactionary in politics, the Jacobins of the Tarn were led to make of their fight on the political reaction an economic as well as a political struggle. By attacking the economic power of the bankers they could win the support of the peasants. In addition, by weakening, perhaps socializing, centralized banking, the Jacobins believed they could undermine the political strength of the entire reaction.

The region also saw the growth of two large-scale industries: a coal-mining and metallurgical establishment, and a bottle works. These industries were an early example of modern capitalist concentration.[10] In the third quarter of the eighteenth century, Gabriel de Solages obtained control of all the coal and iron mines in the Carmaux basin, erected a blast furnace, a bottle works, and a factory for shipbuilding materials. In 1880 the coal mines employed approximately 1,800 men; in 1900, the coal mines employed 3,000, the iron mines at Alban, 3,000, and the metallurgical works, 1,122. As compared with the departments of Nord (home of Marxian socialism), Pas-de-Calais and Meurthe-et-Moselle, this development of heavy industry was relatively unimportant in the total industrial output of France, and it amounted to only about ten percent of the Tarn's industry.[11] Yet, together with the bottle

[9] Valatx, *op. cit.*, p. 40.   [10] *Ibid.*, pp. 24-25, 35.

[11] For example, the entire coal output of Carmaux in 1910 was 666,000 tons, and the entire output of Tarn and Aveyron in 1913 was 1,988,000 tons; but the output of the two departments of Nord and Pas-de-Calais was, in 1913, 27,389,000 tons.—*Ibid.*, pp. 24-25; *Ministre du Commerce: Rapport général sur l'industrie française* (Paris, 1919), I, 9.

works, employing about 1,000 men in 1891 (the year in which a coöperative bottle works was established), the De Solages enterprise was the foreshadowing in the Tarn of modern economic tendencies.

The Chevalier Gabriel de Solages was a member of the aristocracy who had been forced to emigrate during the Revolution.[12] After the Restoration, the head of the family was advanced to the position of Marquis. The contemporary Marquis Gabriel de Solages was related by marriage to the Baron Reille, an imperial noble; and both entered politics, taking positions at the extreme right in the Chamber of Deputies. In short, the large-scale industry of the Tarn was in the hands of the political and aristocratic reaction.

Jaurès became the personal political enemy of Baron Reille and Marquis de Solages. Even while Jaurès held his first academic position as "master of conferences" at the Faculty of Toulouse (1883-85), he began to contribute to *La Dépêche de Toulouse*, the liberal Jacobin paper which included among its regular contributors such eminent left-wing Radicals as Clemenceau, Ranc, Pelletan, and Goblet. In 1885, Jaurès became a candidate for Parliament; and on the *scrutin de liste* (a vote taken in the department as a whole) he as well as Reille and De Solages were elected. The personal rivalry was sharp. In 1887 Jaurès delivered an attack on Baron Reille for his antidemocratic, antireform, proclerical attitude.[13] Two years later, when the *scrutin d'arrondissement* was introduced, Jaurès was defeated for re-election by Baron Reille and the Marquis de Solages. In 1892 it was revealed that the Marquis had won the election of 1889 by exercising political pressure on his workingmen.[14] The Marquis resigned, and Jaurès won the by-election. In 1898 Jaurès again attacked Reille and De Solages, accusing the latter of using corrupt methods in the election

[12] *Revue historique, scientifique et littéraire du Département du Tarn* (1901), XVIII, 241, 244.
[13] *La Dépêche*, June 25, 1887.   [14] See *ibid.*, Sept. 6, 1892.

campaign; and he proclaimed that the struggle against Reille and De Solages was the battle of the Republic against reaction.[15] Jaurès came to believe, as we shall see, that the political strength of the reaction could be weakened only by destroying its economic power through socialism.

Jaurès, as we have seen, entered politics in 1885, when the Monarchists had renewed their attack on the Republic.[16] The republicans themselves had split into three factions. The Opportunists, speaking for the wealthy republicans, favored imperialism and opposed social reform. The middle-bourgeois Radicals also favored imperialism but were anticlerical and less opposed to reforms. The petty-bourgeois Radical-Socialists were opposed to imperialism (in this period); they were anticlerical; and they favored a certain measure of social reform. The strength of the political reactionaries (or Conservatives, as they were now called) on the first balloting in the election of 1885 stimulated the formation of a "Republican Concentration."[17] This union, however, was far from stable. Jaurès was sympathetic to the Radical-Socialists; but because he was primarily interested, as he later explained, in the defense of the Republic, he chose a position from which he could work most effectively for republican unity: the neutral position of left-center (*centre-gauche*).[18] In short, he became a republican-at-large.

Jaurès retained this position during the second pitched battle

[15] *Ibid.*, Apr. 22, May 4, 1898.

[16] For this crisis, see Charles Seignobos, *L'Évolution de la 3ᵉ République* (Paris, 1921), in *Histoire de France contemporaine*, edited by Ernest Lavisse, Vol. VIII, pp. 107-17.

[17] In the election the Conservatives won 201 seats, of which 87 were held by titled descendants of the old nobility. In the preceding Chamber, there were about 45 titled nobles. See *Journal officiel*, 1885.

[18] *L'Humanité*, Aug. 15, 1906. Jaurès admired both Ferry and Gambetta. He was continually quoting the opinions of the latter, while he favored Ferry for president in 1887; and when Ferry died, he declared that he had always admired him for "the vigor of his spirit, the force of his character and courage, the integrity of his life." See *La Dépêche*, Nov. 19, 1890, Mar. 25, 1891, Mar. 20, 1893.

over the democratic Republic in which he participated before joining the socialist movement: the Boulanger crisis leading up to the election of 1889. The Conservatives had allied themselves with the popular General Boulanger, who was rapidly gaining the support of the civil population with a program of constitutional revision, social reforms for the workers and peasants, and a foreign policy of *revanche* against Germany. Although the coalition failed to gain a majority, it obtained a strong representation in the Chamber of Deputies.[19]

During these crises Jaurès fought for the Republic in terms of the whole Jacobin tradition. In fact, he justified all his ideas and activities by the touchstone of the French Revolution. While addressing the Chamber of Deputies in 1889, he asked: "Is the genius of the French Revolution spent? Do you not find in the ideas of the Revolution the means of meeting all the questions, all the problems, that appear? Did not the Revolution produce an immortal wisdom that could face all the difficulties of the changing *milieu* in which we live?"[20] These questions were purely rhetorical, for regardless of the nature of the question (financial or social reform, national credit, or national defense) Jaurès advised the Chamber to be guided by the lessons contained in the "Revolutionary memories," by the ideal, the spirit, the tradition, of the French Revolution.[21]

Of equal importance in the mind of Jaurès was the French nation, the French *patrie*.[22] Patriotism was at the very root of the Jacobin tradition. The French Revolutionaries, in proclaiming the democratic Republic, had emphasized the impor-

[19] One hundred and seventy-three Conservatives and 38 Boulangists were elected as against 266 Republicans. For a description of the Boulanger crisis, see Seignobos, *L'Évolution de la 3ᵉ République*, pp. 134-45.

[20] Jaurès, *Discours parlementaires* (Paris, 1904), Feb. 11, 1889, p. 130.

[21] See, for example, *La Dépêche*, Oct. 1, 1887, July 23, 1890; *La Petite République*, Oct. 5, 1893.

[22] The term *patrie* is used by the French to denote their "country"—the land, the nationality, and the state. The use of *patrie* does not necessarily imply an invidious attitude toward other nations such as is contained in the French term *nationalisme*.

tance of the nation from which the Republic derived its authority. Hence, in the eyes of the Revolutionaries, devotion to the Republic was synonymous with patriotism. This identification of republicanism with patriotism was intensified by the attack on the Republic by the neighboring monarchies. The Revolutionaries defended the nation with cries of *"Vive la République!"*

Jaurès inherited not only the French Revolutionary tradition of patriotism but also the nationalistic thought developed in the nineteenth century, particularly by German conservative philosophers. He followed these philosophers in assembling real or fancied differences as criteria for determining the distinctions between nationalities. In his opinion, nationalities are groups united "by community of spirit, of language, and of history, by common memories and common hopes, by certain dates of public mourning and public joy"; they are groups with "moral individualities fashioned by history, with their own language, literature, sense of life, memories, their own particular form of hopes and particular turn of passions, souls and genius," possessing "the consciousness of their collective right to live."[23]

Jaurès also followed the nineteenth-century political theorists who anthropomorphized the nation into a living organism, a collective person with all the attributes of human beings.[24] The nationality, as it appeared to Jaurès, possessed instincts, sentiments, a heart, a conscience, and a soul.[25] His articles and speeches were filled with admiration for this great metaphysi-

[23] See, for example, Jaurès, *Alliance française: association nationale pour la propagation de la langue française dans les colonies et à l'étranger; conférence de Jean Jaurès* (Albi, approximately 1886), p. 3; *L'Humanité,* May 29, June 29, 1905.

[24] Professor Dunning showed how the collective works of Hegel, Fichte, Dahlman, Waitz, Stahl, and Bluntschli, prepared the way for the idea that the nationality has the attributes of a collective person. See William A. Dunning, *Political Theories from Rousseau to Spencer* (New York, 1926), pp. 299-301.

[25] For example, *La Dépêche,* June 4, 1887, Feb. 10, 1889; *Discours parlementaires,* Feb. 8, 1893, p. 383.

cal entity, for France's "genius, virility, and power"; for the fertility of her labor; for her thrift and her initiative.[26] Jaurès also followed the practice of ascribing general characteristics to Frenchmen as a group. He found them distinguished by their gaiety, cordiality, intelligence, and "heroism in war and peace."[27] Above all, he believed that the French nation was exceptionally idealistic; and he felt that "her native generosity" and the "humanity with which her soul is full" would make of her the champion of social justice for all humanity.[28]

Jaurès had great admiration for France's "flame of genius," expressed in the "tradition of great French classic art," in the "French Rennaissance," in the painting of Puvis de Chavannes, and in the scientific discoveries of Becquerel and Curie.[29] He loved French literature, "the simple and great beauty of the masterpieces of our language"; and he wanted all Frenchmen to be able to grasp, "in all its beauty, power, richness, subtlety of shading, this French language—created by the genius of thinkers, of writers, of artists."[30] Even the less spiritual aspects of French life—the beauty of the countryside, the climate, the customs, "the good wine of France"—received his enthusiastic praise.[31]

French history was both a joy and a sorrow for Jaurès. He declared that he loved "the profound past of France," be-

[26] La Dépêche, Jan. 6, 1889, June 2, 1891.
[27] See ibid., Sept. 10, 1887, Sept. 16, 1888, Apr. 23, 1890; Discours parlementaires, Oct. 27, 1894, p. 797.
[28] Alliance française . . . , op. cit., p. 11; La Dépêche, Nov. 4, 1888, Nov. 3, 1889, Jan. 9, Feb. 19, Apr. 16, 1890.
[29] La Dépêche, May 12, 1889, Jan. 1, 1891; L'Humanité, Sept. 7, Oct. 17, 1905. At times, Jaurès took great pride in the culture of the Midi; but this tendency toward regionalism was retarded by a greater admiration for the culture of France in general. Thus, although he spoke of "the artistic glories" of Toulouse, of "its creative genius in painting, sculpture, music," he added that Toulousian art was "more precious in that it is not only Toulousian, but French, and occasionally universal." La Dépêche, May 27, 31, 1891.
[30] Jaurès, Action socialiste (Paris, 1899), p. 28; Pages choisies (Paris, 1922), pp. 65-66.
[31] For example, La Dépêche, Mar. 19, 1890, May 8, 1893.

lieving it to be "the longest and most glorious past in Europe," a past filled with grandeur and difficulties.[32] The difficulties which Jaurès himself experienced are to be found in the events of 1870. At the impressionable age of twelve, he had lived through the invasion of German troops and the loss of Alsace-Lorraine, which affected him as a personal disaster. When France recovered from the effects of the War, rapidly developing her economic and military strength, Jaurès exulted because "on every side to which one turns, France, whom they have wanted to destroy and whom they have believed destroyed, recovers herself in defeat, more living, more ardent, and more reverberating than before; the old tree—from which they have been able to cut some branches, but of which they have not been able to touch the root—has new sap; it has grown leaves again; it is going to bloom again, and again shower the world with the fruits of justice and liberty."[33] Jaurès was indeed "a citizen of France who is proud of being a citizen of France."[34]

Over France Jaurès placed the halo of the French Revolution. It was the French Revolution, he explained, that ushered the nation into the world. The monarchy had slowly assembled the pieces of France, but the experiences of the Revolution had fused them together.[35]

Jaurès believed that "a sincere patriotism" brings a true exaltation of the individual, for it permits him to work for something which continues beyond himself.[36] "France, when we have disappeared, will not have manifested all her resources; but short as our life may be, we can participate, by our work and our hope, in the unlimited future of our country." True patriotism, Jaurès insisted, demands that the individual sub-

[32] *Ibid.*, Dec. 31, 1887, Nov. 4, 1888, Aug. 27, 1891; *Journal officiel*, May 10, 1907, p. 958.
[33] *Alliance française* . . . , p. 14.
[34] Jaurès, *Diplomatie et démocratie* (Paris, 1906), p. 10.
[35] *Discours parlementaires*, Feb. 17, Nov. 5, 1894, pp. 557, 893.
[36] *Alliance française* . . . , pp. 13-14.

ordinate his interest to that of the nation and serve the nation beyond the limits of what duty alone requires.[37]

Patriotism is an abstract concept, the definite content of which varies according to the interests of individuals and groups. Frenchmen of the 1880's differed as to what ideas a patriot should hold and what activities the nation should pursue. For Jaurès, the supreme patriotic necessity was the existence of the Republic.

In the eyes of Jaurès the Third Republic was the "supreme expression" of the French Revolution and the fulfillment of its basic ideas; it was the "logical and definitive form of democracy"; and as its universal suffrage permitted the nation to impose its will, it was synonymous with *la patrie*.[38] Similarly, for Jaurès the enemies of the Republic still represented the alliance of the monarchy, the aristocracy, and the Church (plus the *haute bourgeoisie*) against the Revolution; and because they were bent on restoring, "under a hypocritical and still more odious form, the Old Régime," they were the mortal enemies of the nation.[39] Because Boulanger, too, was striving to deprive the nation of its political liberty, he was guilty of *lèse-nation*.[40]

But the nation was also threatened by external dangers. Jaurès feared that Bismarck, faced with the opposition of the German Socialists and the French sentiment in Alsace-Lorraine, would heed the militarists and resort to war—as he had done in 1870.[41] He also feared that Germany, worried by "the astonishing and happy revival of our country," would take advantage of some pretext, such as the increase of the French army, to attack France.[42] France's "first duty," Jaurès warned,

---

[37] *Ibid.*, pp. 2-3; *Discours parlementaires*, Nov. 5, 1894, p. 893.
[38] *La Dépêche*, Feb. 26, Nov. 12, 1887, Mar. 11, Apr. 1, 1888, Aug. 18, Oct. 6, 1889, Oct. 22, 1890, Sept. 19, 1892; "Discours de Jaurès à Amsterdam," *La Revue socialiste*, 1904, XI, 292-93.
[39] *La Dépêche*, June 9, July 28, Oct. 6, 1889; *Discours parlementaires*, Introduction, pp. 17-19.
[40] For example, *La Dépêche*, Apr. 1, July 1, 1888, Sept. 10, 1890.
[41] See *La Dépêche*, Feb. 26, 1887.   [42] *Ibid.*, May 28, June 11, 1887.

must be to improve the national defense; and she "must always be ready to rise to the last man in the defense of her soil . . ."[43] He therefore demanded that the technical equipment of the army be modernized with the advancement of science; that the budget be balanced to insure France's credit in time of war; and that the exemption of priests and university students from military service be abolished.[44]

Jaurès became an ardent partisan of the Republic's Three-Year-Service Law, passed in 1889. He argued that France must follow the ideal of the "nation in arms" of the French Revolution.[45] France must instill into the army the nation's moral principle—"the republican and the democratic spirit." This was especially important, he added, because the next war would be political as well as military, and France must be in a position to ally herself with the republican and democratic movements in all European countries. The fusing of the army with the democratic nation could be effected only by the provisions in the Three-Year Law guaranteeing equality in the service.[46] Jaurès was also interested in eliminating the aristocratic officers by filling the military schools with men from the ranks and by abolishing fees for attending Saint-Cyr.[47] His first speech in the Chamber of Deputies was on behalf of establishing a preparatory course for the Naval School at a lycée in Paris.[48]

Jaurès, however, drew a sharp line between preparation against attack and the bellicosity of militarism. He firmly believed in "the holy war for la patrie" if France were attacked, but he denounced "the foolish war of an adventurer."[49] In

[43] Ibid., Feb. 12, Apr. 13, Dec. 31, 1887, May 12, 1888.
[44] For example, ibid., Apr. 2, May 7, 1887, May 26, 1889.
[45] See ibid., March 26, June 25, July 9, 1887, July 21, 1889, Aug. 21, 1890; La Petite République, Oct. 15, 1893.
[46] Jaurès also argued that the law would give France a million trained soldiers with less expenditure of money.—La Dépêche, July 21, 1889, Aug. 27, 1891.
[47] Ibid., Aug. 21, 1890.
[48] Discours parlementaires, Jan. 25, 1887, p. 187.
[49] La Dépêche, Apr. 23, 1887.

repudiating aggressive warfare he argued that peace would permit France to complete her work of restoration; that it would give German democracy an opportunity to control the German government and therefore lessen danger of an attack on France; and that in an offensive war, France would lack the *élan* necessary for victory, and would lose the moral support of the outside world.[50]

Jaurès held the reaction responsible for "the tearful tragedy of 1870, a war, declared in the interests of a single family, which caused the ruin and dismemberment of *la patrie*."[51] He unceasingly accused the reaction of wanting—in order to crush the Republic and regain its privileges—to gamble with France's future in an aggressive war.[52] On the other hand, he praised the Republic's policy during the Schnaebele crisis of 1887-88, caused by the arrest of a Frenchman by German troops. The Republic, he said, had preserved peace, peace "without weakness and without humiliation."[53]

During this early period, Jaurès regarded "simultaneous disarmament" as a "criminal chimera," holding that it would weaken the Republic's defense against the reaction and invite an attack by Germany.[54] He did not accept the argument that large armaments necessarily engendered international suspicion. "For a long time to come," he said, "the nations can carry, not without fatigue, but without peril, the enormous budgets of national defense."[55] Moreover, in his opinion, the best guarantee for peace was a powerfully armed France that would be respected by her neighbors.[56]

Jaurès accepted the Franco-Russian Alliance as part of this policy of patriotism and peace. While negotiations for the Alliance were under way, he held that such an alliance implied

[50] *Ibid.*, Feb. 12, 1888, Jan. 9, 1890, Sept. 3, 1891.
[51] *Ibid.*, Sept. 16, 1889.
[52] For example, *ibid.*, Apr. 1, Aug. 10, 1888, Feb. 3, 1889, Oct. 29, 1893.
[53] *Ibid.*, Feb. 26, Dec. 31, 1887, Feb. 12, 1888, Feb. 10, 1889.
[54] *Ibid.*, Dec. 31, 1887.
[55] *Ibid.*, Dec. 31, 1887, Feb. 12, 1888.
[56] *Ibid.*, May 28, 1887.

aggressive intentions and might lead to weakening the Republic.[57] But three years later, in 1891, Jaurès was entirely won over. The Franco-Russian Alliance now appeared to him as a guarantee of peace and of France's security, for in counterbalancing the Triple Alliance it worked against "the domination of odious Prussian militarism."[58]

But to be strong, "France" must be prosperous. Jaurès was greatly concerned with "national activity" along economic lines, believing that national prosperity was essential for military power.[59] He advocated protective tariffs to further "national economic interests." An unfavorable balance of trade, he argued, indicated a weakening of France's economic energy, and "it is necessary to protect French property and French labor against excessive foreign competition."[60]

Jaurès, along with other Jacobins, looked with favor upon commercial and colonial expansion. The Tonkin expedition was unpopular, he thought, not because it represented capitalist imperialism, but because it was too costly, inefficiently conducted, and added a new humiliation to a France anxious to recover her glory.[61] In default of colonial expeditions between the Tonkin expedition and the time Jaurès joined the socialist movement, he emphasized the extension of French commerce and the propagation of French ideas in foreign countries. Jaurès enthusiastically complimented the *Alliance française* for its work in spreading the French language, for assisting the "glorious efforts to extend our legitimate influence abroad."[62] The spread of the French language would help make public opinion favorable to France, particularly useful in time of war; it would help to bring favorable commercial treaties, and perhaps defensive alliances to protect French colonies; in short, it would contribute to "our profit and our honor."

---

[57] *Ibid.*, Feb. 26, 1887. [58] *Ibid.*, Aug. 6, 27, 1891.
[59] *Ibid.*, Mar. 19, 1890.
[60] For example, *ibid.*, Dec. 11, 18, 1889, July 10, 1890.
[61] *Ibid.*, Feb. 10, 1889, Nov. 19, 1890.
[62] *Alliance française* . . . , *op. cit.*, pp. 2, 8-12.

Jaurès praised efforts to spread French culture in the colonies.[63] He remarked that as the emigration of Frenchmen to the colonies was small, language was "the necessary instrument of colonization." The spread of the French language would make the natives of Algeria, Tunis, Annam, and Tonkin, "French in intelligence and feeling." The natives must be taught—particularly by a study of French history—that the French have always been motivated in their colonial enterprises by "justice and goodness." Thus would be completed the work of "moral conquest and assimilation."

The interest of Jaurès in Alsace-Lorraine never waned. He referred to the Treaty of Frankfort as "a treaty of violence and spoliation," by which Bismarck "tore millions of men from the fatherland to which their souls were attached."[64] "It is impossible," he said, "for French democracy to accept this mutilation."[65]

Jaurès adopted Gambetta's proposal for a peaceful restoration of the lost provinces.[66] Because an aggressive war would be dangerous for France, her formula must be "no war, no renunciation." A triumphant democracy in Germany would return the provinces seized by the Emperor William I, and this triumph would be hastened by the maintenance of peace and by the preservation of the French Republic as the inspiration for German democracy. The French, therefore, must all the more strengthen the Republic, "keep ourselves well armed, speak little of Alsace-Lorraine, and think of it much . . ."

So absorbed was Jaurès in the concept of national unity, that he was willing, when he conceived the welfare of the nation to be at stake, to regard the reactionaries as friendly enemies. He remarked, for example, that the community of spirit, lan-

[63] *Ibid.*, pp. 5-9.
[64] For example, *La Dépêche*, Dec. 31, 1887, Dec. 4, 1889, July 2, 1890.
[65] *La Dépêche*, Dec. 31, 1887.
[66] For Jaurès's ideas on the solution of the problem of Alsace-Lorraine, see *La Dépêche*, June 11, Dec. 31, 1887, Jan. 9, 1890.

guage, memories and hopes, "revives in the midst of our quarrels the touching unity of the French family, and two fellow-citizens who agree on nothing are nevertheless closer to each other, and at certain times, dearer to each other, than to foreigners with whom they agree. No struggle can prevail against the profound union of hearts. Therefore, what does it matter if we are divided on certain points as long as we can unite on others?"[67] He congratulated the Conservatives on their willingness to coöperate with the republicans to strengthen national defense.[68] At times, however, Jaurès made "unanimous acceptance of the Republic" a positive requirement for national unity.[69] And this concept of national unity based on democratic republicanism, was one of the spearheads of his attack on the Church.

The secularization of education was the aspect of anticlericalism most closely bound up with the problem of national unity. Jaurès, holding that la patrie "needs a cult," was concerned with the problem of teaching patriotism to the masses. He thought that the army partially performed this service, but he expected still more from the school.[70] The school, he said, prepared "the unity and community of all classes from one end of the social scale to the other." The school, therefore, must teach "national fraternity" and "the moral and intellectual grandeur of humanity and la patrie." It must especially teach the children, through the study of geography and history (that of Michelet, Lamartine, and Blanc), to know France and to exercise their duties as French citizens.[71]

The Church, Jaurès held, could not fulfill these functions. The Jacobins had always regarded the Church as the most

[67] Alliance française . . . , op. cit., pp. 3-5.
[68] La Dépêche, Feb. 12, July 9, 1887.
[69] Ibid., Apr. 30, 1887, May 20, 1891.
[70] Ibid., Oct. 22, 1887, Apr. 15, 1888, June 16, Sept. 29, 1889; Action socialiste, op. cit., p. 32.
[71] See La Dépêche, Jan. 15, 1888, Feb. 6, 1893.

despicable element in the reactionary alliance against the Republic. Under feudalism, Jaurès asserted, the Church was a religious despotism, and in the past century the Church had been the "core of counter-revolution."[72] He accused the Church of lack of patriotism, of having sided with France's enemies.[73] Now the Church was guilty of rekindling religious passions and instigating a religious war that was "cutting in two the soul of the country."[74]

Jaurès argued that religious instruction in the schools was harmful.[75] Questions of religion divided the students, and religious instruction prevented the teachers from treating the students as "little Frenchmen, all receiving the same education."[76] Lay education, on the other hand, worked for "accord among all Frenchmen, not only on political issues, but also on the questions of the Republic's vital institutions and of the moral direction of modern societies."

To the teachings of the Church Jaurès opposed the rationalism of the eighteenth century and the higher criticism of the Bible. Like other Jacobins of his time, Jaurès had great respect for "reason" and an almost mystical regard for science. Education, he held, should develop the reasoning capacities of the students and introduce them to the conclusions of science. But the Church, holding to dogma based on authority, could not fulfill these requirements.[77]

Finally, according to Jaurès, the Church was incapable of

[72] Ibid., June 16, Oct. 6, 1889; Jaurès, La Constituante, 1789-1791 (Paris, 1901), in Histoire socialiste, edited by Jean Jaurès, Vol. I, pp. 24, 533.

[73] Ibid., June 25, 1887.

[74] Ibid., Sept. 29, Oct. 6, 1889.

[75] At first, Jaurès did not object to the teaching of religion in private schools; and he often declared that he was primarily interested in keeping religious instruction out of state schools—in order to ensure the neutrality of the state in religious matters.—Ibid., June 23, Oct. 6, 1889. He came, however, to oppose all religious teaching and any control of schools by the Church.

[76] For example, ibid., June 16, Sept. 29, 1889.

[77] Ibid., Apr. 28, June 16, 23, Oct. 6, 1889, Sept. 10, 1891, July 4, Aug. 23, 1892, Aug. 22, 1894; Action socialiste, op. cit., pp. 11, 279-80.

teaching religion itself.[78] Religious instruction should emphasize "the high spirituality and divine tenderness which fills the work of Christ"; it should teach the "pure, inner religion of sweetness, of pity, of resignation, of infinite hope," the essentials of religion as understood by Renan, Michelet, Lamennais and Hugo. The Church, however, now contained only "a hateful, narrow clericalism, avid for domination and revenge"; and the religion which it taught consisted only of "arbitrary dogmas and rotten theologies" that had been undermined by the development of Biblical criticism, the study of other religions, and "the positive and naturalist conception of the world."

Jaurès demanded the separation of the Church and the state in order to free the government from clerical influences, to replace religious persecution with "freedom of conscience," and to fulfill the ideal of an absolutely secular society proposed by the French Revolution.[79] He also advocated that the clergy be required to submit to universal military training; that religious organizations be forced to support themselves; and that extensive social reforms be instituted in order to loosen the hold of the Church on the people.[80]

Most of the views on the Republic and patriotism expressed by Jaurès in this period (from his entering politics in 1885 until the Dreyfus Affair in 1898) were retained by him until his death. Some of these views underwent modification after 1898, particularly in the direction of a greater emphasis on peace and internationalism. This emphasis arose particularly from his acceptance of socialism and his personal contact with its protagonists.

[78] See *La Dépêche*, Apr. 28, 1889, Sept. 24, 1890, Aug. 21, 1891; *Pages choisies*, Jan. 7, 1892, pp. 43-45; *Action socialiste*, July 4, 1892, pp. 160-67; *Discours parlementaires*, Nov. 1, 1893, p. 492.
[79] *La Dépêche*, Oct. 7, 1888, June 16, Oct. 6, 1889.
[80] *Ibid.*, Oct. 7, 1888, June 23, 1889.

III

FROM JACOBINISM TO SOCIALISM

TO JAURÈS, the Republic meant more than political liberty; it was also an instrument of social welfare. From the very outset the French Revolution had established the tradition of using political power for the advancement of social aims. The Convention period was characterized by radical legislation favorable to the lower middle classes, the workers, and the poor peasants. At one point the Revolution sighted socialist goals; and the conspiracy of Babeuf, in its own confused way, was the historic forerunner of French Socialism. Thus there gradually arose the conception of the *République sociale*, which, while not socialist, held out the hope of piecemeal social amelioration through liberal and democratic political forms.

It was this *République sociale* that was expected to solve the new problems created by large-scale capitalism. The lower middle classes faced economic extinction through financial concentration. The peasants, forced off the land, were migrating into the cities and competing with the factory workers. The peasants and the industrial proletariat threatened to desert the Republic for a "social" monarchy or for revolutionary socialism. Moreover, the power of the reaction was being augmented by the wealth of capitalism; some of the reactionary aristocrats acquired a large share in the ownership of industry, and at the same time, many of the big bourgeois capitalists (the *haute bourgeoisie*) sided with the reaction against a threatening democracy.

Faced with such problems in the Tarn, Jaurès at first followed the lead of the left-wing Jacobins (Clemenceau, Ranc, Pelletan, Goblet) who attempted to reform capitalism rather than abolish it. In the early period of his career, Jaurès denounced not capitalism but specific groups of capitalists. He was particularly hostile to the "clerical industrialists" in the Tarn, those large capitalists whom he accused of having formed an alliance with the Church against democracy.[1] He charged that in return for the Church's moral support of the industrialists, who amassed large fortunes by compelling their workers to labor twelve, thirteen, fourteen hours a day, the industrialists gave the clergy access to the factories.[2]

After his defeat for re-election to the Chamber by the Marquis de Solages in 1889, Jaurès accused the reactionary industrialists of using economic pressure and corruption in order to win elections; and he contended that the poor must have "a part in the economic power, for such power will become the living expression and the practical guarantee of their political sovereignty."[3] In 1892, the strike of the workers at Carmaux against the political pressure of De Solages occasioned the assertion that the merging of the reaction and capitalism was a menace to universal suffrage and the Republic.[4]

Jaurès also accused the "financial oligarchy," the bankers, of working hand in hand with the reaction in order to protect their wealth from an aggressive democracy.[5] The bankers, he charged, were responsible for the economic difficulties of the peasants: the high interest rates on mortgages, high taxes, and high railway rates.[6] These burdens, together with the speculation of the bankers in commodities, particularly wheat, deprived the peasants of their land and built up large estates. In his opinion, also, the *haute banque* was the power behind the ex-

[1] *La Dépêche*, July 21, 1889, Feb. 24, June 21, 1892.
[2] *Ibid.*, June 21, 1892.   [3] *Ibid.*, Jan. 1, 1890.   [4] *Ibid.*, Oct. 4, 1892.
[5] *Ibid.*, Nov. 11, 1888, June 16, 1889, Dec. 19, 1892; Jaurès, *Discours parlementaires*, pp. 19-20. Jaurès claimed that the Church supported the bankers in their oppression of the peasantry; that the reaction aided the bankers in their attempt to renew the railway concessions and the charter of the Bank of France; and that the reactionaries did not attack the bankers for their part in the Panama Affair.
[6] *La Dépêche*, Jan. 29, 1887, Jan. 25, 30, 1893, Feb. 6, 1895.

ploitation of labor and the concentration of industry and commerce which was crushing the small and middle bourgeoisie—
those who lived less by the return from their investments than
by their own labor.[7] The economic power of the financiers, in
reality, constituted a "feudalism of the new régime."[8] To economic evils they had added political evils; for the Panama
Affair indicated how they augmented their power through corruption of the government and the press.[9] Jaurès warned that
the financiers, by discrediting democracy, were responsible for
the sinister growth of anarchism.[10]

In the meantime, Jaurès was faced with the necessity of
satisfying the demands of the workers. Early in his career,
he remarked: "It is necessary that the Republic, by showing its
affection for the workers of the cities and the workers of the
fields and by giving benefits to both groups, attach them to
itself."[11] Jaurès was troubled by the threat of violent revolution uttered by the Marxists and the Anarchists. He feared
the "dangerous ruptures" and "the upheavals to which future
society will be exposed if a pacific revolution does not calm
the world of labor."[12]

The divisions among the bourgeoisie mentioned in the preceding chapter also troubled Jaurès, for they permitted the reaction to accomplish "the most dangerous maneuvers against
the Republic."[13] He decided that "Republican Concentration"
could best be achieved by uniting all the republicans upon a
program of social reform.[14]

The program offered by Jaurès was similar to that sponsored
by the left-wing Radicals. To aid the peasants he favored the

[7] *Ibid.*, Nov. 11, 1887, Mar. 3, 17, 1889.
[8] *Ibid.*, Mar. 17, 1889, Apr. 24, 1894.
[9] *Ibid.*, Feb. 14, 1893; *Discours parlementaires*, Feb. 18, 1893, pp. 383-84.
[10] *Discours parlementaires*, July 25, 1894, pp. 754-81. Jaurès, it may be
noted, was outraged by the assassination of President Carnot by an Anarchist.
[11] *La Dépêche*, Dec. 10, 1887.
[12] *Ibid.*, Nov. 18, 1891; *Discours parlementaires*, Apr. 8, 1886, p. 369.
[13] *Discours parlementaires*, pp. 5-15, 175.
[14] *La Dépêche*, Sept. 23, 1888.

reduction of taxes on land, on vines, and on sugar, such taxes to be replaced by graduated income and inheritance taxes and by government monopolies of alcohol and tobacco; the reduction of railway rates; the suppression of the *octroi* and reduction of the tax on beverages; and the imposition of a tariff on agricultural products.[15] To help particularly the peasants of the Midi he wanted a tariff on wheat and wine.[16] Jaurès believed that these reforms, if supplemented by the establishment of agricultural credit by the government, would lower the cost of production for the peasants, increase the consumption of their goods, and facilitate their acquisition of more land.[17] He also proposed the legalization of unions for agricultural workers: to obtain reforms for the laborers such as higher wages and sickness insurance; and, at the same time, to raise the production costs of the large capitalist landowners and the agricultural nobility.[18] Finally, for the *fermiers* and *métayers* (tenants of the large landowners) Jaurès advocated compensation for improvements; suppression of payment in kind; and generally, a larger share of the produce.[19]

In addition Jaurès favored the reduction of food taxes to compensate the workers for the increased tariffs on agricultural products; measures to prevent accidents in factories; laws to regulate the hours of labor for women and children, particularly at night; the eight-hour day; and a complete system of social insurance to counteract "the consequences of illness, accident, old age, prolonged unemployment."[20] The young Jaurès

[15] *Ibid.*, June 18, Dec. 10, 1887, Apr. 15, Oct 7, 1888, Sept. 1, 1889, May 16, 1890.
[16] *Ibid.*, Feb. 26, 1888, Mar. 8, 1890, July 19, 1893.
[17] *Ibid.*, Oct. 7, 1888, Feb. 5, Mar. 18, May 16, 1890.
[18] *Ibid.*, Dec. 30, 1891. Jaurès contended that much of the misery of the peasants was caused by the possession of land by the agricultural nobility (the *hoberaux*), which they had inherited from their forefathers of the *Ancien régime*. He charged that the *hoberaux* and the big capitalist landowners held two-thirds of the land of France. See *ibid.*, Feb. 5, June 18, 1887, June 16, 1889; Jaurès, *La Constituante, 1789-1791*, p. 519.
[19] *Ibid.*, June 18, 1887.
[20] For example, *ibid.*, June 17, 1888, Feb. 19, July 10, 1890.

was greatly interested in the miners who were a powerful electoral force in his district and were working in the mines of the reactionary De Solages. He advocated many safety devices, such as an improved system of lighting; the right of the miners to choose their own safety-inspection delegates, supported by the state; pensions for miners; and accident and death insurance, the charges to be born by the owners.[21]

Jaurès, however, came to feel that these reforms were insufficient to solve the politico-economic problems raised by the growth of large-scale capitalism. The continuing political struggle with the industrialists and bankers, together with the increasing demands of the workers, led Jaurès gradually to a program of complete socialization.

As early as 1886, when Jaurès was troubled by the prospects of violent revolution and the Republic's loss of labor and peasant support, he set forth a plan for a "definite emancipation of labor by association and collective capital."[22] Capital, he pointed out, possessed the instruments of production and thereby constituted an "aristocracy of privilege" which eventually must be destroyed. His plan proposed that the workingmen use money supplied by the state for pensions and insurance, to purchase industry.[23] The workers, he explained, would thus possess a large part of the instruments of production in less than a century.

While Jaurès first enunciated these proposals as early as 1886, he did not press for their enactment, and it was the jolt of the Boulanger affair that catapulted him into socialism. Political signs just before the election of 1889 indicated to Jaurès the strength of General Boulanger among the workingmen and peasants.[24] Jaurès warned the workers that Boulanger would

[21] For example, ibid., Mar. 19, 1887, Aug. 13, 1890.
[22] Discours parlementaires, Apr. 6, 1886, pp. 365-76.
[23] Ibid., p. 374. Jaurès gave Louis Blanc and Proudhon credit for this plan. La Dépêche, June 28, 1892. Barbaret had favored socialization of industry through funds raised by the workers themselves. See Samuel Bernstein, The Beginnings of Marxian Socialism in France, pp. 60-62.
[24] La Dépêche, Mar. 4, 1888, Feb. 10, 1889.

give them only "the humiliating alms of a hypocritical master."[25] But, at the same time, he warned that the Republic, in order to win popular support, would have to concede the social demands of the masses.[26]

Jaurès now came to regard labor as the source of wealth and to feel that "the arrogant, idle rich" gave nothing to society in return for "the product of labor they have taken from the worker."[27] He extended the concept of the proletariat to include not only the city worker and the agricultural laborer, but also the *métayer* in debt, and the peasant proprietor with limited capital.[28] All these groups, he explained, labored and were unable to save enough to own their tools; they were thus reduced to "a state of perpetual uncertainty and perpetual dependence." He demanded a "profound transformation" that would free the proletariat from the "yoke of capitalism" and would allow the proletarian to retain "the whole product."[29]

As the crisis sharpened, Jaurès wondered whether the ideal of socialism would prevent the working class from falling into "Cæsarian temptations and reactionary ambushes."[30] "The entire problem," he stated, "is to know whether or not socialism will be sufficient to strengthen and rally the workers; and whether or not, at the same time, socialism can reach, without shock and trouble, to the foundation of French society." And Jaurès replied in the affirmative.

Slowly Jaurès began to gravitate toward socialist political activity. He was still dissatisfied with the various socialist parties, but he found praise for individual Possibilists (Basly and Camelinat, for example), and he viewed them as allies in the defense of the Republic.[31] He was attracted by Malon's synthesis of republicanism and socialism.[32] When defeat in the

[25] *Ibid.*, Feb. 17, 1889.
[26] *Ibid.*, Apr. 8, 22, Oct. 7, 1888, Feb. 10, 17, 1889.
[27] *Ibid.*, Aug. 19, 1888.   [28] *Ibid.*, Mar. 3, 1889.
[29] *Ibid.*, Aug. 19, 1888, Mar. 31, 1889.   [30] *Ibid.*, Oct. 27, 1889.
[31] *Ibid.*, Mar. 25, 1888, Oct. 27, 1889.
[32] At the end of his thesis on German socialism Jaurès bowed to Malon, in whose work socialism became an "image of humanity, of eternity."—

elections of 1889 sent Jaurès back to the academic world, he wrote a doctoral dissertation on the origins of the German socialist movement. Finally, when he won a by-election against De Solages in 1892, he formally joined the socialist group in Parliament, and then the *Parti ouvrier français*. Henceforth Jaurès devoted his tremendous energy, his controversial skill, and his oratorical genius, to furthering the cause of the socialist ideal.

Jaurès, however, did not take kindly to Marx's view of class struggle and violent revolution. The socialist movement, as he conceived it, was to be a continuation of the democratic movement of the French Republic; it would be based on a united Third Estate, embracing small producers and shopkeepers as well as peasants and proletarians; and it would overthrow capitalism by using the same democratic government that the French Revolution had used to overthrow feudalism. Socialism, he said, would result "not from the violent and exclusive agitation of a social fraction, but from a kind of national movement."[33]

Jaurès, therefore, sought collaboration between the liberal bourgeoisie and the proletariat. His original plan had been to socialize industry by "trade associations," in which capital and labor worked together in harmony.[34] In 1891, he proposed that the state itself nationalize all credit facilities and use them to purchase industry from the capitalists;[35] and he supplemented

---

"Les Origines du socialisme allemand," *La Revue socialiste,* 1892, XVI, 167. He related that when he turned to socialism, he tried to establish relations with Malon.—*Discours parlementaires,* pp. 177-78. Years later, Jaurès stated that Malon "had been, at the period when my mind was seeking its way, one of the intellectual influences that led me in the socialist direction"; and he added that his interest in Malon was inspired by the manner in which Malon "combined a respect for the revolutionary tradition with a sense of daily, reforming, and progressive action."—"Discours à l'inauguration de monument Benoît Malon," *La Revue socialiste,* 1913, LVIII, 547.

[33] *La Dépêche,* Mar. 17, 1889.
[34] *Ibid.,* Jan. 13, 1888, Mar. 31, 1889.
[35] *Ibid.,* Feb. 11, 1891, June 28, 1892.

this plan with governmental reforms to increase immediately the security and well-being of the workers and peasants.[36]

Jaurès was a staunch and consistent supporter of trade unionism. He defended the miners' strikes at Carmaux as attempts at organization, and he attacked the government for interfering in the strike at Rive-de-Gier in 1893.[37] Credit coöperatives received his support, as did the attempt to establish a coöperative bottle works at Carmaux.[38] But, like the Possibilists, he maintained that the activities of the trade unions and coöperatives could obtain only partial results; that the democratic conquest of political power and the use of the state were indispensable elements in the socialist method.[39]

Jaurès felt certain that this conquest of the state would be aided by the republican bourgeoisie, who would arrive at socialism "partly through necessity, partly through persuasion."[40] He remarked that the French bourgeoisie were, in general, "liberal and humane"; and that they deprecated reforms only because their timidity often overcame their "native generosity."[41] He admitted that many bourgeois (the financial oligarchy and reactionary industrialists) were definitely hostile to reforms; but he explained that this group, of whom Casimir-Périer was a good example, were descendants of those wealthy bourgeois who had abused the French Revolution to place themselves in the position of the nobility, and who had themselves oppressed their workers. But the real republicans were the descendants of those bourgeois who, filled with the spirit of the *Encyclopédie*, had really worked during the revolutions

[36] For example, *ibid.*, Nov. 13, 1890, July 29, 1891, July 4, 31, 1893.

[37] *Ibid.*, Jan. 14, 1891, Nov. 8, 1892, Sept. 25, 1895; *Discours parlementaires*, Feb. 28, 1893, p. 395.

[38] *La Dépêche*, Dec. 18, 1895. For Jaurès's part in the founding of the coöperative bottle works, see Albert Thomas, *Histoire anécdotique du travail* (Paris, n. d.), pp. 265-70.

[39] *La Dépêche*, Apr. 18, 1893, Aug. 5, 12, 1896.

[40] *Ibid.*, May 7, 1890.

[41] *Ibid.*, Mar. 19, 1887, Feb. 19, Nov. 11, 1888, July 21, 1889, May 7, 1890, Sept. 24, 1891; *Discours parlementaires*, Nov. 5, 1894, pp. 883-97.

of 1789, 1830, and 1848 for the welfare of the nation as a whole.

Nevertheless, this very republican bourgeoisie was, as a matter of fact, opposed to socialism; and Jaurès toiled to convince it that socialism was, after all, the logical outcome of the Jacobin tradition. He sugar-coated his defense of socialism with the idealism of the Enlightenment.[42] Rousseau, he argued, dreamed of abolishing the evil effects of property; Diderot and Condorcet wrote of a society in which equality and justice would reign supreme; Diderot called attention to the sufferings of the workers and peasants, and Voltaire, Montesquieu, and Buffon stressed "the social welfare of organized humanity."[43]

Jaurès explained that although the French Revolution was, naturally, not in a position to foresee the growth of modern industry and its peculiar problems, it laid the foundation for later socialism.[44] The Revolution, in the first place, indirectly prepared the future of the proletariat by realizing "the two essential prerequisites of socialism: democracy and capitalism." Through the Declaration of the Rights of Man the Revolution proclaimed the principles of justice and equal rights—the underlying principles of socialism. The Revolutionaries made several applications of the socialist principle of equality, particularly in the organization of public education; in the "admin-

[42] Jaurès constantly argued that socialism was the only means of realizing social justice, of insuring equality and true liberty, of utilizing reason and science for the progress of mankind. See, for example, *La Dépêche,* July 23, 1890, Apr. 29, June 3, 1891, June 15, 1892, Jan. 30, Sept. 24, 1893, June 25, 1894; Jaurès, "L'Organisation socialiste," *La Revue socialiste* (1895), XXI, 265.

[43] See *Pages choisies, op. cit.,* pp. 192-201; Jaurès, "La Doctrine Saint-Simonienne et le socialisme," *La Revue socialiste,* 1903, XXXVIII, 832-37; *Discours parlementaires,* Nov. 5, 1894, pp. 883-84; *La Dépêche,* Sept. 16, 1900.

[44] For Jaurès's ideas on the relation of socialism and the French Revolution see *La Dépêche,* Oct. 22, 1890, Feb. 26, Apr. 8, 1891; *Pages choisies,* pp. 228-31; *Etudes socialistes* (Paris, 1902), pp. 136-40; *La Constituante, 1789-1791, op. cit.,* p. 136; Jaurès, *La Convention, 1793-1794* (Paris, 1902), in *Histoire socialiste,* edited by Jean Jaurès, Vol. III, pp. 324-47, 358-64, Vol. IV, 1486-1576, 1595-1622, 1646-59, 1699-1706, 1747-51, 1786-98, 1820-24.

istration of public possessions and the public domain"; in the destruction of monopolies granted to individuals. The Revolution, moreover, set the example for concerted proletarian action; and the proletariat often exercised decisive influence on the government. Finally, Babeuf brought the first glimmerings of real "modern and industrial communism."

The "right of property" proclaimed by the French Revolution stood athwart Jaurès's demonstration that socialism was the progeny of the Revolution. But he argued that the concentration of industry and finance was depriving the workers, peasants, and petty bourgeoisie of their property; and resorting to Marx, he declared that concentration of ownership was inevitable under capitalism.[45] While capitalism deprived the masses of property, socialism would restore it by adapting it to the "new economic conditions," and allowing everyone to share in collective ownership. The Convention, Jaurès explained, had pointed to the socialist solution by permitting the social control of property in order to prevent it from endangering security and liberty; by proclaiming that society must guarantee to all men subsistence and the right to work; by curbing the property rights of the father in order to insure the equality of the children.[16] Thus, the Revolution introduced the principle of socialism into the family; and the Socialists would complete this work by giving equal rights, not only to all children, but to all men.

To Jaurès the establishment of the Republic was the most convincing proof of the socialist tendency of the Revolution.[47] Economic sovereignty, he contended, logically follows political sovereignty; for, as Diderot pointed out, "what is intolerable is to have slaves and call them citizens." Citing the pressure of the capitalists on the workers, Jaurès declared that there could be no real political democracy until the workers had obtained

[45] La Dépêche, Nov. 4, 1893, Oct. 15, 1894.
[46] Ibid., Oct., 22, 1890; Études socialistes, pp. 214-20.
[47] La Dépêche, Oct. 22, 1890, Jan. 29, 1891, Nov. 6, 1892.

the instruction, well-being, and security, which would enable them to realize their political will.

Jaurès's reconciliation of socialism and the Jacobin tradition appeared so convincing to himself that he believed, in this early period, that even the Moderates or Opportunists would accept socialism; and he declared that he would rather work with the whole republican party, including the Moderates, than with a socialist party exclusively.[48] Jaurès soon perceived that the Opportunists—under the leadership of President Casimir-Périer and Premier Méline—were becoming even more reactionary; but this only led him to conclude that resentment against the reactionaries would throw the remainder of the republicans into the socialist camp.[49]

For a short time Jaurès waited to see the Radicals migrate *en masse* into the socialist movement.[50] He was, however, beginning to realize that the Radicals were interested in political rather than social reforms, and that the Radical-controlled Parliament was guilty of "lassitude, indifference, and political somnolence."[51] He admitted that his ambition to bring all the republicans into a socialist party was "evidently the error, the slightly naïve illusion of youth."[52] He decided that the proletariat was the only class vitally interested in social emancipation, and that the Socialists should have a separate organization—"while working for the evolution of the entire country toward the Republic, and the entire Republic toward socialism."[53]

When about 1892 Jaurès reluctantly gave up the idea of the Radicals' joining a separate socialist party, he substituted party alliance for out-and-out fusion. He hoped for an alliance uniting separate organizations for common action against financial

[48] *Ibid.*, Oct. 22, Nov. 27, 1890.
[49] *Ibid.*, Feb. 24, Sept. 28, 1892, May 1, 1894, Aug. 7, 1895, Jan. 21, 1897. *Discours parlementaires*, Apr. 20, 1894, pp. 592, 618.
[50] *La Dépêche*, Apr. 2, July 23, 1890.
[51] *Ibid.*, Apr. 2, 29, July 23, 1890, Apr. 23, 1891.
[52] *Ibid.*, Jan. 11, 1893.
[53] *Ibid.*, Apr. 23, May 7, Nov. 18, 1891, Jan. 11, 1893.

oligarchy and clerical reaction and for the program of minimum socialist reforms—those reforms "which, although not touching the bases of the existing order, will do much to ameliorate the lot of the workingmen and to pave the way for a social transformation."[54] Jaurès decided that Socialists must not enter a bourgeois ministry, for they would be "captives," and might consent to dangerous compromises; but this would not prevent the Socialists from supporting ministries which were made up entirely of republicans.[55]

The Marxian Socialists, as well as the republican bourgeoisie, balked at Jaurès's plan for a national movement to defend the Republic and to achieve socialism at the same time. Not only did the Marxists refuse to join a "Republican Concentration," but their talk of class struggle and violent revolution alienated the republican bourgeoisie.

Jaurès attacked the Marxian program as "revolutionary romanticism," dangerous to socialism because it identified socialism with the violence of the Anarchists and thus prevented the liberal bourgeoisie from joining the socialist movement.[56] Like Malon, he argued that violent revolution was "an impotent folly" leading only to reactionary repression and prolonging injustice. Especially for France, violent revolution was an anachronism, for France possessed universal suffrage—"the revolutionary instrument of the modern period."

Faced with the Marxian repudiation, on the basis of economic determinism, of class collaboration, Jaurès turned to a more elaborate defense of humanitarian idealism than that of the Possibilists.[57] In debating with Lafargue, who held that

[54] For example, ibid., Apr. 7, July 26, 1892. For the reforms suggested by Jaurès as the immediate goal of the alliance, some of which were intended to alleviate the condition of the small manufacturer and shopkeeper, see ibid., Apr. 7, 1892, Sept. 10, 1893, Jan. 29, 1896.

[55] Ibid., Sept. 10, 1893.

[56] Ibid., May 7, 1890, May 20, 1891, Nov. 14, 1892, Apr. 18, 1893.

[57] The thesis of Jaurès's dissertation on the origins of German socialism was to show that German socialism was the result of German philosophy, beginning with Luther and ending with Hegel; and he contended that the development of German socialism "indicates, first of all, how events pro-

idealism was a reflection of bourgeois interests, Jaurès argued that belief in the value of idealism in furthering the socialist movement could be reconciled with Marx's materialism.[58] He agreed with Lafargue that ideas are produced by a cerebral process, but he held that ideas are influenced not only by economic conditions but also by a certain "cerebral preformation of humanity" which arose through prehistoric psychological development. In this "cerebral preformation," the most important element is "the sympathetic sentiment of fraternal reconciliation." When economic conditions affect the mind, they set in motion this primitive sentiment. The contradiction between this sentiment and economic conditions accounts for social change; and the fact that the trend of development is from cannibalism to slavery, from slavery to serfdom, from serfdom to the wage system, from the wage system to the socialist régime, indicates that development has taken place in "an intelligible direction with a sense of the ideal."[59]

Passing to concrete policies, Jaurès held that "class struggle" could be interpreted to mean that the proletariat would best serve its interests by forming a separate political party; and a separate political party did not imply that socialism was a class movement or that the socialist party should enter into conflict

---

ceed from ideas, how history depends on philosophy." "Les Origines du socialisme allemand," *La Revue socialiste,* 1892, XV, 643 ff.

[58] Debate with Lafargue (1894), reprinted in *Pages choisies,* pp. 358 ff. Jaurès defined idealism as "the conception that humanity, from its beginning, had a vague idea, a first presentiment of its destiny, of its development. Before the experience of history, before the constitution of such and such an economic system, humanity created in itself a preliminary ideal of history, the ideal of humanity."—*Ibid.,* p. 360.

[59] Jaurès considered this reconciliation of idealism and materialism the basis of his historical writings. In the introduction to his volumes of *Histoire socialiste,* he explained that he was guided by Marx, Michelet, and Plutarch; that he aimed at "understanding and translating the fundamental economic evolution that governed societies; the ardent aspiration of the spirit toward complete truth; and the noble exaltation of the individual conscience defying suffering, tyranny, and death."—*La Constituante, 1789-1791, op. cit.,* pp. 9-10.

with the rest of the nation.[60] On the contrary, if a political party was to win elections, it must make alliances with the bourgeois parties. Hence, the Socialists must abandon the extreme interpretation of the concept of class struggle, to avoid being precipitated into a violent revolution which would fail. They must "strive for the fusion of classes in the common defense of liberty, in the common quest for justice."

But this position led to a special "French Socialism."[61] Jaurès accepted from Marx the idea that the preëmption of surplus value by capital is "a constant levy on the workers"; and the idea that concentration was leading to an ever greater separation of capital and labor, thus rendering inevitable a social transformation. He also accepted from Marx the unity of labor as the condition of emancipation. But, Jaurès added, "all socialism, all collectivism is not in Marx. It comes, in France, from French conceptions and French traditions." The international socialism based on the truths of Marx must "be adapted to our political and economic state, to the traditions, conceptions, genius, of our country."

This "French socialism," according to Jaurès, is idealistic as well as scientific, and (following Fourier, Blanc, and Proudhon) it is based on reciprocal good will, rather than exclusively on class struggle.[62] It attempts to reconcile collectivist organization with individual rights, with individual savings, and with "what is legitimate and essential in individual property." Finally, French socialism "is passionately republican. Never do we separate economic questions from political questions, social justice from liberty, socialism from the Republic."

After instructing the Socialists that their ideal was unrealizable without coöperation by the various classes composing the nation, Jaurès turned to warn the nation that it could not attain unity without binding the proletariat to the other classes

[60] *La Dépêche,* Oct. 27, 1889, July 23, 1890, July 1, Nov. 18, 1891, July 26, 1893.
[61] *Ibid.,* Sept. 25, 1893.　　　　[62] *Ibid.*

through ties of social reform. Jaurès told the bourgeoisie that because capitalism divided the nation "into antagonistic classes filled with hatred," it was a menace to national unity and national welfare.[63] This division between employers and employees, he told them, could be eliminated only by socialism. Indeed, "if I am passionately attached to the socialist idea, it is because socialism, in making all citizens associates, abolishes those struggles which make of present society a barbaric society."[64] Hence, "it is we, we alone, who are the true nationalists, because we alone can bring profound unity to the nation."[65]

Jaurès also tried to convince the bourgeoisie that social justice would give "to our well-beloved France the most glorious position to which a glorious nation can aspire."[66] The Great Revolution had bequeathed to the French Republic the mission of bringing liberty to the world.[67] Upon France now fell the task of leading the world to social justice. By virtue of her tradition of the French Revolution, her "native generosity," her general superior well-being, and her republican institutions which permitted her to achieve socialism without a political revolution, France was "predestined to solve the problem of universal justice."[68] Hence, France alone could, and must, become "mistress of justice and right."

Jaurès assured the bourgeoisie that if France was true to her mission, she would obtain the sympathies of the workers of all countries and her security would be increased.[69] It would become impossible to mobilize the German workers for a war against France. Already the influence of French socialism had

[63] Ibid., Oct. 6, 1889, May 7, 1891; "L'Organisation socialiste," La Revue socialiste, 1896, XXIII, 526; Jaurès, "Le Socialisme (but et moyens)," La Revue socialiste, 1900, XXXI, 259.
[64] La Dépêche, Apr. 10, 1895.
[65] La Petite République, Oct. 4, 1896.
[66] La Dépêche, Feb. 10, 1889, Aug. 5, 1897.
[67] For example, ibid., Feb. 10, 1889, Aug. 21, 27, 1891; Jaurès, La Guerre franco-allemande, p. 40.
[68] For example, ibid., Feb. 19, Apr. 16, 1890, Apr. 8, 1891.
[69] Ibid., Feb. 25, July 2, 1890, Apr. 8, Aug. 27, 1891, Jan. 3, 1893.

increased the strength of the German Socialists; and the latter, in leading the movement to overthrow Bismarck and in voting against German military credits, had weakened German militarism. Eventually, the socialist workers would overthrow the monarchies of the Triple Alliance and end their menace to the security of France.

The growth of German socialism, inspired by the example of France, would bring the liberation of Alsace-Lorraine.[70] Jaurès pointed out that the socialist leaders, Bebel and Liebknecht, were thrown into jail for protesting the annexation of Alsace and Lorraine. Soon the triumph of German socialism, following that of French socialism, would "sweep away Prussian corporalism and the great iniquity of 1870." In short, "socialism is one of the greatest forces of the French *patrie*, and patriotism will win those who through indifference, ignorance, prejudice, or egoism, turn from social justice."[71]

Jaurès's attempt to reconcile socialism and patriotism was handicapped by the Marxists' contention that socialist class struggle and proletarian internationalism logically meant replacing devotion to the nation by devotion to class. But Jaurès had already repudiated the class struggle, and his reformism enabled him to relegate proletarian internationalism to a subordinate position. The aim of international socialist unity, in his opinion, as in the opinion of the Possibilists, was concerted propaganda: to preserve peace, and to press various national parliaments to grant specific reforms—in order to prevent the nation which adopted such reforms from losing competitive advantages.[72] In effect, his tactics, like those of the Possibilists,

[70] For example, *ibid.*, Jan. 9, Feb. 25, 1890, Jan. 14, 1892; *Action socialiste, op. cit.*, pp. 406-10.

[71] *La Dépêche*, July 2, 1890.

[72] For example, *ibid.*, May 7, 1890; Jaurès, "Les Grèves d'Armentières," *La Revue socialiste*, 1903, XXXVIII, 587. Jaurès remarked: "We French Socialists wish to prepare the union of all the workers of the world in order to protect and emancipate labor, in order to lead it to the progressive conquest of industrial capital. We wish it because the great economic and social movements cannot be accomplished in our country without peril; the eight-hour day, for example, must be realized about the same time in

stressed the unity of the different classes of each nationality, rather than the international unity of each of the several classes. Jaurès denounced as "a blind calumny" the charge of his opponents that the Socialists were *sans-patrie* because they were internationalists.[73] He explained that the Socialists intended to federate nations in the future order, "to reconcile all the autonomous nations without abolishing them"; that socialist internationalism, in fighting for peace, was serving the interests of France which needed peace; and that the French Revolution had been "internationalist and patriotic at the same time."[74]

Indeed, Jaurès argued, the pacific attainment of socialism itself required that the Socialists serve the nation and defend it from "all aggressions and all humiliations."[75] *La patrie,* he stated, is for the workers "not only a sacred tradition, it is the natural, immediate field of action where their propaganda for justice must be realized. The nations have nothing to fear from the international solidarity of the workers, and France less than the others. From the political point of view, France's free and flexible institutions permit her to support, without a new revolution, the development of social democracy, which, one day or another, will crush the monarchies. From the economic point of view, as to leisure and wages our workers are in a situation superior to that of the German, Austrian, and Italian workers."[76]

Jaurès believed that these advantages made the French nation necessary not only to the French Socialists but also to the proletarians of all nations. "If we, French Socialists, were indifferent to the honor, to the security, to the prosperity of France, it would not only be a crime against *la patrie* . . . it would also be a crime against humanity. A free, great, strong

---

all the industrial countries, because a people who marches toward the future cannot be isolated from humanity."—*La Dépêche,* Jan. 3, 1893.
    [73] *La Dépêche,* Jan. 3, Sept. 10, 1893.
    [74] *Ibid.,* Sept. 3, 1891, Jan. 3, 1893; *Discours parlementaires,* Feb. 15, 1894, p. 559; *Action socialiste,* pp. 406-10.
    [75] *La Dépêche,* May 29, 1893.   [76] *Ibid.,* May 7, 1890.

France is necessary to humanity. It is in France that democracy has obtained its most logical form—the Republic; and if France falls reaction will rise in the world."[77]

The Marxists, as we have seen, had rejected these patriotic conclusions of the Reformists, in the 1880's; but in the 1890's the concepts of the French Marxists were undergoing a transformation. This transformation resulted, to a considerable extent, from their unexpected successes at the polls. The parliamentary elections of 1889 sent thirteen Socialists of different shades to the Chamber of Deputies.[78] The municipal elections of 1892 resulted in socialist majorities in more than twenty-five municipal councils, including those of such cities as Marseilles, Toulon, and Guesde's stronghold, Roubaix. In the parliamentary elections of 1893, the Socialists won fifty seats. Guesde, who was himself elected, hailed it as "a veritable revolution."[79] These years also witnessed the transition of Jaurès, Millerand, Viviani, Briand, and others, from Jacobinism to socialism. They were welcomed by the Marxists into the socialist movement, but they stressed evolutionary as against revolutionary procedure.

In these circumstances the Marxists between 1893 and 1898 relaxed their emphasis on the class struggle and began to appeal to the bourgeoisie with the slogan that socialism was "the party of social peace."[80] Guesde remarked that "in the present *milieu* the interests of both the employed class and the employing class can evolve peacefully, without sacrifice and without suicide."[81]

Universal suffrage came to be regarded by the Marxists as "the instrument for solving pacifically all questions."[82] They finally promised that they would lay aside revolutionary tactics, insisting, with Guesde, that if the government did not

[77] *Ibid.,* Jan. 3, 1893.
[78] Zévaès, *Le Socialisme en France depuis 1871, op. cit.,* pp. 105, 132-33.
[79] *Ibid.,* pp. 147-48.
[80] *Aux travailleurs; Conseil national du P.O.F., op. cit.,* July 2, 1893, pp. 42-43; Guesde, *Quatres Ans de lutte de classe* (Paris, 1901), I, 211, 214.
[81] *Quatres Ans de lutte de classe,* I, 131.   [82] *Ibid.,* I, 183, 190; II, 21.

force revolution on the Socialists, they would observe "existing legality" and "proceed evolutionarily" toward their goal.[83] In the Chamber of Deputies, Guesde stressed social reforms to make of the proletariat "the conscious and capable instruments of their fundamental and definitive emancipation."[84] This shift to the use of the democratic method was seconded in the manifestoes of the *Parti ouvrier français*.[85]

Guesde now insisted that if the Republic were endangered, the Socialists would at once become a "battalion in the *avant-garde* of the republican army."[86] Likewise Guesde now denounced the reactionaries for calling the French Socialists antipatriotic and insisted that they needed no lessons in patriotism.[87] "The tricolor," he exclaimed, "belongs to us as well as to you, and I forbid you to monopolize it."[88]

Guesde asked the Chamber of Deputies to make real patriots of the proletarians by giving them a stake in property; and he argued that the immediate reforms proposed by the Socialists would arrest the decline of the birth rate, the high infant mortality rate, and the physiological degeneration of the French because of overwork—all of which were injurious to the defensive force of the nation.[89] He agreed with Jaurès in maintaining that the return of Alsace-Lorraine—attached to France "by heart, history, and the future"—would result from the growth of German socialism.[90]

---

[83] *Ibid.,* I, 124-27.
[84] *Ibid.,* I, 46, 103-16, 167, 204-6, 230-31; II, 119-23, 126.
[85] See *Aux travailleurs* . . . , 1893-98, pp. 44-45, 59-62, 73.
[86] *Quatres Ans de lutte de classe,* I, 29-30; *Aux travailleurs* . . . , Apr., 1898, p. 72.
[87] *Quatres Ans de lutte de classe,* I, 99; II, 196-202.
[88] *Ibid.,* I, 200; *Aux travailleurs* . . . , July, 1893, pp. 31-34, 45.
[89] *Quatres Ans de lutte de classe,* I, 49-50, 155, 171, 190, 220, 275, 283; II, 106.
[90] *Ibid.,* II, 171-84, 192, 209. An election notice of the P.O.F. read: "Patriots of Roubaix and Wattrelos! To vote for Eugène Motte is to vote for the Emperor of Germany, whom the political patrons of Von Moltke—the Mélines and the Hanotaux—have had the impudence to acclaim at Kiel with the arms of the French Republic! To vote for Jules Guesde is to vote for Alsace-Lorraine, which, by electing Bebel and Beub have once again

Socialist internationalism was explained away. Like Jaurès, Guesde maintained that this internationalism did not weaken "the patriotic sentiments of the Socialists," for it aimed not to destroy national units, but to establish a régime in which they would all live together in harmony.[91] The Marxists no longer looked to war to unleash revolution, asserting that war would result "only in unprecedented disasters" and an increase of "Asiatic barbarism as represented by Russian Tsarism."[92] Socialist internationalism, by working for peace, operated "not against the nations of today, but for their benefit and their higher development."[93]

In order to explain their patriotism further, the Marxists even dragged out French socialist tradition and the mission of France, which they had formerly called rationalizations of bourgeois exploitation. The Utopian Socialists, the insurrections of Lyons in 1832, of Paris in 1848 and 1871, and the birth of the Second International at Paris, were cited as evidence of France's leadership in the socialist movement.[94] The Socialist party is "the true patriotic party" because it will give France the leadership of international socialism and will trans-

protested against the criminal annexation of these provinces."—Quoted from Léon de Seilhac, *L'Utopie socialiste* (Paris, 1908), p. 65. See also Zévaès, *La Question de l'Alsace Lorraine et le socialisme* (Paris, 1917), p. 62.

[91] *Quatres Ans de lutte de classe*, II, 196, 206-7.

[92] *Aux travailleurs* . . . , Jan. 23, 1893, p. 33.

[93] *Quatres Ans de lutte de classe*, II, 207. A party manifesto explained that nations have been "necessary stages toward the human unity to which we tend and of which internationalism, engendered everywhere by modern civilization, represents a new and also ineluctable stage." But, in the same way that the development of nations from provinces has benefited the provinces by taking away their former antagonism, so the development of *la patrie humaine* will benefit the present nations rather than harm them. In the same way as a Breton, a Burgundian, or a Provençal, does not cease being a Breton, a Burgundian, or a Provençal, while becoming a Frenchman, so a Frenchman, in becoming an internationalist, does not cease being a Frenchman. *Aux travailleurs* . . . , Jan. 23, 1893, p. 32.

[94] *Aux travailleurs* . . . , Jan. 23, 1893, pp. 33-34. Guesde was now much more complimentary to the French Revolution. See *Quatres Ans de lutte de classe*, I, 205; II, 71.

form "discredited, drooping France" into a great "emancipating France."[95]

The Marxists thus pledged themselves to defend France. A resolution of a congress of the *Parti ouvrier français* declared "that France, if attacked, will not have more ardent and more conscientious defenders than the Socialists of the *Parti ouvrier*, convinced of the great rôle that is reserved for her in the next social revolution."[96] Previously the Marxists had rejected the suggestion of the Anarchists that in time of war the proletarians should refuse to respond to mobilization; and the Marxists had argued that this general strike would prevent the arming of the proletarians and their marching upon the state.[97] Now a manifesto of the Marxists declared that their condemnation of the general strike in time of war was evidence that they had always intended to defend the country.[98] Thus, in the years from 1892 to 1898, the emphasis had been shifted from revolution to patriotism. The harmony between Marxists and Reformists, however, was again shaken by the Dreyfus Affair.

[95] *Aux travailleurs* . . . , July 29, 1893, p. 46.
[96] *Quatres Ans de lutte de classe,* II, 196.
[97] See above, pp. 21-22.
[98] *Aux travailleurs* . . . , Aug., 1896, p. 66. See also *Quatres Ans de lutte de classe,* I, 283.

IV

THE SECOND CONFLICT BETWEEN
MARXISTS AND REFORMISTS

THE Dreyfus Affair and its sequel, the entrance of Millerand into a coalition ministry, marked the beginning of the second period of struggle within the ranks of the Socialists. These two events coincided with a reaction against reformism throughout Europe. The Marxists refused to collaborate with the bourgeoisie to save the Republic and to obtain reforms; and they returned, for the moment, to their emphasis on class struggle and revolution. This led to a break with the Reformists, and to a heated controversy lasting six years.

This controversy had several important effects on the subsequent history of the French socialist movement. The bulk of the party was unified; and as the majority was reformist, this unity discouraged revolutionary and antipatriotic minorities, thus helping to prepare the mass of French workers for concerted patriotic action. The extreme right wing of the Reformists, led by Millerand, left the party and proceeded to find a place for itself among the nonsocialist bourgeois parties. At the same time, the successful results of mass pressure during the Dreyfus Affair, together with the meager results of ministerial participation, brought a revulsion against parliamentary methods among many of the workers. This change of attitude gave impetus to the growth of revolutionary syndicalism, the ideas of which penetrated into the unified Socialist Party. The adherence of the Syndicalists to a strict construction of the class struggle and their rejection of the national state led them to an absolute negation of the nation. These three important movements each affected the use of the concept of patriotism in French socialism.

The Dreyfus Affair occasioned the renewal of controversy between Marxists and Reformists. The Affair, entering the political arena as a question of legal justice, became a struggle over the democratic Republic itself. In December, 1894, Captain Dreyfus, an Alsatian Jew, was accused of selling military information to Germany, found guilty, and sentenced to Devil's Island for life.[1] Two years after the conviction of Dreyfus, Lieutenant Colonel Picquart, the new chief of the military intelligence service, charged Major Marie Charles Esterhazy with the crime; but the General Staff, holding that the honor of the army was at stake, refused to reopen the case. The cause of the "Revisionists" who fought for a retrial of Dreyfus was aided by Émile Zola, who in January, 1898, wrote his famous indictment *J'accuse*, and by Scheurer-Kestner, the eminent Alsatian Senator. The General Staff was supported by the anti-Semites (particularly by Edouard Drumont and his organ, *La Libre parole*) who had attacked Dreyfus since the beginning of the Affair. The General Staff was finally forced to try Esterhazy, but he was acquitted.

The movement for "revision" became a serious political question. The "Anti-Dreyfusards" included all the anti-parliamentary groups: politically conservative Catholics; a large part of the Catholic clergy; the anti-Semites; the monarchists; the remnants of the Boulangist group, adopting the name "Nationalist"; and high-ranking army officers.[2] The "Revisionists" or "Dreyfusards" consisted of republican "intellectuals" who either pitied Dreyfus as a victim of injustice or disliked the pretensions of the army chiefs to infallibility; of Protestants, Freemasons, and Jews; of Radical republicans like Clemenceau; and of Socialists and Anarchists. As time went on "the struggle between the two coalitions became a conflict over the

[1] For the details of the Dreyfus Affair, see Seignobos, *L'Évolution de la 3ᵉ République*, pp. 193 ff.; Jaurès, *Les Épreuves* (Paris, 1898). For an account in English, see Matthew Josephson, *Zola and His Times* (New York, 1928), ch. xvi.
[2] Seignobos, *op. cit.*, p. 197.

internal policies of France."[3] It became a fight between the champions and the opponents of the Third Republic.

Zola's *J'accuse* awakened the resentment of Jaurès and he became alarmed over the threat of the anti-Dreyfusard militarists to the Republic. Jaurès had long suspected that nationalist anti-Semitism was a maneuver of the reaction to increase the popularity of the clergy under the guise of religious warfare.[4] He now feared that the "military and clerical reaction" was using anti-Semitism, together with "pretended patriotism and false nationalism," as the mask of a renewed onslaught against the Republic.[5] He warned that if high ranking army officers became familiar with the use of illegal procedures, they would establish a military dictatorship favorable to the Church and the capitalists, but disastrous to the movement for social emancipation.[6]

Jaurès became alarmed at the prospects of a *coup d'état* against the Republic.[7] He saw such a threat in the demonstrations of the nationalist bands, particularly against the new president, Loubet; in the rumors that the reaction was fomenting strikes to provide a pretext for "shooting the republicans and the workers at the same time"; and in the attempt of Déroulède, whom Jaurès considered a reactionary, to seize the presidential palace.[8]

All the reformist Socialists shared his alarm. The Possibilist *Fédération des travailleurs socialistes,* discerning a danger to the Republic similar to the danger they had fought against during the Boulangist crisis, took "their fighting post in the *avant-*

---

[3] *Ibid.,* p. 198.

[4] See *La Dépêche,* Feb. 5, 1890, June 2, 1892.

[5] See *ibid.,* Jan. 22, 28, 1898.

[6] See *ibid.,* Jan. 13, 22, Feb. 16, Nov. 17, 1898, Jan. 26, 1899; *Les Épreuves,* pp. vii-lx, 11-14; "Revue politique", *La Revue socialiste,* 1898, XXXVIII, 387-92.

[7] This danger of a *coup d'état* appeared when Colonel Henry, an intimate friend of Esterhazy, confessed to forging documents attributed to Dreyfus and then committed suicide in prison. See Seignobos, *op. cit.,* pp. 201-5.

[8] See *La Dépêche,* Sept. 15, Oct. 12, 19, 1898, Oct. 5, Nov. 4, 1899; "Revue politique," *La Revue socialiste,* 1898, XXVIII, 517.

garde of the republican army."[9] The followers of Allemane organized mass demonstrations of workers to counteract the nationalist bands.[10]

The Marxists, though aware that the danger to the Republic was considerable, feared to fall into the trap of collaboration with bourgeois liberals on a common platform of republicanism. In July, 1898, an election manifesto of the *Parti ouvrier français* cautioned the workers to fight anti-Semitism, but to shun the war between Dreyfusards and Anti-Dreyfusards as a family quarrel of bourgeois factions, "both equally enemies of our class and of socialism."[11] In October, 1898, however, they became so disturbed over the danger of a *coup d'état* that they joined with the other socialist groups to form a permanent Committee of Vigilance for united action in anticipation of "all eventualities."[12] Guesde, as well as the Reformists (Jaurès, Millerand, Briand, Brousse, Allemane, Fournière, and Viviani) took part in forming the Committee. A proclamation of the Committee stated that "it will not permit the militarist conspiracy to touch the too few republican liberties, and it will not leave the street to the reaction and its violences."[13] Jaurès hailed this meeting as an indication that "the socialist proletariat is ready to fight for the safety of the Republic"; and he suggested that further unity be obtained by means of a socialist congress.[14] This congress actually met, but the unity of the Socialists was short-lived; for the Marxists were not willing to fight for the Republic to the extent of uniting with the bourgeoisie in a common ministry.

The Court of Cassation revoked the sentence against Dreyfus on the grounds of technical illegality and inadequate evi-

[9] Humbert, *Les Possibilistes*, pp. 78-79.
[10] Charnay, *Les Allemanists*, pp. 92-101.
[11] See *Aux travailleurs; Conseil national du P.O.F.*, July 24, 1898, pp. 75-76.
[12] Zévaès, *Le Socialisme en France depuis 1871*, pp. 293-94; Charnay, *op. cit.*, p. 101; Humbert, *op. cit.*, p. 81.
[13] Zévaès, *op. cit.*, pp. 293-94.
[14] *La Dépêche*, Oct. 19, 1898; Humbert, *op. cit.*, p. 82.

dence, and ordered a new trial. As a result, the danger of a *coup d'état* became still more acute.[15] Loubet appointed Waldeck-Rousseau, a moderate Republican, to form a "ministry of republican defense." The ministry consisted largely of Moderates, but it also included two Radicals, a Socialist (Millerand), and General Gallifet, "The Butcher" (commander of the Versailles forces sent against the Paris Commune of 1871), who was to offset the presence of Millerand and to assure the bourgeoisie of the safe and sound character of the ministry.[16]

Jaurès had, since the beginning of the Dreyfus Affair, desired to work in harmony with the Republican bourgeoisie.[17] He had welcomed the formation of the "League for the Defense of the Rights of Man and of the Citizen," made up of Socialists and republican bourgeois intellectuals. And although he had previously frowned on the prospect of "captive Socialists," he was now happy that Millerand entered the cabinet to help avert the growing danger of a *coup d'état*.[18] The dangers of sharing responsibilities with the bourgeoisie, he explained, could be overcome if the action of the socialist minister was regulated by a unified socialist party.[19]

The Marxists, however, unqualifiedly rejected the participation of a Socialist in the ministry. In the first place, they heartily detested Gallifet. Then, the question of ministerial participation became involved in the general question of reform versus revolution. Millerand, like Jaurès, approached socialism from the point of view of a radical Jacobin;[20] and he had long been regarded as the spokesman for the right wing of the

[15] Seignobos, *op. cit.*, p. 206.   [16] *Ibid.*, pp. 206-7.
[17] *La Dépêche*, Oct. 26, 1898.
[18] *Ibid.*, June 29, July 13, 28, 1899.   [19] *Ibid.*, July 13, 1899.
[20] Millerand explained that he had accepted socialism because it was necessary to win the support of the workingmen to the Republic; to prevent violent revolution; and to fulfill the aims of the French Revolution by abolishing classes in the social sphere as the Revolution had abolished them in the political sphere. Millerand, *Le Socialisme réformiste français* (Paris, 1903), pp. 6, 31, 62-64.

socialist movement.[21] He pointed out that he entered the ministry to help save the Republic and to secure reforms increasing the liberty and well-being of the workers.[22]

Millerand at once began to enact, by executive decree, regulations to improve factory hygiene; to prevent industrial accidents; to ameliorate conditions of work for women and children; to secure a shorter working day and a weekly day of rest for employes of companies serving the government; and to provide an eight-hour day for government functionaries in the Department of Postal Service, Telegraphs, and Telephones.[23] He obtained from Parliament laws limiting the working day to ten and a half hours in factories employing both sexes, and a law to abolish private employment agencies charging fees. To achieve through arbitration a "régime of peace and growing harmony," Millerand reorganized the Superior Council of Labor, admitting representatives of trade unions and employers; increased the participation of workers in existing trade-arbitration boards and strengthened their power to settle labor disputes; proposed legislation to enforce a majority vote in all strikes and to provide compulsory arbitration in all disputes.[24] In short, Millerand's activities seemed a step toward the achievement of socialism along reformist lines.

Toward the end of the eighteen nineties, however, there appeared throughout the European socialist movement a growing reaction against reformism. A world-wide controversy between Marxists and Reformists (or "Revisionists," as they were called at this time) began in Germany with the attempt

[21] At the famous banquet of Saint-Mandé in 1896—at which all branches of the party were assembled to celebrate an electoral victory, Millerand's speech was accepted as a delimitation of the socialist frontier on the right. Orry, Les Socialistes indépendants, op. cit., pp. 26-27.

[22] Le Socialisme réformiste français, pp. 13-17, 49-56; "Le Congrès de Bordeaux," La Revue socialiste, 1903, XXVII, 541, 547-50.

[23] For the reforms of Millerand, see A. Lavy, L'Œuvre de Millerand (Paris, 1902), pp. 7-47, 91-138, 175-85, 189-215, 262-74.

[24] Ibid., pp. 27-84, 141-47, 152-70, 236-48.

of Eduard Bernstein to revise Marx. Bernstein held that since the concentration of wealth, the decline of the middle class, and the pauperization of the masses, were not occurring as Marx and Engels had predicted, the Socialists should discard the ideas of class struggle, violent revolution, and a dictatorship of the proletariat and should look to achieving socialism by the action of universal suffrage, supplemented by trade unions and coöperative societies.[25] Karl Kautsky, opposing Bernstein, insisted that no advance toward socialism could be made before the Socialists conquered the state; and that parliamentary reforms, as well as trade-union and coöperative action, were incapable of bringing about the social transformation.[26] Kautsky, however, believed it possible to arrive at the socialist domination of the state—the beginning of the socialist realization—without a violent revolution.[27] It remained for a third group, led by Rosa Luxemburg and Karl Liebknecht, to uphold complete Marxism by advocating the seizure of the state by revolution and the establishment of a dictatorship of the proletariat.[28]

Rosa Luxemburg, in an article attacking Millerand, stated that from Bernstein's point of view ("the *progressive infiltration* of socialism into bourgeois society") the entrance of a Socialist into the ministry was desirable.[29] But, she argued, from the point of view of those who expected to achieve

[25] For the ideas of Bernstein, see his *Evolutionary Socialism* (trans. by E. C. Harvey, New York, 1911); *Socialisme théorique et démocratie pratique* (Paris, 1900); "Démocratie et socialisme," *Le Mouvement socialiste*, 1899, II, 324 ff.; "La Révision du programme social-democrate," *La Revue socialiste*, 1909, XLVIX, 507 ff.

[26] For the ideas of Kautsky, see his *Le Marxisme et son critique Bernstein* (Paris, 1900); *Le Programme socialiste* (Paris, 1910); "Démocratie et lutte de classe: réponse à Bernstein," *Le Mouvement socialiste*, 1899, II, 385 ff.

[27] *Le Marxisme et son critique Bernstein*, pp. 289, 315-39.

[28] For the ideas of this group (the nucleus of the later Spartacans), see Rosa Luxemburg, *Réforme ou révolution* (Paris, 1932).

[29] Rosa Luxemburg, "Une Question de tactique; le cas Millerand," *Le Mouvement socialiste*, 1899, III, 132-37.

socialism only by breaking down the capitalist order, the Socialists should accept only those positions which would enable them to attack capitalism. As long as bourgeois society existed the Socialists must remain a *"party of opposition"*; and they must refuse to accept positions within the ministry.

The French Marxists, led by Guesde and Lafargue, accepted the thesis of Luxemburg. They argued that the class struggle forbade the alliance of the proletariat "with any section of the bourgeoisie whatsoever"; that participation in a bourgeois cabinet divided the proletariat, dissipated its energies, and threw the blame for the repressive activities of the bourgeois government on the Socialists.[30] Lafargue pointed out that the Waldeck-Rousseau ministry had sent troops against the striking workers at Nantes; and that Jaurès, feeling forced to support the ministry, had cautioned the socialist congress not to vote a hasty motion of censure against the government.[31]

Guesde and Lafargue admitted that ministerial participation was a logical consequence of the reformist policy, but they now repudiated this policy as a deviation from the class struggle; and they stressed the idea of violent revolution and a dictatorship of the proletariat.[32] The concept of the class struggle, Lafargue argued, meant that the Socialists must remain a party of "irreducible opposition."[33] Guesde added that all attempted changes before the revolutionary conquest of the state were not only useless but tended to delay the revolutionary advance; that Millerand had accomplished nothing but "lies

[30] Guesde and Jaurès, *Les Deux Méthodes* (Lille, 1900), pp. 10 ff.; *Cinquième Congrès socialiste international, Paris, 1900*, pp. 145-53; *Congrès générale des organisations socialistes françaises, Paris, 1899*, pp. 114-17, 177-87; Lafargue, *Le Socialisme et le conquête des pouvoirs publics* (Lille, 1899), pp. 14, 23.

[31] *Congrès générale* . . . *1899*, pp. 29-30, 117-19.

[32] *Ibid.*, pp. 111-14; *Cinquième Congrès socialiste international, 1900*, pp. 146-48; Lafargue, *Le Socialisme et les intellectuels* (Paris, 1900), pp. 28-30; *Le Socialisme et la conquête des pouvoirs*, pp. 3, 11-18, 24-31; *Les Deux Méthodes, op. cit.*, pp. 13-14.

[33] *Le Socialisme et la conquête des pouvoirs publics*, pp. 11-25.

of reforms"; and that this experience had proven conclusively the sterility of a socialist minister in a bourgeois cabinet.[34]

The most sinister of all the dangers inherent in ministerial participation, in Guesde's opinion, was that it divided the international proletariat. Guesde, again concerned with the idea of international class revolution, held that the international class was the social unit to which the Socialists owed supreme devotion; and that the international proletariat must be united not only by a common aim but also by a uniform method.[35] When, he asserted, Jaurès and the other Reformists, intent on ministerial participation in France, declared that in different countries Socialists must evolve different methods, and that the International must not submit the French Socialists to a uniform system of tactics, these Reformists divided the international proletariat. And Jaurès was "declared guilty, whether he likes it or not and in spite of the horror he professes to feel for the word, of being a nationalist of a new variety, a variety that is more dangerous than the other."

Guesde, moreover, charged that ministerial participation would tie the workers of each nation to the bourgeoisie and thus divide the international proletariat. Ministerial participation, he warned, would destroy socialist opposition to war and pit the various socialist groups against one another; for when each nation had a Millerand, each proletariat would have to support its government against the proletarians of other nations.[36]

Siding with the Guesdists were a group of Socialists who followed the ideas of Auguste Blanqui.[37] This group was

[34] *Congrès générale . . . 1899*, pp. 182-83; *Cinquième Congrès socialiste international, 1900;* pp. 146-47; *Les Deux méthodes*, pp. 13-14; Guesde, *Socialisme au jour le jour* (Paris, 1899), Preface, p. ii; Guesde, Bebel, Vaillant, *Discours de Jules Guesde, Auguste Bebel, Edouard Vaillant à Amsterdam* (Paris, 1904), pp. 3-7.

[35] *Discours de Jules Guesde . . .* , pp. 9-11.

[36] *Congrès générale . . . 1899*, p. 188; *Cinquième Congrès socialiste international, 1900*, pp. 149-50.

[37] See Samuel Bernstein, *The Beginnings of Marxian Socialism in France, op. cit.*, pp. 10-17.

small, but in Edouard Vaillant, a prominent member of the Paris Commune of 1871, they possessed one of the foremost socialist leaders. Vaillant and the other Blanquist leaders who had fought in the Commune escaped to London. Here they became acquainted with Marx, accepting many of the latter's conceptions.[38]

Returning to France at the end of the seventies, the Blanquists organized a secret society, dedicated to avenging the suppression of the Commune and to establishing socialism by violent revolution.[39] They came into the open in 1881, and organized the *Comité révolutionnaire central*, which later became the *Parti socialiste révolutionnaire*. Vaillant became a Municipal Councillor of Paris, holding the position from 1883 to 1897. In 1897, he was elected to the Chamber of Deputies, where he remained until the outbreak of the War. The extent of Vaillant's prestige is illustrated by his leadership of the annual demonstration at Père-Lachaise Cemetery, on May 21, in memory of the executed Communards.

Vaillant had returned to Paris a thoroughgoing revolutionary.[40] But the Blanquists, like the Marxists, turned towards reformism during the eighteen-nineties. They, too, were lured by the electoral victories of 1892 and 1893. They, too, won to their views a number of young middle-class intellectuals, including Marcel Sembat, a brilliant and wealthy lawyer, Pierre Renaudel, Maurice Allard, Eugène Baudin, and Jules-Louis Breton. The whole attitude of the group in the years from 1892 to 1898 was summed up by Vaillant when, at the Banquet of Saint-Mandé in 1896, he approved of Millerand's reformist position as marking the boundary of the party on the

---

[38] Charles Da Costa, *Les Blanquists* (Paris, 1912), p. 42.
[39] A manifesto of the group, issued in London in 1874, stated that the Blanquists believed that all bourgeois parties, including the Radicals, were alike; that the class struggle would permit no collaboration with any of them; that universal suffrage was a "dupery"; and that violent revolution was necessary to overthrow capitalism.—Quoted by Da Costa, *op. cit.*, pp. 46-49.
[40] See *Ni Dieu, ni maître*, Nov. 26, 28, Dec. 8, 9, 11, 1880, Mar. 6, 1881.

right.[41] When the conflict over ministerial participation arose, however, Vaillant again emphasized the class struggle, upheld revolution, and denounced ministerial participation as a menace.[42]

Jaurès, faced with the opposition of the Marxists and Blanquists, argued that the concept of the class struggle implied only the formation of a separate socialist party and therefore did not eliminate ministerial participation.[43] Defending reformist strategy, he maintained that there was no longer any truth in Marx's analysis of the conditions in capitalism leading to revolution. There would be no more bourgeois revolutions or international wars which the proletariat could utilize for its revolution.[44] Social reforms and trade unions now prevented the possibility of revolutions resulting from an increasing pauperization of the proletariat; and there was no real possibility of a universal economic cataclysm sufficient to cause the proletariat to revolt.[45] As for the revolutionary dictatorship of the proletariat, Jaurès insisted that the Reformation, the Renaissance, and the French Revolution had filled the people with a consciousness of their rights; and that

[41] Orry, op. cit., pp. 26-27.

[42] See Congrès générale . . . 1899, pp. 90-95; Cinquième Congrès socialiste international, 1900, pp. 158-60.

[43] Congrès générale . . . , 1899, pp. 57-63; Les Deux Méthodes, pp. 2-3.

[44] The bourgeoisie, Jaurès argued, were already in power in most countries, and where they were not yet in power, they possessed the elements of democracy necessary for their peaceful accession. Moreover, Marx expected international wars would result from the attempts of Tsarist Russia to stifle the democratic and national movements in Europe. But Italy and Germany had become unified, and these two nations, as well as England, France, and Belgium, had obtained democratic constitutions. The possibility of Russian intervention had been still further reduced by the growth of liberalism in Russia and the advance of socialism throughout Europe. See Études socialistes, op. cit., pp. xiv-xix, xxvi-xxvii, xxxiii-xxxiv, 37-41. In 1905, when the Russian Revolution emerged from the Russo-Japanese War, Jaurès was forced to admit that revolutions do come from wars; but he fell back on his argument that such revolutions engender overwhelming reactions. Œuvres de Jean Jaurès (Edited by Max Bonnafous. Paris, 1931-35), II, 434.

[45] Études socialistes, pp. xxxviii-1; Quatrième Congrès générale du Parti socialiste français, Tours, 1902, pp. 139-42.

they would not permit a minority of the people to rule.[46] Besides, Jaurès argued, the task of constituting a new social order would necessitate a discipline and coördination attainable only by having the support of the majority.[47] Socialism, in short, would be achieved only by the will of the majority expressed through universal suffrage.[48]

A socialism based on the use of democracy, Jaurès thought, would greatly profit by ministerial participation. Such participation would help defend the democratic Republic; it would hasten the passage of reforms increasing the liberty and wellbeing of the workers, insure the execution of those already passed, and obtain for the socialists the credit of having passed them.[49] Jaurès, unlike Guesde, was impressed by the reforms Millerand accomplished.[50] Then, too, the activities of Socialist ministers would give evidence that the Socialists had in their ranks men capable of administration.[51] Indeed, Jaurès concluded, ministerial participation was so much a consequence of the parliamentarism which the Marxists themselves had accepted, that they would also have accepted ministerial participation if they had not been antagonized by the inclusion of Gallifet in the Waldeck-Rousseau ministry.[52]

[46] *Études socialistes*, pp. 86-88; *Discours parlementaires, op. cit.,* p. 50.
[47] *Études socialistes*, pp. 89-94.
[48] *Ibid.,* pp. xxxvii-1, 43, 89-96 *La Dépêche,* May 21, 1900. At the Congress of Tours in 1902 and the Congress of Bordeaux in 1903, Jaurès declared that the Socialists should not exclude entirely the hypothesis of possible revolution. At the same time, however, he argued against revolution as energetically as he did before and after these two congresses. His acceptance of the revolutionary hypothesis may justifiably be regarded as an attack on the extreme right wing under Millerand, and as a concession to the Marxists for the sake of regaining the unity which he so ardently desired. See *Quatrième Congrès générale, . . . 1902,* p. 143; "Le Congrès de Bordeaux," *La Revue socialiste,* XXXVII, 596-97.
[49] *La Dépêche,* Oct. 27, 1899, Sept. 16, 1900; *Congrès générale . . . 1899,* pp. 55, 59-61; "Discours de Jaurès à Amsterdam," *La Revue socialiste,* 1904, XL, 289-94.
[50] For example, *La Dépêche,* Jan. 21, 1900, June 25, 1901.
[51] *Ibid.,* June 30, 1900.
[52] Jaurès, "L'Entrée de Millerand au ministère," *Le Mouvement socialiste,* 1901, V, 452 ff.

This divergence of opinion over ministerial participation aroused keen antagonism at the Congress of Paris in 1899—the first general socialist congress since the split of the Marxists and Possibilists in 1882.[53] A compromise was reached after bitter debate. The motion adopted declared that in general a Socialist could not enter a bourgeois ministry; but, that under exceptional circumstances the Socialists would pass on the advisability of a temporary participation.[54] Shortly after this congress, an international congress met at Paris and passed the Kautsky Resolution, a further compromise. The Resolution declared that socialism would be achieved not by a *coup de main* but by a long process of organization; and it concluded that a Socialist should not enter a bourgeois ministry except under extraordinary circumstances.[55]

The ambiguity of this so-called "India-rubber Resolution" was soon apparent at the second general congress of the French Socialists at Paris in 1900. Again the main discussion centered on ministerial participation; for the Marxists had been further antagonized by the refusal of some Socialists to vote an investigation of the government's repressive activities at Châlons and by their having voted for a ministerial declaration that repudiated socialism—all because they feared to overthrow a ministry of which Millerand was a member.[56] The conflict became so heated that one of the members of the P.O.F. was stabbed, and the Marxists left the Congress.[57] The socialist schism was completed when the Blanquists left the Congress of Lyons in 1901, after the majority had refused

---

[53] In the preparation for this congress Jaurès was the guiding spirit, for he believed that socialist unity was useful, generally, to aid the social transformation, and, specifically, to frame the conditions for ministerial participation and to draw up a reform program. See *La Dépêche*, July 13, Oct. 27, 1899.

[54] *Congrès générale . . . 1899*, p. 410.

[55] *Cinquième Congrès socialiste international, 1900*, pp. 101-2.

[56] Zévaès, *op. cit.*, pp. 182-83.

[57] *Deuxième Congrès générale . . . 1900*, pp. 158-60.

to expel Millerand from the party.[58] In November, 1901, the Guesdists and Blanquists organized the *Parti socialiste de France*; and at Tours, in 1902, the Reformists formed the *Parti socialiste français*.

The antagonism between the two groups was increased by the support given the government by Jaurès and the members of the *Parti socialiste français*, and by their participation in the left bloc (*Délégation des gauches*). Under Waldeck-Rousseau, the Socialists had been a part of the republican bloc; that is, they abstained from voting against the ministry—even though that ministry was dedicated to fighting social revolution as well as the reaction.[59] Likewise, in the municipal elections of 1900 and in the parliamentary elections of 1902 Jaurès favored the coöperation of the Socialists with "sincere and democratic republicans," to forestall the reaction and advance the movement for social reforms.[60]

When in 1902 Ernest Combes formed a ministry, less conservative than that of Waldeck-Rousseau, the republican bloc became the left bloc, and the members of the *Parti socialiste français* were included in it until 1905. After Combes's declaration of policy, Jaurès announced that the basis of the Socialists' alliance with the Radicals would be the progressive income tax, national organization of education, workingmen's pensions, the Two-Year Army Law, and the separation of Church and state.[61] With the support of the Radicals Jaurès was elected vice-president of the Chamber of Deputies in 1902.[62]

In justifying his position Jaurès stressed the gains for re-

[58] Vaillant proposed that Millerand be regarded not as a socialist, but as a bourgeois minister; but the De la Porte resolution which contained this idea was rejected by the congress. *Troisième Congrès générale . . . 1901,* pp. 241-42, 381-84; Louis, *Histoire du socialisme en France,* pp. 283-85.

[59] Seignobos, *L'Évolution de la 3ᵉ République,* p. 210.

[60] *La Dépêche,* May 21, Aug. 23, 1901.

[61] Orry, *op. cit.,* p. 60.

[62] *Ibid.*

form and for security of the Republic.[63] He particularly pointed to the Radicals' drive on the Church. The Marxists considered anticlericalism as a "deviation" from class struggle policies;[64] but Jaurès, having regarded the Church as the "principal inspirer and organizer of the whole anti-Republican campaign" during the Dreyfus Affair and as the greatest enemy of socialism, became ever more anxious to curb the Church.[65] He called for a fourfold attack: (1) secularization of the wealth of the Church and the return of its mortmain to the nation; (2) suppression of the religious orders; (3) substitution of education by the state for all education by the Church; (4) separation of Church and state.[66] For Jaurès, the finest fruit of political collaboration between the Radicals and the Socialists was the anticlerical legislation carried through by Briand in the Combes ministry.[67]

Nevertheless, Jaurès lost the battle. This was due, to a considerable extent, to the action of Millerand and his right-wing colleagues, for they moved so far to the right that the majority of Reformists themselves felt that the Millerandists had virtually ceased to be Socialists.

The position of the followers of Millerand was set forth by Joseph Sarraute, the theorist of the faction. Unlike most of the Reformists, who paid lip-service to the concept of the class struggle, Sarraute called it "a consecrated cult" and a "mysterious idol."[68] He argued that the class struggle had been definitely destroyed by universal suffrage and the reform-

[63] *La Dépêche*, June 25, 1901, Aug. 8, 1903; Jaurès, etc., *L'Action du Parti socialiste* (Paris, 1902), pp. 34 36.

[64] See *Discours de Jules Guesde* . . . , pp. 5-6.

[65] *La Dépêche*, Nov. 30, 1898, May 28, 1900; Jaurès, *La Constituante, 1789-1791*, p. 640.

[66] *Ibid.*, Nov. 24, 1900, Mar. 21, Apr. 15, 1900, Aug. 9, 1902, June 19, Aug. 15, 1903; Jaurès, "L'Action socialiste," *La Revue socialiste*, 1904, XXXIX, 675.

[67] For example, *La Dépêche*, Aug. 15, 1903; "L'Action socialiste," pp. 675-78.

[68] Sarraute, J., *Socialisme d'opposition, socialisme de gouvernement, et lutte de classe* (Paris, 1901), p. 10.

ist procedure which arose from it: universal suffrage negated the idea that the state was the instrument of the capitalist class; and the reformist method demolished the concept that the class struggle absorbed all of social life to the exclusion of general interests between classes.[69] Revolutionary socialism could disregard the interests common to both bourgeoisie and proletariat, but since universal suffrage made it possible to further the movement toward socialism within contemporary society, the Socialists had to take into account those interests which united them to other parties.[70] Among such common interests were the defense of the Republic and its institutions of universal suffrage, free speech, and free press; the furtherance of "the normal and regular development of production"; and the protection of "national interests."[71] Because reforms depended on the ability of national industry to provide an abundance of goods, the proletariat must ally itself with the bourgeoisie to further "the economic prosperity and greatness of the nation."[72] In short, the Socialists must abandon the class struggle concept for "the national point of view."[73]

Millerand found Sarraute's doctrine a convenient defense of his actions when he was attacked by the French Reformists.[74] At the Congress of Bordeaux, he was rebuked for having approved the government's prosecution of the *Manuel du soldat*, the antipatriotic pamphlet of the Syndicalists; for having

[69] "Le Congrès de Bordeaux," *La Révue socialiste,* 1903, XXVII, 531-35.
[70] *Socialisme d'opposition* . . . , pp. 11-19, 22-25, 71.
[71] *Ibid.,* pp. 13, 30-55, 71-87.
[72] *Ibid.,* pp. 56-68-69; "Le Congrès de Bordeaux," p. 535.
[73] *Socialisme d'opposition* . . . , p. 56.
[74] Millerand stated: "In his remarkable book *Socialisme d'opposition* . . . my friend M. Joseph Sarraute has demonstrated with exceptional power that the notion of the class struggle attached to the present social régime is, if one isolates it from its complement, the solidarity of classes, as false as it is dangerous."—*Le Socialisme réformiste français,* p. 56. Starting with the idea of "no money, no reforms," Millerand held that the attainment of socialism necessitated a strong and prosperous France; and this in turn necessitated commercial expansion, a powerful army, alliance with Russia, and the return of Alsace-Lorraine. See *ibid.,* pp. 12-14, 17, 40, 46-47, 56 ff.; "Le Congrès de Bordeaux," pp. 605-6.

approved the government's order forbidding the soldiers to enter the *Bourses du travail*; for having abstained from voting the Socialists' resolution for simultaneous disarmament; and for having voted both for the religious budget and for the maintenance of the French ambassador at the Vatican.[75] These actions had so angered the Socialists that even some of the *Parti socialiste français*, notably Hervé and Renaudel, wanted to expel Millerand from the party.[76]

Jaurès opposed the resolution for Millerand's expulsion, but he objected to the attempt of Millerand and Sarraute to replace "class struggle," as Jaurès understood it, by fusion of classes. Jaurès contended that the Socialist Party could *collaborate* with other parties, but because it had its specific aim, it could not *fuse* with them; and because the Socialist Party was based on the proletariat, it was, "in this sense, a class party."[77] Moreover, although he agreed with Sarraute that class struggle did not prevent the proletariat from influencing the contemporary state, he argued that the state had been only partially conquered by the proletariat, and therefore, that it was partially open to proletarian influence and partially hostile to the proletariat at the same time.[78] Hence, although the Socialists must be concerned with the general interests of the nation—its liberty, security, prosperity—they must consider these general interests in the light of the proletariat's specific ideal; and this Millerand failed to do.[79]

Jaurès was anxious to bring the two factions of the party together, so that Guesde could act as a counterpoise to Millerand.[80] Ardently desiring unity, Jaurès was willing to beat a retreat on the new forms of class collaboration. At the Congress of Tours in 1902 he declared that in view of the fact that ministerial participation had divided the party, it had become necessary that no more Socialists accept portfolios in

[75] Orry, *op. cit.*, p. 61.   [76] See "Le Congrès de Bordeaux," pp. 523 ff.
[77] *Études socialistes*, p. x; *La Dépêche*, May 21, 1900.
[78] "Le Congrès de Bordeaux," pp. 551-55.
[79] *Ibid.*, pp. 555-69.   [80] *Ibid.*, p. 568.

the ministry.[81] The following year Jaurès held that a Socialist must enter a bourgeois ministry only for a specific purpose, and that he must not bind the party to continual support of that ministry.[82]

At the Congress of Amsterdam in 1904 Jaurès made his last attempt to gain socialist support for ministerial participation. He pleaded with the International to permit each socialist party to determine a procedure that would fit the institutions, traditions, race, temperament, and habits of each particular country.[83] Jaurès was defeated, for the Congress passed the Dresden Resolution—accepted by the German Social-Democratic Party and upheld at Amsterdam by Guesde, Vaillant, and Bebel. This resolution condemned "revisionist tendencies"; it insisted that the Socialists should do nothing to uphold a bourgeois government or "to mask the always growing class antagonism"; and it declared that there should be no participation of a Socialist in a bourgeois government.[84] The adoption of this resolution finally settled the question of ministerial participation.

Jaurès, eager for socialist unity, accepted the Amsterdam decision, and together with a few other important leaders such as Albert Thomas, Edgar Milhaud, and François de Pressensé—former foreign editor of *Le Temps*, who had joined the socialist movement during the Dreyfus Affair—gave up ministerial participation and the left bloc and joined with the Marxists and Blanquists to form the unified Socialist

[81] *Quatrième Congrès générale . . . 1902*, p. 162.
[82] "Le Congrès de Bordeaux," pp. 557-58.
[83] "Discours de Jaurès à Amsterdam," *La Revue socialiste*, 1904, XL, pp. 289 ff. Jaurès accused the German Socialists of trying to force on the French Socialists a method which was suitable only to Germany. He argued that as France had a real revolutionary tradition and universal suffrage, both of which Germany lacked, the French Socialists could use universal suffrage to attain their goal. And ministerial participation was a necessary part of the method based on democracy.—*Ibid.*, pp. 289, 291, 308-12. See also *La Petite République*, Jan. 3, Sept. 10, 1903.
[84] "Le Congrès d'Amsterdam," *La Revue socialiste*, 1904, XL, pp. 266-67.

Party.[85] For the Marxists, however, this was a fruitless victory. They were forced to grant concessions to the Reformists in return for the sacrifices of the latter. These concessions paved the way to the triumph of reformism in the unified Socialist Party; and the triumph of reformism, exalting the Social Republic, led to the eventual triumph of patriotism.

A second result of the period of the Dreyfus Affair and the conflict over ministerial participation was the defection and gradual assimilation into the bourgeois parties of a large number of socialist leaders. Many of the Reformists, including Millerand, Briand, Viviani, Sarraute, Zévaès, Augagneur, Clovis-Hughes, and Gérault-Richard, refused to accept the Amsterdam Resolution and organized a separate party dedicated to the principles of reformist socialism.[86] In time, however, they ceased to be socialist in anything but name. Briand, once a partisan of the general strike, earned the title of "The Scab" (*Le Jaune*) for his part in the suppression of strikes and demonstrations. Millerand devoted himself almost entirely to such activities as the expansion of French trade and the increase of France's military strength.[87] It remained for the events of 1914 to make Viviani the war premier and to remind the group that it was time to drop the name Socialist. This defection of 1905, the first of numerous defections that have marked the French socialist movement in the twentieth century, was a serious setback for reformism within the uni-

[85] Orry, *op. cit.*, pp. 73 ff.; Zévaès, *op. cit.*, pp. 211-13.

[86] In their congresses the group continued to look forward to the eventual attainment of socialism by means of the Republic, that "indispensable instrument of economic and social progress," and by collaboration with those republican parties "which have always stated their willingness to support economic and social reforms."—Quoted in Orry, *op. cit.*, pp. 80-81.

[87] A speech by Millerand in 1908 illustrated the extent to which he had become preoccupied with increasing the "grandeur and prosperity of the country," "our rank and our influence," by the expansion of French trade. See the reprint of the address in Baudin, etc., *Les Forces productives de la France* (Paris, 1909), pp. 173-83. In 1913 Millerand became one of the foremost supporters of the Three Year Army Law, which all the Socialists and many of the liberals regarded as a victory of nationalist militarism.

fied Socialist Party; but in the long run the defection was a
step toward insuring the patriotism of the French workers
and peasants.

A third result of this period of conflict was the rise of
revolutionary syndicalism. Appearing as a protest against reformist tactics, syndicalism strengthened, temporarily, the opponents of socialist patriotism. To resist syndicalism and its
antipatriotic doctrines was the most urgent problem confront-
ing Jaurès and his reformist allies in the few years immediately following the formation of the unified Socialist Party
in 1905 and preceding the World War.

V

REVOLUTIONARY SYNDICALISM

WITH the rise of revolutionary syndicalism at the turn of the nineteenth century came the sharpest attack on reformist socialism and national patriotism in the pre-War era. The Syndicalists rejected the concepts of national unity and national interests. They depreciated the value of the state for proletarian emancipation, ridiculed democratic political action, and repudiated the French Republic. Hence, they vehemently opposed every form of national and republican patriotism.

The syndicalist rejection of political action in favor of trade-union activity was caused, in the first place, by the fact that many Socialists felt that the electoral successes of both Reformists and Guesdists had failed to bring substantial improvement in the condition of the proletariat. The association of Millerand with the bourgeois ministers indicated to the more revolutionary Socialists that political action was turning the socialist organizations into bourgeois political parties. Further, the experience of the Dreyfus Affair, in which the street agitation of the reactionaries was opposed by the mass demonstrations of republican workingmen, revealed the powerful effect of direct mass pressure.

Another factor in the growth of syndicalism was the development of the trade unions as a potential instrument of class struggle. By 1894 there were more than 400,000 French workers organized in trade unions; and in 1904, this number had increased to 715,576.[1] Some of the unions were organized under the auspices of the Social Catholic movement; others harbored views similar to those prevailing in the Ameri-

[1] J. A. Estey, *Revolutionary Syndicalism* (London, 1913), p. 33.

can Federation of Labor; and still others (less than one-half of the total number) were under the influence of the Socialists and of the Anarchists.

The trade unions that were under socialist and anarchist influence were grouped by industries into national federations.[2] These federations, together with some individual unions, were united in the *Conféderation générale du travail*. The socialist and anarchist trade unions were also coördinated locally by the *Bourses du travail*, which united them by communities for the purpose of job placement, education, propaganda, and struggle against the employers. In 1892 these *Bourses du travail* were organized nationally in a *Fédération des Bourses du travail*. Finally, in 1902, this *Fédération* joined with the *Conféderation générale du travail*, taking the name of the latter, which became popularly known as the C.G.T.

The trade unions affiliated with the C.G.T. had been under the influence of the socialist movement since the Congress of Marseilles in 1879, when the delegates of a large number of unions adopted the principle of the social ownership of the instruments of production and distribution.[3] From 1879 to 1894 that part of the trade-union movement under socialist influence was dominated by the Guesdists.[4] After a national organization of trade unions was formed in 1886, its congresses were held at the same time and in the same town or region as those of the Guesdist *Parti ouvrier français*; and both congresses were composed of the same delegates.

This hegemony of the Guesdists in the socialist trade-union movement was challenged by the Communist-Anarchists. The French Communist-Anarchists—following the doctrines of Kropotkin and, to a certain extent, of Proudhon—held an

[2] Louis Lorwin, *Syndicalism in France* (second edition, New York, 1914), pp. 73-90.
[3] *Ibid.*, pp. 51-53.
[4] See *ibid.*, pp. 53-55; A. Humbert, *Le Mouvement syndical* (Paris, 1912), p. 75; David J. Saposs, *The Labor Movement in post-War France* (New York, 1931), in *Social and Economic Studies of post-War France*, edited by Carlton J. H. Hayes, Vol. IV, pp. 4-5.

ideal of a collective economic society somewhat similar to that of the Marxists. But, unlike the Marxists, they preached the immediate destruction of the state as the first step in the revolution and refused to take part in political activity of any kind.[5] The struggle of the Communist-Anarchists and the Marxists resulted in the victory of the former, who were completely in control at the Congress of Nantes in 1894; and the Anarchists dominated the C.G.T. almost down to the World War.[6]

Even though the official relations between the central trade-union organization and the political Socialists were severed, there remained a large amount of interpenetration, personal and doctrinal, between the socialist parties and the trade-union organization. A large number of trade-union members, opposing the revolutionary views of the anarchist leaders and calling themselves "Reformist Syndicalists," were active members of the socialist parties.[7] Some of the largest and strongest trade unions, such as the important *Fédération de textile*, were led by the Guesdists.[8] Although most of the *Bourses du travail* were under anarchist influence, many of them officially acknowledged their adherence to the socialist parties.[9] In 1910 three members of the Federal Council of the C.G.T. were socialist deputies [10] Likewise, important figures in the unified Socialist Party, notably Gustave Hervé, inclined toward syndicalism. Finally an attempt was made by several theorists, led by Georges Sorel, to show that syndicalism was the true practical expression of Marxian socialism.

[5] For the doctrines of the Communist-Anarchists and their points of difference with the Marxists, see S. Bernstein, *The Beginnings of Marxian Socialism in France,* pp. 166-73.
[6] Humbert, *op. cit.,* pp. 22-26; Saposs, *op. cit.,* p. 5.
[7] For the doctrines of the Reformist Syndicalists, see below, pp. 168-70.
[8] Humbert, *op. cit.,* p. 76.
[9] Pelloutier admitted that three *Bourses du travail* were Blanquist, twelve were Allemanist, and five were Guesdist. F. Pelloutier, *Histoire des Bourses du travail* (Paris, 1902), p. 151.
[10] Saposs, *op. cit.,* p. 13 n.

The leading theorists of the communist-anarchist group of Syndicalists were Ferdinand Pelloutier, and the workingmen, Paul Delesalle, Victor Griffuelhes, Georges Yvetot, Louis Niel, and Émile Pouget. All of them held important official positions in the trade-union movement.[11] The Marxist group of Syndicalists differed from the anarchist group chiefly in its approach to socialism through the theories of Marx rather than of Kropotkin, Bakunin, and Proudhon. In addition, the leading members of this group, Georges Sorel, Hubert Lagardelle, and Edouard Berth, were intellectuals interested in a philosophy of syndicalism rather than trade-union organizers.[12]

In repudiating political activities within the state, the Syndicalists substituted direct economic action through the trade unions. If the Reformists tended to exalt state institutions, the Syndicalists grouped all their activities and policies with the trade union as the integrating center.

The Syndicalists believed that trade-union activities alone could fulfill the class struggle—which for them, too, was the basic concept of socialism.[13] Pouget, for example, argued that the trade unions satisfied the fundamental requirement of the class struggle: the emancipation of the workers by their own action and without the aid of nonworkers.[14] The trade unions,

[11] Pelloutier was secretary of the *Fédération des Bourses du travail*; Delesalle, a mechanic, succeeded Pelloutier; Griffuelhes, a shoemaker, was secretary of the C.G.T.; Yvetot, a printer, was secretary of the C.G.T. for the *Fédération des Bourses du travail*; Niel, a printer, was secretary of the *Bourse du travail* of Montpellier, and later of the C.G.T.; Pouget, a traveling salesman, was also secretary of the C.G.T. See *L'Action directe*, Aug. 1904, p. 136; Humbert, *op. cit.*, p. 92.

[12] Sorel, a retired government engineer, spent the last thirty years of his life writing treatises on economics, politics, and socialism. His two major disciples were also intellectuals: Lagardelle, founder of *Le Mouvement socialiste*, was an ex-professor of law at the *École Libre des sciences politiques* at Paris and at the University of Brussels; and Berth was a free-lance journalist.

[13] See, for example, Pouget, *Le Parti du travail* (Paris, 1907?), pp. 5-7; Griffuelhes, "Les Deux Conceptions du syndicalism," *Le Mouvement socialiste*, 1905, XV, 2-5; Berth, "Les Discours de Jaurès," *Le Mouvement socialiste*, 1904, XIV, 216-17.

moreover, united the workers by the most substantial of all common interests, economic interests, and thereby created the solidarity upon which the class struggle depended. Thirdly, as the trade unions had their roots in industry, and as the class struggle was waged over economic interests, the trade unions revealed the class struggle to the workers and made clear the necessity for a social transformation.

For Pouget, as for the Marxian Socialists, the contemporary state was but the defender of capitalist privilege against the proletariat; and, in his opinion, changes in the form of government would not alter its primary function.[15] Democracy meant only a change in the façade of a state, a change contrived to paralyze the effective action of revolutionary minorities. The insidious evil of democracy, according to Pouget, was that it led the proletariat to accept political institutions and the action of political parties as a means of its emancipation. The Socialist Party, Pouget insisted, differed little from other political parties: because the Socialist Party accepted the parliamentary terrain as the field of combat and became filled with humanitarian capitalists and with politically ambitious "deserters from the bourgeoisie," it also was doomed to sterility.[16] Pouget pointed to the Socialist-controlled municipalities, and he contended that instead of aiding the proletariat, they had "absorbed those energies that should have been expended on syndical organization,"—the sole instrument of emancipation.[17]

[14] Pouget, Le Syndicat (Paris, n.d.), pp. 7 10, 13-15; Les Bases du syndicalisme (Paris, 1907), pp. 18-20.

[15] Les Bases du syndicalisme, pp. 3-5, 16-18; Le Parti du travail, p. 3.

[16] Le Parti du travail, p. 3; Les Bases du syndicalisme, pp. 9, 16-22. For the denunciation by the other Syndicalists of the state, democracy, and the Socialist Party, and their exaltation of the trade union, see Yvetot, A.B.C. syndicaliste (Paris, ed. of 1911), pp. 30-31; Delesalle, L'Action syndicale et les anarchistes (Paris, 1900), pp. 7-12; Les Deux Methodes du syndicalisme (Paris, n.d.), pp. 3, 7-8; Pelloutier, Le Congrès générale du Parti socialiste français (Paris, 1900), p. vi; Griffuelhes and Niel, Les Objectives de nos luttes de classe (Paris, 1909), pp. 14-22.

[17] Les Bases du syndicalisme, pp. 17-18.

Disgust with political democracy was the fundamental theme of the Marxian Syndicalists, Sorel, Berth, and Lagardelle. They pointed out that the Socialist Party by using democratic procedure attracted non-proletarian elements and then proceeded to ally itself with the bourgeois parties to the point of amalgamating with them "more or less openly."[18] Even the Guesdists lost their vigorous notion of the class struggle upon coming into contact with democracy; and their acceptance of reformism resulted from democratic contamination.[19] According to Lagardelle, the aim of the Marxian Syndicalists was to revise socialism to the left by bringing back the class struggle and by suppressing the use of democracy.[20]

The state must, in the opinion of the Syndicalists, disappear in the future order, and its place be taken by free associations of producers organized along the same economic lines as the present trade unions.[21] This meant that the workingmen must be emancipated through their present corporate groups. The Syndicalists, according to Pelloutier, by making the trade unions the basis of emancipation, "sow in capitalist society the

[18] For the analysis of Jaurès and reformism by the Marxian Syndicalists, see Sorel, *Matérieux d'une théorie du prolétariat* (Paris, ed. of 1919), pp. 250, 262-72; *Introduction à l'économie moderne* (Paris, 1906), pp. 9-10, 373; Lagardelle, "Révolutionnairisme électorale," *Le Mouvement socialiste,* 1905, XVII, p. 384; Berth, "Les Discours de Jaurès," *op. cit.,* pp. 214 ff., 302 ff.; "Notes bibliographiques," *Le Mouvement socialiste,* 1905, XV, p. 69.

[19] Berth, *Les Derniers Aspects du socialisme* (Paris, 1923), pp. 51-56; Lagardelle "Notes bibliographiques," *Le Mouvement socialiste,* 1906, XVIII, pp. 103-4.

[20] Lagardelle, "Le Socialisme ouvrier," *Le Mouvement socialiste,* 1904, XIV, pp. 1-5. The dislike of Sorel and Berth for democracy was so intense that they were almost carried into the ranks of the royalist group centering around Léon Daudet and Charles Maurras. See P. C. M. J. Perrin, *Les Idées sociales de Georges Sorel; thèse pour le doctorat* (Algiers, 1925), pp. 30-31. They were saved from this by the War; and the Russian Revolution, in spite of the dictatorship of the proletariat, brought them back to socialism. See *ibid.,* p. 34; Berth, *Les Derniers Aspects du socialisme,* pp. 32-33, 105 n.

[21] See Pelloutier, *Histoire des Bourses du travail, op. cit.,* pp. 54-59, 169; Delesalle, *L'Action syndicale et les anarchistes, op. cit.,* pp. 9-10; Pouget, *Le Syndicat, op. cit.,* pp. 19-21.

germs of the free groups of producers necessary to realize our communist and anarchist ideal."[22] The complete rejection of the state by the anarchist Syndicalists raised difficulties for the Marxist group. In attacking Guesdism, Sorel maintained that Marx, as well as Proudhon, considered anarchy a necessary feature of future society; and that if the Socialists intended to abolish the state, they must not plan to use it to establish socialism.[23] Sorel, however, was forced to admit that Marx believed the revolution would produce a dictatorship of the proletariat; but, he countered, unfortunately Marx did not possess the necessary knowledge of capitalist development to reason about the potency of labor organization; and it was therefore necessary to make a distinction between the bourgeois leanings of Marx and his theories that are specifically socialist and therefore specifically Marxist.[24]

Sorel explained that trade-union action, rather than a dictatorship of the proletariat, followed from Marx's conception of historical materialism and the class struggle; for applied to capitalism, this conception meant that the proletariat would develop its own mechanism of revolt and would acquire the "juridical and political capacity" needed to establish a new order without borrowing from bourgeois ideology.[25] The trade unions enforced the habits of labor discipline and collective effort needed for socialized production; they destroyed bourgeois juridical concepts of property and developed the "new juridical relationships which must take the place of the old"; they would fulfill the demands of historical mate-

---

[22] Pelloutier, *Le Congrès générale du Parti socialiste français, op. cit.,* p. viii.

[23] Sorel, Preface to Pelloutier, *Histoire des Bourses du travail,* pp. 22-28; *L'Avenir socialiste des syndicats* (Paris, ed. of 1901), p. 59-60; Berth, "Notes bibliographiques," *Le Mouvement socialiste,* 1905, XV, 70-71.

[24] See Sorel, "Réflexions sur la violence," *Le Mouvement socialiste,* 1906, XVIII, 270, 283, 423-27; *La Décomposition du Marxisme* (Paris, 1908), pp. 12, 57-64; *Matérieux d'une théorie du prolétariat,* pp. 2, 252-53.

[25] See Sorel, *L'Avenir socialiste des syndicats,* pp. 3-4, 27, 36-39, 59-60; *La Décomposition du Marxisme,* pp. 48-61; "Le Syndicalisme révolutionnaire," *Le Mouvement socialiste,* 1905, XVII, 273-79.

rialism for new organizations, and would themselves provide the cells of the future order.

The "direct action" of the Syndicalists consisted of mass demonstration, the simple strike, the general strike, sabotage, the union label, and the boycott.[26] The simple strike was considered as the basic form of daily direct action because, they explained, it turned the workers into revolutionaries; that is, it ruptured the relations between workers and employers, negated the authority of the latter in the eyes of the former, led the former to realize that their labor was the essential element in society, and strengthened the bonds of solidarity among the workers.[27] Sabotage, boycott, the union label, mass demonstrations against the employers or the state—all were considered to be of "revolutionary essence," because they trained the workers to fight and they strengthened the bonds of solidarity.[28] All these forms of direct action would prepare the workers for the revolutionary general strike, which would bring the final overthrow of capitalism.[29]

Sorel credited the saving of socialism to direct action during the Dreyfus Affair, explaining that it was "direct action, with its frequent accompaniment of acts of violence," which showed the possibilities inherent in the trade-union movement and opened the way to revolutionary revisionism.[30] Sorel sometimes considered the general strike valuable as a social myth; that is, as a collection of images which related partial strikes to the ultimate catastrophe and therefore kept alive the idea

[26] See, for example, Yvetot, *A.B.C. syndicaliste,* pp. 30-37; Griffuelhes and Niel, *Les Objets de nos luttes de classe,* pp. 23-25; Pouget, *Le Syndicat,* p. 19.

[27] See Griffuelhes and Niel, *Les Objets de nos luttes de classe,* pp. 23-27, 32, 51-52; Pouget, *Le Syndicat,* pp. 6, 17-18; *Le Parti du travail,* pp. 14-15; Yvetot, *A.B.C. syndicaliste,* pp. 39-40.

[28] Griffuelhes and Niel, *Les Objets de nos luttes de classe,* pp. 29-32; Pouget, *Le Syndicat,* p. 19; Yvetot, *A.B.C. syndicaliste,* pp. 34-37.

[29] See, for example, Griffuelhes and Niel, *Les Objets de nos luttes de classe,* pp. 23-25, 33-35; Griffuelhes, "Les Deux Conceptions du syndicalisme," p. 17.

[30] Sorel, *Matérieux d'une théorie du prolétariat,* pp. 284-86.

of revolt.[31] At other times, however, he indicated that he regarded the general strike as a positive reality.[32] Berth considered the general strike the "final hand-to-hand struggle," and the "decisive test" upon which the fate of the working class rests.[33]

The revolutionary aspect of direct action was still further clarified by the Syndicalists' acceptance of violence, particularly in the general strike. Pouget argued that a class will never surrender its privileges without being forced to do so; that the capitalist class will be no exception; and that the general strike must entail violence because "it is impossible to suppose that this supreme blow can be struck without producing a revolutionary conflagration."[34] Sorel further attacked the moral basis for opposition to violence, and demonstrated its revolutionary utility.[35]

The Syndicalists, like the Marxists in the 1880's, looked to revolutionary action on an international scale. Delesalle, for example, declared that when the workers realized that regardless of frontiers they were the same exploited class, "capitalism will not have long to live."[36] A report of the *Bourse du travail d'Alger* stated: "We are internationalists. Internationalism is our *raison d'être*, the means which will unify the aspirations of the workers of the entire world and will permit them to attempt common action to attain, simultaneously, the same end. To establish international relations between all the organized workers—that is, to effect a union of the feeble in order to resist and break the rule of the powerful—is the capi-

[31] See Sorel, "Réflexions sur la violence," pp. 263-82; *La Décomposition du Marxisme*, pp. 59-60.
[32] See Sorel, *L'Avenir socialiste des syndicats,* Preface, p. vii. This is particularly evident in Sorel's discussion of the superiority of the revolutionary general strike over the political general strike favored by the Socialists. See "Réflexions sur la violence," pp. 399-404, 415-18.
[33] See Berth, *Les Derniers Aspects du socialisme,* pp. 65-66.
[34] Pouget, *Le Parti du travail,* pp. 13-15; Yvetot, *A.B.C. syndicaliste,* p. 41.
[35] See Sorel, "Réflexions sur la violence," pp. 12-57, 253.
[36] Delesalle, *L'Action syndicale et les anarchistes,* p. 15.

tal point, the center of action toward which all our efforts must converge."[37] Delesalle suggested the use of internationalist propaganda and "practical internationalism"; that is, the establishment of international federations of trades and industries.[38]

In actual practice, the Syndicalists worked for the internationalizing of the unions. By 1900 powerful international federations had been formed, including the federations of miners, metallurgical workers, printers, tailors, and railway workers.[39] These international unions fulfilled the duties of national federations on an international scale. They collected money for strikers, established unemployment and sickness insurance, and exerted simultaneous pressure on parliaments for such reforms as the eight-hour day.[40] Moreover, the unions of one country helped the strikers of another. For example, the striking French longshoremen were aided by the longshoremen of other countries; and the unemployed printers of Belgium and Switzerland refused to accept the positions of the striking French printers in 1896.[41]

The unions also planned a general international organization to embrace the unionized workers of all countries. International congresses met regularly after 1900, and an International Secretariat was established in 1902.[42] According to Paul Louis, an historian of French socialism, the object of this action was "to further the destruction or the transformation of the capitalist régime by enlarging the offensive of the working-class to include all continents."[43] And he adds that the aim of the Syndicalists was the universal general strike. The French Syn-

[37] Quoted in Kritsky, op. cit., p. 293.
[38] Delesalle, L'Action syndicale et les anarchistes, p. 15. See also Yvetot, A.B.C. syndicaliste, pp. 28-29.
[39] Paul Louis, Histoire du mouvement syndical en France, 1789-1906 (Paris, 1907), pp. 258-62.
[40] Ibid., pp. 262-63. The Syndicalists were not averse to agitation for parliamentary reforms that might be useful to the proletariat. See Yvetot, A.B.C. syndicaliste, p. 37; Pouget, Le Syndicat, p. 19.
[41] Louis, op. cit., pp. 254-55. [42] Ibid., pp. 266-68. [43] Ibid., pp. 252-53.

dicalists played an active part in sponsoring the International Bureau and the meetings of international congresses;[44] and when these congresses refused to discuss the formulation of a general policy for all countries, the French Syndicalists threatened to withhold their participation.[45]

In short, the Syndicalists added unity of the proletariat across the national frontiers to class division within the nation. The first rejection of *la patrie* in the trade-union congresses appeared in a motion which argued that because capitalism is everywhere the same, the workers of all countries must unite for common action and must disregard the idea of *la patrie*.[46]

Events were not lacking to convince the Syndicalists that *la patrie* was not precisely the *patrie* of the workers. In 1899, for example, a large strike occurred in the Creusot plant when the workers tried to form a union; three thousand workers were dismissed; and in the resulting disorder, government troops were brought in.[47] In 1900, when six thousand textile workers at Vienne went on strike, clashes between soldiers and the strikers resulted in the wounding of several workers.[48] During the strike of the Haviland workers at Limoges in 1905, the troops killed two strikers and wounded several.[49] These events tended to crystallize antipatriotism and led to the publication of the *Manuel du soldat* in 1901 by the *Fédération des Bourses du travail*.[50] Issued to the soldiers, its chief purpose was to denounce national patriotism in order to persuade the young recruits not to fire at the strikers.

The *Manuel du soldat* distinguished between official patriotism and "true" patriotism—devotion to "a common and harmonious life"; and it explained that this true patriotism was

[44] See *XIIe Congrès national corporatif . . . 1900*, pp. 133, 205-7; *XIIIe Congrès national corporatif . . . 1902*, p. 63.
[45] See *XVIe Congrès national corporatif . . . 1908*, pp. 61 ff.
[46] See *XIe Congrès national corporatif . . . 1900*, p. 205.
[47] Kritsky, *op. cit.*, pp. 271-72. [48] *Ibid.*, p. 300. [49] *Ibid.*, pp. 354-55.
[50] The *Manuel du soldat* and *Le Nouveau Manuel du soldat* were unsigned, but were often referred to by the Syndicalists as the work of Yvetot. See Bidament's statement in *XVIe Congrès national corporatif . . . 1908*, p. 186.

not accepted by "our rulers and prominent thinkers" because they needed "a narrow patriotism which will have the brutalizing effect of a religion; they need a fanatical patriotism, for fanaticism is an excellent means of government."[51] *La patrie,* the *Manuel du soldat* proceeded, was a magic word that permitted all kinds of crimes and glorified those who committed them. It was especially used to justify low wages, long hours, high taxes, the export of French products, and above all—its "most frightful consequence"—militarism. The army, justified by "the religion of patriotism," was but "a means of enslavement," an institution to protect the property of the capitalists by using workers to assassinate other workers.[52]

The *Manuel* advised the conscripts to desert if they could not "stand the vexations, the insults, the imbecilities, the punishments, and the evils of the barracks."[53] It also pleaded with the conscripts not to fire at strikers; "for your enemy is only he who exploits you, oppresses you, commands you, and deceives you." Little wonder that the government proscribed the *Manuel du soldat* and forbade the soldiers to enter the Bourses.

As time went on the Syndicalists became more and more antipatriotic. This was demonstrated by the answers to a questionnaire on the relation of socialism to patriotism sent out by Lagardelle's *Le Mouvement socialiste* in 1905. Of the forty-one answers, given by provincial labor militants as well as the prominent officials of the C.G.T., all but one was definitely antipatriotic; and that one was presented by a man who disagreed with the principles of revolutionary syndicalism.

The first question was: "Have the workers a *patrie* and can they be patriots? To what does the idea of *patrie* correspond?"[54] The answer was almost unanimously that the workers had no *patrie* and that they could not be patriots. Several reasons were given. One was that patriotism implied a com-

[51] *Le Nouveau Manuel du soldat* (Paris, ed. of 1908), pp. 3-6.
[52] *Ibid.,* pp. 6 ff.   [53] *Ibid.,* pp. 29-32.
[54] The questions are in Lagardelle, "Enquête sur l'idée de patrie et la classe ouvrière," *Le Mouvement socialiste,* 1905, XVI, 435-36.

munity of interests which did not exist, particularly in view of the class struggle and of class interests.[55] A second reason was that patriotism had been identified with the defense of the larger measure of liberty afforded by some countries, whereas in reality the workers everywhere were equally deprived of liberty and subjected to the same exploitation.[56] A third was that the idea of *patrie* was associated with the possession of property, and that as the proletarian had no property, he could not have a *patrie* and must not be patriotic.[57] Almost all the responses to the first question agreed that patriotism was an instrument of exploitation and oppression, justifying the capitalist régime and the maintenance of the army.[58]

The second question was: "Does *labor internationalism* recognize frontiers other than those which separate classes; and is not the aim of labor internationalism to organize, across geographic and political divisions, *the war* of the workers of all countries against the capitalists of all countries?" The consensus of opinion was contained in the statement that the workers, in their war on capitalism, "must organize internationally with their class brothers and must defy all the prejudices of language, of customs, of races. There are two absolutely distinct classes: the class of the exploited, and that of the exploiters; that of the producers, and that of the parasites. The former must kill the latter in order to live. This is the sole war which can occupy the workers, and if the rulers, if the bourgeoisie wish to declare another, it is for the workers to profit by the occasion to declare their war also. . . ."[59]

---

[55] See the replies of Griffuelhes and Graizely, secretary of the *Bourse du travail* of Besançon, *ibid.*, XVI, 443-44; XVII, 326.

[56] See the replies of Griffuelhes and A. Clerc, a printer, and secretary of the *Bourse du travail* of Bourges, *ibid.*, XVI, 440, 444-45.

[57] See, for example, the replies of Delesalle and Yvetot, *ibid.*, XVI, 466; XVII, 202.

[58] See, for example, the reply of Gabriel Beaubois, an employee of the State Railway, *ibid.*, XVII, 321-23.

[59] See the replies of Yvetot, Delesalle, and L. Robert, secretary of the *Fédération des syndicats de peinture, ibid.*, XVI, 467, XVII, pp. 204-22.

The third question was: "Is not *labor internationalism* to be identified not only with the international organization of workers but also with *antimilitarism* and *antipatriotism*? Is not the real progress of labor internationalism in direct relation to the progress of antimilitarist ideas and of antipatriotic sentiments in the laboring masses?" The consensus of opinion was that "the workers must be antimilitarist because the army is the negation of the internationalist ideal," and because its immediate rôle is "internal repression."[60] Labor internationalism must be identified with antipatriotism because "militarism is the support of capitalism, and patriotism is the recruiting office for militarism."[61]

To the fourth question—"What do you think of the military general strike?"—the replies gave almost unanimous approval. There was, however, some difference of opinion as to what a general strike of the soldiers against a war would accomplish. Some answers stressed the efficacy of the military general strike in preventing war.[62] Others emphasized that the military general strike meant that the proletarian would turn his arms against the bourgeoisie "in the name of social revolution"; and that it must accomplish "the end of exploitation of man by man."[63] A few, however, feared that the sentiment for a general strike in time of war had not sufficiently penetrated the masses, and that the general strike would be impossible in the near future.[64] But these replies favored an incessant internationalist, antimilitarist, and antipatriotic propaganda to prepare for a military general strike.

[60] See the reply of Lenoir, a miller, and secretary of the *Fédération des syndicats d'ouvriers mouleurs, ibid.*, XVI, 448.

[61] See, for example, the replies of Yvetot, and Bousquet, a baker, and secretary of the *Fédération des travailleurs de l'alimentation, ibid.*, XVI, 438, 467.

[62] See, for example, the reply of P. Guilbert, a mechanic, and secretary of the *Chambre syndicale des Constructeurs-mécaniciens* of Rouen, *ibid.*, XVII, p. 46.

[63] See, for example, the reply of Delesalle, *ibid.*, XVII, 205.

[64] See the replies of Niel; A. Morel, an agricultural laborer; Joucaviel, a miner; *ibid.*, XVI, 462, XVII, 52, 61.

The fifth and final question was: "What do you think of Socialists who consider themselves patriots and internationalists at the same time?" The answers almost unanimously condemned such Socialists as "obscurantists," "arrivists," "imbeciles," "clowns," "sinister scoundrels," "shameless politicians," "ignoble mystifiers," and "counterfeiters of the great socialist idea."[65] Many of the replies stated that the Socialists were patriotic because they had to obtain the good favor of the voters.[66] Others attributed the patriotism of the Socialists to their possession of property.[67] One opinion was that socialist patriots who professed to be internationalists were neither internationalists nor socialists, but patriots only.[68]

This question of the patriotic Socialists particularly interested the Marxian Syndicalists Sorel and Berth attributed the patriotism of the Socialists to their acceptance of the state. Sorel contended that the political Socialists, in anticipating their dominance of the state, "must have an army, they must pursue a foreign policy, and consequently, they must also promise devotion to *la patrie*."[69] In attacking the patriotism of Guesde, Berth offered a different explanation: that Guesde intended to make the state the depository of all political, social, and industrial life; and, as the state had been identified with the nation and the army since the French Revolution, Guesde was forced to accept the army and devotion to *la patrie*.[70]

Lagardelle connected patriotism, not with states in general, but with the democratic Republic and the reformist method.[71]

[65] These titles were applied by Bousquet, Clerc, Yvetot, Bonin, Cazaux, Albin Villeval fils, Porcq.—*Ibid.*, XVI, 439, 442, 469-70, XVII, 39, 41, 71, 335.

[66] See, for example, the replies of Cazaux and Torton, *ibid.*, XVII, 41-42, 231.

[67] See, for example, the reply of Delesalle, *ibid.*, XVII, 205.

[68] The reply of Niel, *ibid.*, XVI, 463.

[69] Sorel, "Réflexions sur la violence," *op. cit.*, pp. 162-63.

[70] Berth, *Les Derniers Aspects du socialisme, op. cit.*, pp. 48-49.

[71] Lagardelle, "L'Idée de patrie et le socialisme," *Le Mouvement socialiste*, 1906, XIX, 5-22; "Antimilitarisme et syndicalisme," *Le Mouvement socialiste*, 1906, XVIII, 124-26; "Révolutionnairisme électorale," *Le Mouvement socialiste*, 1905, XVII, 385.

He explained, first of all, that the French Revolution identified patriotism with the state by giving political sovereignty to the nation; and it identified patriotism with the army because the latter was used to defend the Republic. As the democratic state was based on the nation and the army, and as the parliamentary Socialists had a Jacobin partiality for the Republic, they were naturally patriotic. Moreover, as long as socialism was based on class struggle, it was irreconcilable with patriotism, which meant "union of classes"; but when the Socialists accepted the use of democracy and began to act "on the terrain where classes meet," they surrendered class struggle; and just as class collaboration had replaced class struggle, so patriotism had replaced internationalism.

The Syndicalists had nothing but contempt for the opposition of Jaurès and the reformist Socialists to war. Lagardelle remarked that although the Socialists preached opposition to war, this opposition was but "pure sentimentalism," for it was divorced from the desire to abolish the state which was constituted by wars and of which war was still the true vocation.[72] Lagardelle, Sorel, and Berth insisted that real opposition to war and to militarism could come only from the Syndicalists: the Syndicalists alone repudiated the state, and with the state, patriotism and the army.[73] The Syndicalists replaced national warfare by social warfare; "life will not sink into a pacifist morass; there remains a school of heroism and a field of permanent battle; it is the labor struggle."[74]

Thus, the revolutionary syndicalist movement was a potential obstacle to patriotism and to patriotic adventure in France. Indeed, it is quite possible that if the movement had continued to grow after 1906, the year when the very revolutionary Congress of Amiens was held, socialist antipatriotism might have effectively counterbalanced socialist patriotism. After 1906,

[72] Lagardelle, "Notes bibliographiques," *Le Mouvement socialiste*, 1905, XVI, 402-6.
[73] For example, *ibid.*, p. 415.   [74] For example, *ibid.*, p. 416.

however, the revolutionary syndicalist movement began to slacken, and organized workers veered toward "reformist syndicalism," a moderate trade unionism under the influence of the politically-minded Socialists. The fate of antipatriotism in the trade-union movement was to a considerable extent bound up with its fate in the ranks of the newly-formed unified Socialist Party.

VI

CONFLICT IN THE UNIFIED PARTY

UPON the formation of the unified Socialist Party in 1905, Reformists and Guesdists were confronted with the doctrines of revolutionary syndicalism as a practical party question. The Marxian Syndicalists were for a time directly represented in the Socialist Party by Lagardelle, who believed that the party might do useful work in clearing away the legal obstacles to trade-union progress.[1] When the party refused to accept his recommendations, Lagardelle lost interest.

It was left to Gustave Hervé (1871-   ) to inoculate the party with the virus of revolutionary syndicalism. The son of Breton parents, and an instructor of history at the lycées of Rodez, Alençon, and Sens, Hervé became prominent in the socialist movement after 1902. At first, Hervé represented the typical reformist attitude.[2] When the Socialists split over ministerial participation, he joined Jaurès and Millerand in the Parti socialiste français.[3]

In this early period, Hervé sought to reconcile patriotism and socialism by stripping patriotism of its nonrepublican and

---

[1] See Hubert Lagardelle, "Révolutionnairisme electoral," Le Mouvement socialiste, 1905, XVIII, 390-91; "Le Socialisme ouvrier," Le Mouvement socialiste, 1904, XIV, 6-7; 4e Congrès national . . . 1907, pp. 455 ff.

[2] In this early period Hervé believed in the efficacy of partial reforms; he held that the concept of the class struggle was not exact and that the support of the liberal bourgeoisie could be won by moderation; and he was proud of having defended the Republic during the Dreyfus Affair. See Quatrième Congrès général . . . 1902, pp. 129-31.

[3] When Hervé sided with Renaudel in demanding Millerand's expulsion from the Party, he explained that he did so not because the latter was a Reformist but because he tried to suppress every possibility of revolutionary action. That is, although Hervé repeatedly showed himself to be a Reformist in this period, he was loath to burn the bridges to revolution behind him. See "Le Congrès de Bordeaux," La Revue socialiste, 1903, XXXVII, pp. 523-24.

aggressive aspects. At the Congress of Tours in 1902, Hervé criticized the cult of the flag, a flag that had been abased by "the tricks of Napoleon" and by "colonial brigandages," and "the cult of ancestors" which included Louis XIV and Napoleon.[4] He asserted that the Socialists were internationalists like "the patriots of '93": they denounced colonial wars and a war of revenge against Germany; they demanded arbitration; and if the French government undertook an aggressive war, the Socialists would revolt. But Hervé said that "in case of aggression coming from any country whatsoever, the Socialists will participate in the defense of the Republic."[5]

In 1904, however, Hervé came under the influence of the Revolutionary Syndicalists, particularly the Anarchists;[6] and he became the champion within the Socialist Party of the C.G.T. He praised syndicalism because it combined the tendencies of Marx and Bakunin, and because, in his opinion, the organization of the proletariat for trade-union activity was really political action as Marx had conceived it.[7] He showed supreme contempt for the political method of democracy. He

[4] *Quatrième Congrès général . . . Tours, 1902*, pp. 131-35.

[5] *Ibid.*, p. 131. Even Hervé's famous "flag on the dunghill" article, written about the anniversary of Wagram, was not an antipatriotic tirade (as it was then considered), but an attack on Napoleon which was patriotic, pacifist, and internationalist in a republican sense. In the article, he declared that the anniversary of Wagram was "a day of shame and sorrow" because it re called that the great nation which had proclaimed the Rights of Man had been infatuated with the "uniformed bandit" who had strangled the Republic. He then went on to explain that such celebrations fostered "the cult of the saber" and prepared the country for colonial and international wars and for the overthrow of the Republic. And he recommended "in order to dishonor militarism and wars of conquest in the eyes of the soldiers," that on the anniversary of Wagram the flag be ceremoniously planted in a dunghill. See Hervé, "L'Anniversaire de Wagram," July, 1901, reprinted in Hervé, *Mes crimes* (Paris, 1912), pp. 23-29. Hervé later explained that he had intended not to dishonor the flag but to attack the Napoleonic tradition. See Hervé, *La Conquête de l'armée* (Paris, 1912), pp. 137-38.

[6] When Hervé founded *La Guerre sociale*, his chief collaborators were such men as Victor Méric, Eugène Merle, and Miguel Almeyreda, all of whom had been collaborators on the anarchist journal, *Libertaire*. Hubert-Rouger, *La France socialiste* (Paris, 1912), in *Encyclopédie socialiste*, edited by Compère-Morel, Vol. III, pp. 131-35.

[7] *3e Congrès national . . . 1906*, pp. 159-64.

contended that universal suffrage in France was corrupted by the financiers; that the Republic was a "label" hardly different from the Empire; and that a gulf separated the working classes from the Radicals who had "defied, abused, imprisoned, sabered, and shot" their faithful socialist allies.[8] The Republic was rebaptized by Hervé as "Marianne number 3"; and in the hands of Hervé's cartoonists in *La Guerre sociale*, Grassier and Poncet, Marianne underwent a plastic transformation from the incarnation of Gallic beauty into a fat, slovenly woman in a revolutionary *bonnet rouge*.

Hervé now styled himself an "insurrectionary Socialist," oscillating between the political insurrectionary tradition of Blanquism and the "insurrectionary general strike" of syndicalism.[9] He devised a "revolutionary militarism" to prepare the workers for the great coup. He even outlined in detail a plan for winning the army by undermining the loyalty of the officers.[10]

Hervé likewise accepted the antipatriotic doctrines of syndicalism and propagated them with obstinacy and contempt for authority. He lost his position at Sens; he was barred from the practice of law; from 1906 to 1912 he was sentenced to a total of eleven years in prison and actually served two years.[11] Hervé became the symbol of antipatriotism in France. It was due to his efforts that patriotism was treated as a major problem at the socialist congresses at Limoges in 1906 and Nancy

[8] *4e Congrès national . . . 1907*, p. 296; *6e Congrès national . . . 1909*, pp. 501-4.

[9] See *6e Congrès national . . . 1909*, pp. 366-70; *7e Congrès national . . . Nîmes, 1910*, p. 408.

[10] See Hervé, *La Conquête de l'armée, op. cit.*, pp. 121-36.

[11] In 1905 Hervé was sentenced to four years in prison for taking part in a syndicalist proclamation to the recruits. He was liberated after six months by an amnesty. He was again sentenced in 1908 to one year in prison, a sentence which he served in full. In 1910 he received four years and in 1911, two years, both sentences ending by amnesties after a few months. In 1912 he was sentenced to three months, serving the full time. *Mes Crimes, op. cit.*, pp. 45, 47, 223, 229, 285, 335.

in 1907, and at the congress of the International held at Stuttgart in 1907.

Hervé's most intensive attack on patriotism began in 1905, when war seemed imminent between France and Germany over the Moroccan question. He bluntly declared that the members of the *Fédération de l'Yonne*, to which he belonged, refused to die for "the French nation."[12] He explained that he had been a patriot, a devotee of the "religion of patriotism," and would have died to defend the French nation or to recover Alsace-Lorraine, but now he had become a "heretic," an "antipatriot."[13]

Antipatriotism, in Hervé's opinion, was a logical consequence of revolutionary socialism: it was necessary to win the peasants in the army from loyalty to the present régime, and to prepare them to refuse to suppress a workers' insurrection.[14] Antipatriotism, he also argued, resulted from the class struggle and proletarian internationalism.[15] Socialism meant class cleavage within the nation and international proletarian solidarity; it grouped "poor against rich, class against class, regardless of differences of race, language, and the frontiers traced by history." Patriotism, on the other hand, grouped men by "countries of origin"; it united the rich and poor in each country; and it meant that the French proletariat and French bourgeoisie formed a "bloc against the stranger." If the Socialists were patriotic, they would have to fight side by side with the capitalists of their nationality against their fellow Socialists of another nationality: "Bebel on the one side, Jaurès on the other, each with a rifle, one dying for the German nation, the other for the French nation." Indeed, "it is necessary to be a subtle rhetorician to reconcile these irreconcilables: internation-

[12] See *3e Congrès national . . . 1906*, p. 214.

[13] *Ibid.*, p. 215; Hervé, *Leur Patrie* (Paris, 1905), Preface, p. 5; *Mes Crimes*, p. 52.

[14] *6e Congrès national . . . 1909*, pp. 368-69.

[15] See *Leur Patrie*, pp. 6-7, 138-43; Hervé, *L'Internationalisme* (Paris, 1910,) p. 101; *3e Congrès national . . . 1906*, pp. 215, 298; *4e Congrès national . . . 1907*, pp. 220-22, 303; *L'Humanité*, May 29, 1905.

alism and patriotism, the class struggle and the communion of classes in a common *patrie*."

To Jaurès's argument that it was necessary to defend France because socialism would develop more easily under the French Republic than under the German monarchy, Hervé replied that as far as the proletariat was concerned, "all *patries* are of equal value."[16] In all nations, regardless of political structure, the governments were controlled by the capitalists, and the proletarians suffered from long hours of labor, low wages, insecurity, evil living conditions, poor food, little education, vulgar pleasures, and prostitution. In France, universal suffrage was "oppressed, corrupted, adulterated by all kinds of pressure"; and in France, as elsewhere, freedom of the press, of meeting, and of organizing unions was restricted. In France, too, the government sent troops against the striking workers. Hence, the conquest of France by Germany should be a matter of indifference to the proletariat.[17] Indeed, instead of losing by annexation, the proletariat would gain, for the wiping out of the frontier between the two countries would unite the French and German proletarians in the struggle against capitalism.[18]

Hervé argued that the only reason why the German, French, Japanese and Russian workers stupidly fought one another, instead of the capitalists, was that they had been corrupted by the religion of patriotism.[19] This faith, he said, had its fanatics —the nationalists and imperialists; its priests—professional patriots and military men; its Bible and catechism—historical

[16] *Leur Patrie*, pp. 7, 19-30; declaration at Hervé's trial, *L'Humanité*, Dec. 30, 1905.
[17] *L'Humanité*, Dec. 30, 1905; *Leur Patrie*, pp. 30, 107-8, 144-50. Hervé also denied the contention that conquest would mean the loss of France's language and national characteristics. He argued that the failure of the attempts in Alsace-Lorraine, German Poland, and the Baltic provinces of Russia, had proved that languages could not be extirpated; and, he added, even if the masses did lose their language, they would receive another one "equally rich in idiom." As for "national characteristics," they could not be lost by annexation because they did not exist. See *Leur Patrie*, pp. 144-46.
[18] *Ibid.*, pp. 150; *L'Humanité*, May 29, 1905.
[19] *Leur Patrie*, pp. 37-95.

manuals; an impressive array of vestments, hymns, and ritual —military uniforms, patriotic songs, martial music, reviews, parades, and military celebrations; finally, the blessed sacrament of the flag. Like religion, patriotism was inculcated "by continual suggestion, by a poisoning that begins in the cradle." Toy soldiers for the child, patriotic songs and history books for the youth, newspapers and theaters for the adult—all inculcated hatred for France's neighbors, the belief in France's superiority, "the idolatry of the saber," the evils of arbitration, and other patriotic dogmas. After his training is completed, after "having arrived at this degree of intellectual deformation, the patriot is an animal ready for killing; he is now ready for the slaughterhouse."

This elaborate religion, Hervé contended, had been consciously built up by the ruling classes to serve their interests.[20] Patriotism, by uniting "the wolves and the sheep within each nation," blinded the proletariat to the class struggle and prevented the growth of socialism; it gave the bourgeoisie a pretext for maintaining a standing army to crush a socialist uprising; and it sponsored capitalist imperialism.

To the religion of patriotism, Hervé opposed the conception that nations would be melted in the evolutionary process and would give way to internationalism. The future order, composed of federated proletarian countries, with an international language (perhaps Esperanto) was already being prepared by the growth in the means of communications and by the international solidarity of the proletariat.[21] The twentieth century, he insisted, would be the era of internationalism as the nineteenth century had been that of nationalism.

To combat the effects of patriotism and militarism, Hervé

---

[20] *Ibid.*, pp. 95-116; *4e Congrès national . . . 1907*, p. 215; Hervé, *Histoire de France pour les grands* (Paris, 1910), pp. 389-90.

[21] *L'Internationalisme*, pp. 1-89, 165-73; *3e Congrès national . . . 1906*, p. 215. Hervé acknowledged that the future order would be federative, but he asked Jaurès "why these autonomous 'groupings' of the future must be precisely the present *patries* such as the chances of war have distributed them . . . ?" *Leur Patrie*, pp. 208-9.

proposed, first of all, that the Socialists agitate for a militia, which would lower the period of service for the proletariat, reduce the financial burden of the army, insure protection from a possible invasion of Europe by Asia, and eliminate the use of the army in strikes.[22] Before 1905, it is important to note, Hervé stressed the advantage of a militia in defending France from an invader;[23] but after 1905 he insisted specifically that agitation for a militia must in no sense imply the defense of the nation against advanced European nations.[24]

Hervé's program in case of war coincided with that of the Syndicalists; namely, to bring about a general strike and a socialist insurrection. The heart of the motion of the Yonne, proposed by Hervé at the Congress of Limoges, was that "the Congress repudiates the bourgeois and governmental patriotism which falsely affirms the existence of a community of interest among all the inhabitants of a country; the Congress affirms that the duty of the Socialists of every country is to fight only in order to institute a collectivist or communist order and to defend it when they have succeeded in establishing it; and the Congress, confronted by diplomatic incidents which, from different sides, threaten to disturb European peace, calls on all citizens to reply to a declaration of war, from whatever side it comes, by a general strike and by insurrection."[25]

Hervé offered two different plans for insurrection.[26] According to one proposal, the workers would enter the army, receive their arms, and then revolt, seizing industry and turning it over to the *Bourses du travail*. According to the second plan, the workers would refuse to join the army, and the conscripts already in the army would desert. He favored the latter plan because he feared that once the workers had entered the bar-

[22] *L'Internationalisme*, pp. 156-59.
[23] See Hervé, "Le Pioupiou de l'Yonne," 1901, reprinted in *Mes Crimes*, pp. 31-35; "Le Congrès de Bordeaux," *op. cit.*, p. 526.
[24] *L'Internationalisme*, p. 159.
[25] *3e Congrès national . . . 1906*, p. 260.
[26] *Ibid.*, p. 216; *4e Congrès national . . . 1907*, pp. 216-17; *Leur Patrie*, pp. 170-72.

racks, it would be difficult for them to leave; and besides, if the workers refused to join the army, the support of their families would be won for the insurrection.

Hervé rejected the proposal of Jaurès and Vaillant that the Socialists should have recourse to the general strike and insurrection if France were the aggressor, but should defend France if she were attacked. The resolution to defend a country against attack, he argued, was tantamount to the resolution to defend it at all times; inasmuch as the governments controlled the telegraph and could influence the newspapers, "it is almost impossible to know who is the true aggressor at the moment when the conflict breaks out."[27] Hervé recalled that in the Franco-Prussian War, the Boer War, and the Russo-Japanese War, the real aggressors were not known at the time. The general strike and insurrection should therefore be employed in all cases of war.[28] The country should be defended by the proletariat only after a socialist régime had been established; after the workers had become co-proprietors of the country's wealth and had acquired a real interest in defending it.[29]

Hervé denied Guesde's contention that the country with the strongest socialist movement would be the most weakened by a military general strike; and that if such a country were defeated, the strongest socialist movement would be crushed.[30] He explained that antipatriotism would be made international, and therefore each socialist movement would be protected from the conqueror.[31] Instead of being reactionary, Hervé told Guesde, the insurrection in time of war was the best means of attaining socialism. War would be the most opportune time

[27] *Leur Patrie*, pp. 140-42; *3e Congrès national . . . 1906*, p. 218; *L'Humanité*, May 29, 1905.
[28] *Leur Patrie*, p. 143; *3e Congrès national . . . 1906*, pp. 218, 257-58; *4e Congrès national . . . 1907*, pp. 299-303. In reply to a question by Jaurès, Hervé declared that even if France accepted arbitration in a dispute with Germany, and the latter refused and proceeded to attack France, the French proletariat should not defend France but should revolt and try to establish socialism.—*4e Congrès national . . . 1907*, p. 302.
[29] *Leur Patrie*, pp. 8, 106-7.   [30] For Guesde's argument, see below, p. 164.
[31] *Leur Patrie*, pp. 211-16.

for revolution: the army—"watchdog of capitalism"—would
be otherwise engaged; and the proletarians, facing death in
battle, would prefer to die for socialism.[32] The threat of the
general strike would be so formidable that it would frighten
the government and prevent war.[33]

Hervé received little support from the leaders of the Socialist Party.[34] Only Lafargue, who differed with Hervé on
certain points, agreed with his revolutionary approach.[35] Lafargue was still a revolutionary Marxist;[36] and on questions
of revolutionary procedure, he disagreed with Hervé mainly
in the matter of relations between the Socialist Party and the
C.G.T. Holding to his early Marxism, he expected trade unions
and coöperative societies to serve as primary schools of socialism; and whereas Hervé wanted the Socialist Party to please
the C.G.T. by making no effort to control it, Lafargue believed
that the political, syndical, and coöperative organizations
should not be autonomous, but should unite their forces for
common action under the leadership of the Socialist Party.[37]

Lafargue, although differing with Hervé on the practical

[32] *Ibid.*, pp. 141, 222-23; *3e Congrès national . . . Limoges, 1906*, pp.
244-46.

[33] *4e Congrès national . . . 1907*, p. 217.

[34] Hervé's chief allies, aside from Lagardelle, were the only two women
prominent in the party, Madame Sorgue and Madeleine Pelletier. For their
ideas on revolution and patriotism, see Sorgue, *L'Unité révolutionnaire*
(Paris, 1901); Pelletier, *Idéologie d'hier: Dieu, la morale, la patrie* (Paris,
1910), pp. 54-87; *3e Congrès national . . . 1906*, pp. 146-48; *4e Congrès
national . . . 1907*, pp. 169-70, 244-45, 526-35; *6e Congrès national . . .
1909*, pp. 467-70.

[35] Hervé, embittered against Guesde, was very friendly to Lafargue. See
his statement in *7e Congrès national . . . Nîmes, 1910*, p. 406. In 1911,
Lafargue recommended Hervé for the high honor of secretary to the editorial board of *L'Humanité*. See *8e Congrès national . . . 1911*, p. 389.

[36] Lafargue still maintained that universal suffrage was a "dupery"; that
parliamentarism was the form of government best suited to the interests of
the bourgeoisie; that reforms of amelioration and "public services" were
unable to improve the lot of the workers. And he still looked forward to
revolution. See *5e Congrès national . . . 1908*, pp. 134-40, 330; *8e Congrès
national . . . 1911*, p. 335; *L'Humanité*, Nov. 4, 1907.

[37] *7e Congrès national . . . Nîmes, 1910*, pp. 302-3; *7e Congrès national
. . . Paris, 1910*, pp. 106-10. For Hervé's ideas on the relation of trade-
unions and the Socialist Party, see *3e Congrès national . . . 1906*, pp. 162-63.

application of the antipatriotic principle, supported the principle itself. He asserted that the very word *patrie* had always denoted possession of property; and the proletarians would remain *sans-patrie* until they had expropriated the wealth of the capitalist class.[38] Instead of giving up their antipatriotism in the face of attacks by the bourgeoisie, the Socialists should counter these attacks by showing that the patriotism of the bourgeoisie has always been motivated and limited by their economic interests.[39] In defending desertion as advocated by the *Manuel du soldat*, Lafargue declared that the bourgeoisie had always practiced desertion; indeed, they had "elevated desertion to the dignity of a class principle."[40] All the bourgeois patriots who were of conscription age during the Franco-Prussian War, such as Clemenceau, Ribot, Drumont, Fallières, Grévy, Gambetta, Rochefort, served not at the front, but in "the regiment of patriotic desertion." Hence, "to inveigh against the antimilitarism and desertion that the Syndicalists, the Socialists, and the Anarchists preach to the conscripts, demands a seldom-encountered effrontery."

Lafargue, like Hervé, was opposed to the resolution to defend France if she were attacked, declaring that "it is impossible for a Socialist to be a patriot and a militarist."[41] Lafargue, however, had three main objections to Hervé's motion.[42] First, this motion could not be proposed as a resolution for an international congress, for as the German Socialists were more severely punished for their antipatriotism than the French Socialists, such a resolution would place the German Socialists in a dangerous position. Secondly, the motion concentrated on international wars, which, Lafargue believed, had been replaced by colonial wars. Thirdly, a general strike and insurrection

[38] *L'Humanité*, Aug. 12, Nov. 4, 1907; *4ᵉ Congrès national . . . 1907*, pp. 200-201.
[39] *L'Humanité*, May 27, 1907; *4ᵉ Congrès national . . . 1907*, p. 200; Lafargue, *Le Patriotisme de la bourgeoisie* (Paris, 1906), pp. 3 ff.
[40] *L'Humanité*, May 27, 1907.
[41] *4ᵉ Congrès national . . . 1907*, p. 201.
[42] *Ibid.*, pp. 198-204; *L'Humanité*, Aug. 13, 1907.

would be unsuccessful at the beginning of a war. Lafargue argued that in 1870 the people were filled with patriotic fury; and this meant that at the outbreak of a future war "a similar idiotic enthusiasm will appear." Lafargue's own solution did not, however, differ greatly from Hervé's. He advised obstructing the use of troops for colonial wars; and he pointed to the example of the Italian women who lay down on the railroad tracks in order to prevent troops from leaving on colonial expeditions.[43] He also recommended that antipatriotic and antimilitarist propaganda be directed primarily toward the overthrow of the government during a war.[44]

The rise of syndicalism, the penetration of the Syndicalists into the Socialist Party, the revolutionary intransigence of Lafargue, and the desertion of Millerand and his right-wing supporters, made the position of the Reformists within the Socialist Party extremely difficult. Under the leadership of Jaurès they continued their struggle to win the unified party back to their views.

Although Jaurés had surrendered to the International on the question of ministerial participation, he made no further concessions to revolutionary principles. On the contrary, he fought to turn the syndicalist movement into a tractable supplement to the work of the socialist deputies in achieving a gradual, peaceful inauguration of socialism. Jaurès became the foremost champion of the C.G.T. in Parliament and defended the organizational efforts and strike activities of the postal employees, the teachers, the arsenal workers, the electricians, the railway workers, and the sailors of the merchant marine.[45] In 1908, when the leaders of the C.G.T. were arrested after bloody clashes between troops and workers at Dravail and

---

[43] *L'Humanité,* Aug. 12, 1907.

[44] *4ᵉ Congrès national . . . 1907,* pp. 204-5. Lafargue embodied these ideas in a motion he presented to the Congress of Nancy. See *ibid.,* p. 205.

[45] For example, *L'Humanité,* Nov. 16, 1905, Mar. 11, Apr. 19, 30, 1907, May 16, 1909, Apr. 1, July 9, 1911, Apr. 6, June 24, Sept. 22, 1912; *Journal officiel,* May 10, 1907, pp. 954-56.

Villeneuve-Saint-Georges, Jaurès was in the forefront of the agitation against the government. Moreover, he fought the attempts of the Guesdists to subject the trade-union movement to the Socialist Party, and upheld the autonomy of the C.G.T.[46]

Jaurès, however, demanded that the Syndicalists surrender their revolutionary views and settle down to a "peaceful reformist action," to a "continuous action for immediate objectives."[47] The function of the trade union, in his opinion, was to provide a transition period in the evolution from capitalism to socialism by limiting the power of the employer through such syndical activities as factory inspection; to educate the workers for collective action and for actual management of socialized industry; and to win reforms to increase the well-being and security of the workers.[48] The Syndicalists, therefore, should abandon both violent direct action and the revolutionary general strike, for these could result only in the triumph of reaction.[49] To prevent violence in strikes, Jaurès recommended the legal strengthening of the right to organize trade unions and to strike; the adoption of proportional representation in order to give the workers a greater field for political action; the compulsory arbitration of labor disputes, and the use of the majority vote in decisions to strike.[50]

As against Hervé and the Syndicalists, Jaurès contended

---

[46] *3e Congrès national . . . 1906*, pp. 164-67; *9e Congrès national . . . 1912*, p. 355; *L'Humanité*, Sept. 14, 1912.

[47] *L'Humanité*, Sept. 4, 5, 1913.

[48] For example, *ibid.*, Sept. 27, 1908, June 7, 13, 1909, Dec. 11, 1911, Feb. 25, 1912, Sept. 4, 12, 1912.

[49] Jaurès, *Études socialistes, op. cit.*, Aug. 29, 1901, pp. 104-21; *L'Humanité*, Sept. 8, 1908, Nov. 7, 1910. Jaurès approved the occasional peaceful use of the general strike to force the government to grant a specific reform. See *L'Humanité*, Mar. 18, 1907, Aug. 24, Sept. 9, 1908.

[50] *La Dépêche*, Oct. 11, 1899; *L'Humanité*, Aug. 12, 1908; Jaurès, "La Réglementation des grèves et l'arbitrage obligatoire," *La Revue socialiste*, 1901, XXXIII, pp. 533-37. Jaurès particularly favored compulsory arbitration, but realizing that organized labor was bitterly opposed to this reform, he withdrew his support. He continued, however, to advocate a referendum in all strikes.

that because the state was the "most alive of associations," it must be conquered from the bourgeoisie by universal suffrage and used for a social transformation.[51] Moreover, electoral and parliamentary action was necessary to counteract the political force which the employers used against the trade unions and to obtain governmental reforms which would enhance the workers' power of resistance; namely, public assistance for school children, old-age pensions, and unemployment insurance.[52] To Jaurès, the Socialist Party was essentially a party of workers, appealing to the petty bourgeoisie only in order to prepare the way for the triumph of the proletariat.[53] He recalled that the trade unions, as well as the Socialist Party, had their scabs and traitors; and he insisted that the evil could be remedied if the workers took a greater interest in politics.[54]

Jaurès's program for the Socialist Party remained the same as before 1905: the attainment of immediate reforms, the conquest of the state by democratic action, and the socialization of industry by "repurchase." During the period from 1905 to 1914 he was a staunch advocate of several social reforms that were being considered in Parliament—a five-and-one-half day week, a minimum wage, an income tax, and a government monopoly of alcohol; and he gave unstinted support to two reforms that were finally realized—the government's purchase of the West Railway in 1908, and the old-age pension law of 1910.[55]

Jaurès continued to advocate collaboration between the proletariat and the liberal bourgeoisie. He favored electoral coalitions with the Radicals on the second balloting during the

[51] See La Dépêche, Dec. 17, 1900; 5e Congrès national . . . 1908, pp. 384-89; L'Humanité, May 2, 1909.
[52] 3e Congrès national . . . 1906, pp. 174-75; L'Humanité, Aug. 17, 1908.
[53] 3e Congrès national . . . 1906, pp. 173-76.
[54] L'Humanité, May 3, 1912.
[55] Ibid., May 22, 1907, Apr. 8, May 30, 1908, June 8, 1909, Apr. 1, 1910, Feb. 19, 20, 1911, Feb. 10, 1912, Nov. 14, 1913; 5e Congrès national . . . 1908, pp. 312-13; 7e Congrès national . . . Nîmes, 1910, pp. 362-77. For Jaurès's ideas on the "repurchase" of industry, see L'Humanité, Oct. 11, 1905.

parliamentary elections of 1906 and the municipal elections of 1907.[56] In 1908, Jaurès declared war on the Clemenceau ministry for its failure to achieve reforms; for its indecisive foreign policy; for its suppression of strikes, and for the shooting of workers at Dravail, Villeneuve-Saint-Georges, and Narbonne.[57] This did not, however, prevent him from favoring the continuation of the policy of electoral coalitions with the Radicals in the parliamentary elections of 1910.[58] In 1912, he again favored coalitions with the Radicals, making the reservation that the Radical candidate must accept proportional representation.[59] Jaurès favored this reform particularly because it would eliminate conflicts between the Radicals and Socialists on the first balloting, and thus open the way to more complete coöperation between them.[60] In 1914 Jaurès proposed that the attitude of the Radical candidate toward the Three-Year Service Law rather than proportional representation be the criterion of socialist support.[61]

Jaurès tried to formulate a policy to obtain socialist support of a ministry without actually forming a bloc. Although he detested Clemenceau, Poincaré, Delcassé, and such socialist "deserters" as Briand and Millerand, he still expected much from such Radicals as Goblet, Léon Bourgeois, and Herriot.[62] He therefore held that if a ministry were really reformist or its existence were necessary to prevent the reaction from creating a chaotic situation favorable to a *coup d'état,* then the Socialists, although continuing to attack the ministry for such undesirable activities as imperialistic aggression, should defend it from the assaults of the reaction.[63] In short, he continued

[56] *2e Congrès national* . . . *Chalon, 1905,* pp. 100-102; *L'Humanité,* Aug. 20, 1905, Mar. 28, 1906, June 4, 1907.
[57] *L'Humanité,* July 1, Dec. 28, 1908, May 16, 1909.
[58] *6e Congrès national* . . . *1909,* pp. 473-81.
[59] *9e Congrès national* . . . *1912,* p. 188.
[60] *L'Humanité,* Sept. 23, Dec. 23, 1909.
[61] See below, pp. 138-39, 178.
[62] *L'Humanité,* Sept. 17, 1905, June 12, Dec. 20, 1912.
[63] *Ibid.,* Sept. 23, 1910; *3e Congrès national* . . . *1906,* pp. 50-52; *8e Congrès national* . . . *1911,* pp. 192-96.

to believe that collaboration should continue between the Socialists and the bourgeois parties in Parliament.

Jaurès led the Reformists in their attack on the antipatriotism of the Syndicalists, of Hervé, and of Lafargue. In 1901, when syndicalist antipatriotism was expressed in the *Manuel du soldat*, Jaurès defended patriotism; and when Hervé championed antipatriotism in 1905, Jaurès made himself the acknowledged spokesman for the reformist position: that patriotism is necessary for the attainment of socialism—by the reformist method.

In a series of articles written at the end of 1901 and at the beginning of 1902, Jaurès conceded the argument that *la patrie* meant possession of property; but he contended that possession of property was implied in political liberty; and that the term *sans-patrie* could be applied to the proletariat only when it was deprived of the system of political liberty which would enable it to acquire property.[64] He said that before the democratic period of the French Revolution the proletariat was rightly called *sans-patrie* by Marat, inasmuch as at that time the proletariat possessed neither property nor political rights. Likewise, the masses were patriotic after 1792 because they hoped to use universal suffrage in order to gain property, education, a share in the government, and other concessions. When the Revolution failed and the proletarians were weighed down by the excesses of capitalist exploitation, without possessing the counterweight of political liberty, they were again really *sans-patrie*—as the *Communist Manifesto* and the Chartists had declared. But, Jaurès continued, the formula of the *Communist Manifesto*—"the proletariat has no fatherland"—was not a denial of *la patrie*; it was a lament that the proletariat "did not have a *patrie up to the present*." If this formula were detached from its surrounding circumstances, it was "a piece of nonsense."

[64] *La Petite République*, Dec. 24, 26, 28, 1901, Jan. 2, 4, 1902.

This formula, Jaurès held, was an absolute principle only on the assumption of ever-increasing pauperization of the working class.[65] Moreover, Jaurès pointed out, the *Communist Manifesto* also stated that the proletariat "must constitute itself the nation."[66] This contradiction, he argued, could be solved only by the theory of revolution; that is, a sudden revolution could take the proletariat, which is outside *la patrie*, put it in place of the bourgeoisie, and make it the nation before complete fusion with the world proletariat.[67] If, however, the replacement of the bourgeoisie by the proletariat were attained through a gradual acquisition of power by the latter and a gradual transformation of existing institutions, there would be "a long period when the nation would still not be confounded with the proletariat, but when, nevertheless, the proletarian—under penalty of ruining his basis of action—will be obliged to protect and strengthen the nation as such."

Jaurès also contended that the concept of a gradual transformation eliminated the negation of *la patrie* contained in the concept of the class struggle.[68] After socialism was achieved, he said, there would be unity between bourgeoisie and proletariat in a "common administration"; and "at each moment of the struggle, each of the concessions imposed on the bourgeoisie by the growing proletariat is preparatory to this full unity of the future." Moreover, in their struggle against the bourgeoisie, "the proletarians use the fundamental resources of their *patrie* . . . Therefore, even in the immense effort of universal emancipation, the workers remain united

[65] *Ibid.*, Jan. 2, 4, 7, 1902.
[66] The statement in the *Communist Manifesto* referred to by Jaurès is: "The workingmen have no country. We cannot take from them what they have not got. Since the proletariat must first of all acquire political supremacy, must rise to be the leading class of the nation, must constitute itself *the* nation, it is, so far, itself national, though not in the bourgeois sense of the word."—Karl Marx and Friedrich Engels, *Manifesto of the Communist Party*, authorized English translation (London), p. 20.
[67] *La Petite République*, Jan. 4, 7, 1902.
[68] *Ibid.*

to the national life. As proletarians and as [social] revolutionaries, as well as men, 'the workers have a *patrie.*' "[69]

In his debates with Hervé, Jaurès clarified the practical necessity of patriotism. From the point of view of social transformation, he declared, the ideas of Hervé were "the most infantile
and reactionary imaginable," for the social revolution demands "political liberty, economic prosperity, and general education."[70] Of the utmost importance was the question whether
the proletariat would work for socialism "in a nation free or
slave, autonomous or conquered, rich or poor, enlightened or
ignorant." Of the conditions necessary for socialism, Jaurès
stressed political liberty—the Republic. He explained that the
proletariat worked for emancipation in the "national shop";
and in analyzing why the national shop must be defended, he
pointed to the Republic.[71] To Hervé's declaration that the conquest of France by Germany would mean eliminating the
frontier between the two proletariats, Jaurès answered: "Yes,
one frontier gone, but also one Republic gone, one living liberty gone, one resource and one guarantee for the European
revolution gone."[72]

Jaurès cited Hervé's own distinction between the political

[69] *Ibid.* Jaurès contended that Marx later modified the "too abstract ideas
and too simple confections that he had formulated in the *Manifesto.*" He recalled that Marx had scolded the Frankfort Assembly for having failed to
unite Germany; Marx had hoped for the triumph of the democratic traditions
of the French Revolution against autocratic Russia; he had espoused the
national interests and national policy of England against Russia; he had
favored Napoleon III's policy against Russia, but he had condemned Napoleon's policy in Italy because Napoleon, in attacking Austria, was injuring
the power of Germany. Jaurès believed that this signified that Marx had
substituted a realistic utilization of "national forces and national passions
for communist aims, in place of an abstract and narrow interpretation of
socialist internationalism.—*Ibid.,* Jan. 9, 1902.

[70] *L'Humanité,* May 17, 1905, Oct. 6, 1906.

[71] Debate with Hervé, *L'Humanité,* May 29, 1905; *ibid.,* June 16, 1905.

[72] *Ibid.,* Nov. 6, 1905. In order to strengthen his argument that "national
autonomy was confounded with Republican liberty," Jaurès again pointed
out that the two were identified in the French Revolution; and he argued
that the conquest of France in 1871 had meant the triumph of political
reaction, relying on the Prussian troops.—*Ibid.,* June 11, 16, 1905.

régimes of Western Europe and those of Russia and Turkey. Then he remarked that if France had the right to defend herself against Russia and Turkey, she had the right to defend the Republic at all times; for "however iniquitous, however bourgeois, however reddened with the blood of the workers the Republic may be," it is still the "definitive form of democracy" and the régime which all of the European socialists desire.[73]

Jaurès also argued that if Hervé would defend a country after the establishment of a socialist order, he should defend a country which by virtue of possessing a Republic is already on the road to socialism.[74] Hervé, in defending the Russian Revolution of 1905, was not defending an established socialist order, but the Russian Republic from which that order would some day emerge.[75] Either Hervé must disown defending the Russian Revolution, or he must admit that "in Europe a republican and autonomous France is worth more than a France subjected to the Kaiser."

Jaurès denied the argument that because the French Republic as well as the German monarchy oppressed the proletariat the latter had nothing to fear from conquest. He declared that two oppressions, the oppression of the conqueror added to that of the national government, were worse than one; that the oppression of the conqueror, demanding "silence, passivity, inertia," fell most heavily on the workers; that a régime of conquest distracted the attention of the proletariat from the work of social transformation to that of obtaining national independence.[76] Besides, Jaurès argued, the meetings of the German Emperor and the Russian Tsar held the possibility "that the political and social reaction definitely seeks its welfare in the abasement of free peoples."[77] For these reasons, there

[73] Debate with Hervé, *L'Humanité*, May 29, 1905.
[74] *4e Congrès national* . . . *1907*, pp. 270-71.
[75] *L'Humanité*, Nov. 6, 1905.
[76] *Ibid.*, May 29, 1905; *3e Congrès national* . . . *1906*, p. 252.
[77] *L'Humanité*, Aug. 4, 1905.

was no distinction between an international war to defend France and a class war. Hervé's doctrine was, therefore, "a revolutionary abdication even more than a national abdication"; it was a "doctrine of counter-revolution, ominous to socialism, ominous to the working class."[78]

In order to strengthen still further his defense of patriotism Jaurès argued that nations were necessary units of the future order. Time after time, he asserted that in the future order nations would retain their autonomy, and that—as the internationalism of the French Revolution envisaged—they would be federated rather than absorbed into an amorphous humanity.[79] Such autonomy was necessary, in his opinion, to prevent a "colossal and absorbing centralization."[80] The Socialists must choose between "a crushing planetary bureaucracy and the federation of autonomous nations harmoniously associated in the common work of humanity."

Jaurès also believed that nations must be retained in the future order because "the vital instinct of individual conservation" bound the individual "to the group which influences him and which he influences."[81] The basic relationship between the individual and the nation, he explained, was the cultural bond; and because of this relationship "the destiny of the nation becomes the destiny of the individual." If France were conquered, "she could no longer transmit abundantly to her sons the treasures of her language and her literature, from Montaigne to Diderot and from Diderot to Renan; there would also be loss of vitality, psychological weakening, intellectual bankruptcy, and organic suffering of individuals . . ."

The disappearance of the nation, Jaurès proceeded, would

[78] *Ibid.*, May 29, Aug. 4, 1905; *3e Congrès national . . . 1906*, p. 252. See also Jaurès's identification of patriotism and democracy in his *L'Armée nouvelle* (Paris, 1918), pp. 435-42.
[79] *La Petite République*, Jan. 2, 1902; *L'Humanité*, Aug. 15, 1906; Jaurès, *Conférence à Nîmes* (Nimes, 1910), pp. 21-22.
[80] *L'Humanité*, May 29, 1905.
[81] *La Petite République*, Jan. 4, 1902. See also *L'Armée nouvelle, op. cit.*, pp. 449-58.

also mutilate in advance the great communist humanity of tomorrow.[82] Because "humanity has need of the free German genius, as it has need of the French genius," both the German and French Socialists would be "guilty of the crime of lèse-humanity," if they allowed their *patries* to be violated. Jaurès was not always so willing to place "free German genius" on an equal footing with that of France, for his final argument in defense of patriotism was that because France had the "historic vocation" of establishing democracy and of making it the instrument of justice among men, France therefore had "a double right to live: her right as a nation and her right as the initiator of liberty."[83]

Jaurès attempted to circumvent Hervé's argument that if the Socialists were patriotic they would be forced to march against each other at the outbreak of a war. He asserted that permanent peace was possible and that the war which would hurl the proletarians against one another might never come.

Between 1893 and 1898 Jaurès had followed the Marxists in regarding war as a "normal fact" under capitalism; and he had insisted that the only way to abolish war between nations was to abolish the economic struggle between individuals by instituting a socialist régime.[84] During the Fashoda crisis of 1898, however, Jaurès noted that the Socialists were showing a new interest in maintaining peace; and he began to hope that socialist protest in England and France would prevent war.[85] When the conflict between England and France was finally settled peacefully, he joyfully remarked: "From now on, and even before having conquered power . . . socialism contributes to the work of peace . . . and by its ideal of harmony, by the regulating action of the international proletariat, it

[82] *L'Humanité*, May 29, 1905.
[83] *Ibid.*, Aug. 28, Sept. 18, 1905, Mar. 28, 1906; *Journal officiel*, Nov. 17, 1905, p. 3346.
[84] *La Petite République*, July 28, 1898; *La Dépêche*, Sept. 15, 1898; *Action socialiste, op. cit.*, p. 403.
[85] *La Petite République*, Nov. 17, 1898, Jan. 26, 1899.

counterbalances all the forces of disorder, of brutality, of savagery."[86]

To support his belief in the permanence of peace, Jaurès held that the causes of the wars which had occurred from 1815 to 1870—namely, the struggle for political liberty and national self-determination—had been eliminated; that since 1870, there had been no wars between important European nations; and that the few remaining points of dispute could be settled simply "by the progress of democracy and liberty."[87] Peaceful settlement of disputes was assured by the growth of economic ties between nations, resulting in "the internationalism of production and exchange among growing societies, and the internationalism of solidarity and justice of the organized universal proletariat."[88] The new internationalism of the proletariat—with its mass pressure to prevent war—made permanent peace a "profound possibility."[89]

After 1899 Jaurès believed that the advance of disarmament and arbitration would make permanent peace still more certain. In the period before 1899, Jaurès had considered disarmament as a "dangerous chimera";[90] but after 1899 he regarded disarmament as "inevitable," because universal military training and the development of science made war suicidal, while the advance of compulsory arbitration made it unnecessary.[91]

Jaurès admitted that the Hague treaties were narrow and illusory, and that the bilateral arbitration treaties of the first decade of the twentieth century were ineffectual because they excluded questions concerning the honor and vital interests of the conflicting nations; but he asserted that it is "almost always from weak and shapeless beginnings that great institutions develop."[92] These treaties, "the rudiments of a first at-

[86] *Ibid.*, Jan. 26, 1898.   [87] *Ibid.*, Jan. 12, 23, Oct. 9, 1902.
[88] *Œuvres*, Jan. 23, 1903, I, 406.   [89] *Ibid.*   [90] See above, p. 42.
[91] Jaurès, *Discours à la jeunesse* (speech in 1903; Paris, 1926), p. 15; *L'Humanité*, Jan. 24, 1907.
[92] *La Petite République*, Dec. 2, 1900, Oct. 9, 1902.

tempt at the organization of peace against violence and against the menace of unleashed war," would soon be strengthened; a complete set of international rules would be drawn up; and these would make certain the permanence of peace.[93] War, he remarked, might be inherent in capitalism, but there was no iron law of war, just as there was no iron law of wages; and war, as well as the exploitation of labor, could be curbed before the attainment of socialism.[94]

This optimism of Jaurès did not solve the problem of what would happen to proletarian internationalism if a war should nevertheless break out. Jaurès confessed that this is "the most terrible and poignant matter of conscience which still faces humanity in its march forward."[95] But Jaurès evaded the conflict. He stated that the Socialists desired peace, except when "the security, the dignity, the pride of France" were involved.[96] And he insisted that it must "not be peace at any price, not peace at the price of independence."[97]

When Hervé insisted that the problem must be faced rather more concretely, and offered the proposal that the proletariat rebel in case of war, Jaurès countered that Hervé did not solve the problem of how to reconcile national duty with international duty; he merely eluded it by suppressing national duty.[98] Yet the prospect conjured up by Hervé—the German and French proletarians at each others' throats—was too much for Jaurès; and he finally made a concession to international proletarian solidarity, that is, insurrection by the Socialists of an *aggressive* nation. During the Moroccan crisis of 1905, when the forward policy of France evoked in Jaurès a "horrible night-

[93] *Ibid.*, Dec. 2, 1900; Jaurès, "Le Programme socialiste, les organisations ouvriers, et l'action international," *La Revue socialiste,* 1904, XXXIX, 388; *La Dépêche,* Oct. 4, 1905; *L'Humanité,* Aug. 9, 1905, Feb. 2, 1907.
[94] *L'Humanité,* July 9, 1905; *La Petite République,* Sept. 30, 1902.
[95] *L'Humanité,* May 29, 1905.
[96] *Discours à la jeunesse, op. cit.,* pp. 16-17.
[97] "Le Programme socialiste, les organisations ouvriers, et l'action international," *op. cit.,* p. 386.
[98] *L'Humanité,* May 29, 1905.

mare of war," he declared that "it is good for the governments
to know that the war clouds they accumulate can throw out the
flash of revolution which will destroy them."[99] If France were
attacked, Jaurès decided, the Socialists should defend her; but
if the government were the aggressor, the Socialists should resist the war to the point of a general strike and insurrection. In
1906, Jaurès defended the motion presented by Vaillant, the
so-called Limoges Resolution, in which this compromise was
contained.

The first part of the Limoges Resolution stated that the
army is "the organized armament of the state, existing for the
purpose of keeping the working class under the economic and
political yoke of the capitalist class."[100] The Resolution proceeded to "recall to the workingmen of all countries that a government cannot menace the working class of a foreign nation
without assaulting both the working class of that nation and
the international working class; that the menaced nation and
its working class have the duty to safeguard their independence and autonomy against this assault, and in this they have
the right to count on the aid of the working class of all countries; that the antimilitarist and purely defensive policy of the
Socialist Party demands that it strive for the military disarmament of the bourgeoisie and the arming of the working
class through the general arming of the nation."

The second part of the Resolution stated that "the international solidarity of the proletarians and of the Socialists
of all nations is their first duty"; and it advised demonstrations on May 1 on behalf of peace. When a conflict threatened,
the International Socialist Bureau and the Interparliamentary
Conference should arrange to summon their delegates in order
that they, with the help of national and international labor organizations, might decide on preventive measures ranging
"from parliamentary intervention, public agitation, and popu-

[99] *Ibid.,* May 20, June 16, 1905.
[100] *3e Congrès national . . . 1906,* pp. 260-62.

lar demonstration, to the general strike of labor and insurrection."

Jaurès was careful to make clear that he looked upon the threat of insurrection in the event of France's aggression chiefly as a warning to the governments "that in unleashing war, they unleash the revolution."[101] He believed that the threat of insurrection would be sufficient to prevent aggressive action.[102] And he hoped the occasion for an insurrection would not arise; for although he declared that war would interrupt the evolutionary transformation to socialism, and that a revolution against a war might be successful, yet he feared that the revolution would be followed by a long period "filled with crises of counter-revolution, furious reaction, exasperated nationalism, suffocating dictatorships, monstrous militarism—a long chain of retrograde violences and of base hatreds, of reprisals, and of servitudes."[103]

To Hervé's argument that if insurrection could be used in an offensive war, it could also be used in a defensive war, Jaurès replied that if the war were defensive, the revolution would lack the necessary support of the majority, for the people would feel that the revolution was sacrificing national independence.[104] If the war were offensive, the revolutionaries, by attacking "the government of adventure and treason," would appear as the true defenders of the country.[105]

Jaurès also emphasized that insurrection in case of an offensive war did not imply sanctioning antipatriotism; it implied, on the contrary, a more perfect defense.[106] The proletarians must be made to understand that during the revolution, "they must not for a single moment abandon this national independence which is a necessary part of human civilization and

[101] L'Humanité, Dec. 31, 1905, Nov. 11, 1907.
[102] 3e Congrès national . . . 1906, pp. 254-55.
[103] L'Humanité, May 29, July 9, Aug. 4, 1905.
[104] 4e Congrès national . . . 1907, p. 260.
[105] Ibid., pp. 260, 283; L'Humanité, May 20, Sept. 18, 1905.
[106] 4e Congrès national . . . 1907, p. 283; L'Humanité, Sept. 18, 1905; L'Armée nouvelle, op. cit., pp. 459-61.

the necessary organ of proletarian action."[107] But then, Jaurès argued, defending the revolution necessarily meant defending the national existence; and Hervé was really contradicting himself by insisting on defense of the nation during the insurrection but not during the period when socialism was developing out of the Republic.[108]

Finally Jaurès brought forward "a certain sign" by which the aggressor and the victim could be determined: the willingness of the conflicting nations to arbitrate the dispute.[109]

When Clemenceau accused him of being *sans-patrie*, Jaurès summarized his ideas on patriotism and peace as follows: (1) Autonomous nations are necessary to humanity; and the conquest of France, in particular, would be a disaster for European liberty and justice. Therefore, "it is the right and duty of France to defend herself against all violent attacks and to bring the defensive power of France to its maximum." (2) Everyone must work for peace, which is necessary for social progress; and the international union of the workers is the best guarantee of peace. (3) If a war should occur, the proletariat must fight for France's defense; but if France should be the aggressor, the people, although continuing to defend France, would have the right to overthrow the government and the social system that engendered the conflict. (4) The Socialists did not demand social reforms as the price for their defense of the nation, but the people would defend the nation with an ardor in proportion to their share of well-being and right; that is, the more the *patrie* becomes a *patrie* for all, the more it could expect the devotion of the people.[110]

Thus, while Hervé, Lafargue, and the Syndicalists offered a policy of socialist insurrection in every case of international

---

[107] *L'Humanité*, Dec. 31, 1905.
[108] See *ibid.*, Nov. 6, 1905; *3ᵉ Congrès national . . . 1906*, pp. 251-52; *4ᵉ Congrès national . . . 1907*, pp. 270-71.
[109] See *L'Humanité*, Sept. 9, 1907 (address); *4ᵉ Congrès national . . . 1907*, pp. 266-68.
[110] *L'Humanité*, Sept. 18, 1905.

conflict, Jaurès proposed a dual policy: if the government were aggressive, then insurrection; if France were attacked, then patriotism—aid to the government in the defense of the nation against the invader. The Blanquists, Guesdists, and the rank and file of the Socialist Party were asked to choose between these two policies. And the full implications of Jaurès's policy were revealed when this policy was applied to specific problems of twentieth-century international relations.

VII

THE PROBLEMS OF PATRIOTISM

JAURÈS developed the implications of the reformist policy of patriotism and peace, and impressed them upon the
rank and file of the socialist movement. Hervé had warned
that the resolution to fight for France in a defensive war could
easily lead the proletariat into an offensive war. He might have
added that the practice of viewing in a patriotic light such questions as German militarism, rivalry in armaments, the danger of
foreign alliances, French interests in Alsace-Lorraine, and the
problem of Morocco would increase the confusion in which the
French Socialists found themselves when faced with a severe
crisis; for if the Socialists shared the patriotic desires of the
government, the maneuvering of the latter could more easily
obscure the question as to who was the aggressor in any given
case.

The transition from defense of the Social Republic to defense of the interests of the actual Republic was natural and
easy. Socialism, as viewed by the Reformists, necessitated the
development of national prosperity, and in capitalist society,
national prosperity was thought to depend to a large extent
upon commercial and industrial expansion abroad.

Sarraute brought out this relationship lucidly. He remarked:
"Protective tariffs, colonial expansion, conquest of markets,
effective military organization for protecting national interests, a fleet capable of protecting national commercial enterprises—such are the natural consequences of a socialist policy
which today without doubt recoils before these consequences,
but which, admitting the principle [of reformism], must keep
going to the end of this slippery terrain."[1] Sarraute agreed that

[1] Sarraute, *Socialisme d'opposition, socialisme de gouvernement, et lutte de
classe,* pp. 69-70.

these consequences were a severe blow to the ideal of international proletarian solidarity; but, he declared, it "is an inevitable blow, because the policy of reform must concern itself with the economic prosperity of the country as the essential condition of the continuous development of national production."

The conclusion of Sarraute, although an entirely logical consequence of Jaurès's position, was not palatable to the latter. He believed that the attainment of socialism by gradual reform necessitated national prosperity,[2] but to the end he hoped that catastrophe might be averted; and if he strayed after "national interests," he showed loyal devotion to peace and to internationalism. His faith in the necessity for peace and his hatred of war never dimmed. On the contrary, as Jaurès became older, his efforts in behalf of peace became ever more persistent. As each diplomatic crisis rose to the danger point, Jaurès was in the forefront of the struggle against war, striving to marshal the forces of the international proletariat against militarism and aggressive nationalism.

At the same time, and perhaps paradoxically, Jaurès conducted a persistent fight for "national security" and "national interests." In so doing, he played into the hands of the patriots who were willing to settle the problems of Alsace-Lorraine and the colonial rivalry of France and Germany by force of arms. As the foremost socialist leader and as the chief commentator on foreign affairs in L'Humanité, he taught the Socialists to defend France, to view Germany with suspicion, to respect Russia as France's necessary ally, to regard the severance of Alsace-Lorraine as an unpunished crime, to favor French imperialism, and in general to approach the international situation from "the national point of view."

Jaurès's utterances for peace were usually followed by pleas for patriotism. This was true even of his denunciation of the

[2] See above, p. 122.

aggressive nationalism of such men as Déroulède, Delcassé, and Poincaré. From the Boulanger Affair to July, 1914, he constantly denounced the Nationalists for their view of patriotism as an exclusive love for one's nation and a hatred of other nations; for their philosophic justification of war in general and a war of revenge against Germany in particular; for their contemptuous attitude toward arbitration, disarmament, international accord. But as an alternative to the "imbecile chauvinism" of the Nationalists, he offered a "true patriotism" which recognized that other nations were "equally precious portions of the same humanity," and which was, he said, reconcilable with internationalism and the maintenance of peace.[3] When he denied that war was necessary for the nation, he contended that peace would strengthen the nation's defensive energy; that a defensive war would infuse the French masses with the spirit of effective combat; that only a peaceful policy would obtain for France the moral support of the other nations.[4] His often repeated argument in behalf of arbitration was that if France were attacked, she would have a stronger morale and the support of the world.[5]

The welfare of the nation was also to the front in Jaurès's vague idea of a league of nations to prevent war.[6] He said that "it is necessary to harmonize in a magnificent federation of law and peace, the autonomous nations which are incessantly menaced by war and weighed down by crushing militarism."[7] He usually put forth this idea of a European league when he

[3] *L'Humanité*, Aug. 4, 11, 14, 1905; Jaurès, *L'Armée nouvelle*, pp. 453-64.
[4] *L'Humanité*, Oct. 6, 1907, Sept. 27, 1912; *La Petite République*, Jan. 25, Mar. 6, 1902; *L'Armée nouvelle*, pp. 463-64; *Œuvres*, Jan. 23, 1905, I, 392-93; *La Dépêche*, June 16, 1905.
[5] *L'Humanité*, Aug. 15, 1905, Sept. 27, Dec. 10, 1912; *Œuvres*, Dec. 23, 1905, II, 416.
[6] At first this league of nations was, in Jaurès's mind, a "league of peace" made up of individuals. Its object was to exert pressure on the various governments to moderate chauvinistic passions, to maintain the territorial integrity of China, and to regulate differences by arbitration." See *La Dépêche*, Aug. 12, 1900; *La Petite République*, Aug. 5, 7, 1900.
[7] *L'Humanité*, Mar. 28, 1911.

was considering the advantages of peace and the disadvantages to the nation of the current system of heavy armaments.

In his controversy with the Nationalists on the problem of disarmament, Jaurès was guided by solicitude for what he believed to be the welfare and the security of France. He repeatedly argued that the tremendous expense of heavy armaments threatened to ruin "the credit of France, her productive force, and all hope of social reform."[8] But, although Jaurès wanted France to take the initiative in disarmament, he did not intend that she should disarm first. The way to fight the Nationalists, he said, was not by proposing "to deliver a disarmed France to the greed of armed neighbors," but by seizing every opportunity to propose "the simultaneous disarmament of the peoples."[9]

Jaurès's campaign for a militia earned him the nationalist epithet of "traitor," but to him the militia was a patriotic as well as a pacifist necessity. His sponsorship of the militia system grew out of his desire, evidenced as early as 1886, to organize a true "nation in arms" by reducing the period of training in the army and by eliminating inequalities in the service.[10] He asked in *L'Armée nouvelle*, the work which con-

---

[8] For example, *ibid.*, Mar. 15, 1907, Nov. 20, 1909.

[9] Viviani, Briand, Millerand, Jaurès, *L'Action du Parti socialiste* (Paris, 1902), pp. 45-46; *L'Humanité*, Feb. 22, 1911.

[10] It has been shown that Jaurès favored the Three-Year-Service Law because it would organize the "nation in arms." After the passage of this law Jaurès supported the Two-Year Law (finally passed by the Radical-controlled Parliament in 1905) because he believed the expense of the large standing army overburdened national economy and thereby weakened national defense. See *La Dépêche*, Apr. 25, 1893. Upon joining the Socialists in 1893, Jaurès adopted part of their idea of a militia. The socialist view of the standing army as the "watchdog of capitalism" played some part in the adoption; but his most prominent argument was that the national defense demanded the reorganization of the army with a view to developing the reserves. See *Discours parlementaires*, Mar. 7, 1895, pp. 399-401, 411-19, 423; *La Petite République*, July 28, 1898. The Dreyfus Affair, revealing the reactionary tendencies of the officers, gave further impetus to Jaurès's desire to reform the current military system. See *La Dépêche*, Sept. 28, 1898; *Journal officiel*, Sept. 28, 1898, pp. 2285-88; Jaurès, "Revue politique," *La Revue socialiste*, 1898, XXXVIII, 518.

tained his idea of a militia, how, if France "is attacked in spite of her effort and her desire for peace, can her chance of safety and the means of victory be carried to the furthest extent?"[11] His answer was the establishment of "a truly popular and defensive army system"; in effect, a militia.

His plan was modeled after the Swiss system.[12] Every boy from the age of ten to twenty years would be trained in gymnastic exercises, rifle practice, and emulative sports. This training would be followed by six months at the school for recruits, after which the recruit, although returning to his civil occupation, would become part of the army. The army would include all the men from twenty to thirty-four years of age, organized by locality and brought together periodically for maneuvers. The "troops of security" on the Eastern frontier would be replaced by the residents of the Eastern departments; each man would keep his arms at home, and mobilization would be facilitated by an extensive system of railroads and motor transport.

In the system outlined by Jaurès there would be two groups of officers. One group, consisting of one-third of all the officers, would be professional military men acting as permanent teachers. They would be chosen by competition, and would receive a four-year course, with expenses paid by the state, at military departments attached to the universities. The other group, civil officers, would be chosen from among those with a good education who had taken special military courses, or from the noncommissioned officers who had shown special merit.[13]

[11] *L'Armée nouvelle,* pp. 1-4.
[12] For Jaurès's outline of the militia system, see *ibid.,* pp. 214-27, 305-11, 340 484-90, 551-56.
[13] The choice of officers would be made by regimental and divisional committees composed of corps commanders, the representatives of different ranks, and the delegates to the Council of Improvement, the last two groups being chosen by universal suffrage. Promotions would be contingent upon further study periods and competitive examination. The General Staff would be chosen by competitive examination. The non-commissioned officers, appointed for their aptitude shown during the first three months at the

Such an army, in the opinion of Jaurès, would contribute to preserving peace. The men composing the militia, having families, would refuse to leave the country to fight and would revolt against the government if it attempted an aggressive war.[14] But they would fight desperately to defend their homes against an invader; and the militia, by creating a true "nation in arms" similar to that of the French Revolution, would render France "inviolable and sheltered from all menaces and all violences."[15]

To fortify his argument that the militia system was superior for national defense, Jaurès spent months in the *Bibliothèque nationale* studying military science. He reached the conclusion that in a war with Germany France must employ defensive tactics based on the full utilization of her reserves through a militia system, rather than offensive tactics based on a standing or "active" army, composed of the young men of twenty-one and twenty-two—to which most attention was then being given.[16] Clausewitz and Moltke, he said, had advised Germany to do the same; but in the next war Germany would have to take the offensive in order to dispatch France before Russia was ready, and in order to keep French troops out of Alsace-Lorraine. For this offensive against France, Germany would have to use her active army; her reserves, like those of France, would defend their homes, but would not leave their country to engage in offensive warfare. Besides, the German government, being imperial and militarist, lacked the moral force to appeal to the "nation in arms."

If, Jaurès proceeded, France also took the offensive with an active army, she was certain to be defeated. As Germany had the larger population, her active army would always be

---

school for recruits, would be given three months of training at a special school.

[14] *Ibid.*, pp. 45-48; Jaurès, *Conférence à Nîmes* (Nimes, 1910), p. 18.

[15] *L'Armée nouvelle*, pp. 14, 45-47, 157; *L'Humanité*, Feb. 7, 1907.

[16] For Jaurès's strategic arguments on behalf of the militia system, see *L'Armée nouvelle*, pp. 17-143.

greater than that of France. The French active army itself was more reluctant to engage in aggressive action than the German active army, and this reluctance would give the Germans a few days' advantage. Moreover, the French offensive would wear itself out against the Vosges Mountains, the Saar River, and the Rhine. If France did succeed in penetrating German territory, the German masses would be forced to defend their homes; and becoming animated with the spirit of the *Landwehr* of 1813, would overwhelm the French army.

France, therefore, would have to meet the attack of the German army with defensive tactics and with the full use of her reserves. Her troops at the frontier would have to retreat until the reserves were mobilized, and then the whole army would strike a powerful blow. Where the active army would fail, her reserves of 2,000,000 men would easily triumph over Germany's 900,000 troops of the active army. If Russia aided France, these tactics would be still more effective. While Germany's active army was held at bay in France, Russia would attack from the east. Indeed, if France planned to mobilize her whole army immediately, she would be so strong that she would not only be sure to be victorious, but she might even deter Germany from declaring war on her.

Yet while Jaurès was agitating for a reduction in the active service as a step toward the militia, the majority of French politicians, led by Poincaré, Barthou, Reinach, Delcassé, Clemenceau, and Millerand, were demanding the lengthening of service to three years in order to compensate for the declining birth rate of France. During the few years before the World War, Jaurès led the Socialists in a furious battle against the Three-Year-Service Law.

The Three-Year Law, Jaurès argued, would give France only 700,000 active troops, while the German army law of 1913 gave Germany 850,000; and it would distract France from preparing her reserves.[17] It would add 300 million francs

[17] *L'Humanité*, Feb. 20, 25, 1913.

to the 872 millions spent yearly on the standing army, whereas a militia would cost only 700 millions.[18] This financial burden of the army would prevent the execution of social reforms and the payment of government subsidies to improve French industry; it would weaken national credit, especially in time of war; and it would render impossible the construction of a series of necessary fortifications along the eastern and northeastern frontiers.[19]

Jaurès warned that the Three-Year Law, by depriving the factories and fields of man power, would bring a limitation of production, economic disorder, higher prices, postponement of marriage, and a further decline of the birth rate.[20] In addition, the Three-Year Law would intensify the physical and mental diseases inflicted on France: alcoholism, tuberculosis, and the debilitating influence of routine.[21]

The law was passed, and Jaurès inspired much of the opposition to its application. But while he was moved in this whole debate by a passion for peace, he also helped to emphasize the need for military preparation, at least for a defensive war with an aggressive Germany.

During the period from 1896 to 1899, Jaurès's early dislike of the Franco-Russian Alliance had returned. The Opportunist government, under Méline, Félix Faure, and Hanotaux,

---

[18] *Ibid.*, Feb. 20, 1913; *L'Armée nouvelle*, pp. 545-46; *11ᵉ Congrès national . . . 1914*, pp. 372-73.

[19] For example, *L'Humanité*, Feb. 20, Oct. 4, 23, 24, Nov. 2, 1913; *11ᵉ Congrès national . . . 1914*, pp. 372-73. For Jaurès's ideas on fortifications, which he wanted erected on the border of Belgium and Luxemburg as well as on the German border, see *L'Armée nouvelle*, pp. 122 ff.; *L'Humanité*, Oct. 4, 1913.

[20] For example, *L'Humanité*, Feb. 20, Apr. 3, Oct. 20, 1913.

[21] *Ibid.*, May 18, 1913. When the lack of facilities to accommodate the increased number of recruits caused an epidemic of illnesses, Jaurès flayed the government for sending boys to barracks in which food, clothing, and coal were insufficient and in which dampness produced fevers, inflammatory diseases, and tuberculosis. He held that the Three-Year Law was to blame for these evils; and "the lives of young men are paying for the criminal haste with which the charlatans of patriotism have improvised their barracks and their law."—*Ibid.*, Feb. 8, 10, 1914.

appeared to him to be subordinating France's interests to those of Russia; France was lending money to Russia, but Russia refused to further France's colonial interests in return; the reaction was persuading the people that a conservative policy was necessary to please the new ally; and although Russia was raising French hopes of obtaining Alsace-Lorraine, she prevented their fulfillment.[22] After the downfall of the Opportunist government, however, Jaurès again accepted the Alliance. He argued that since the overthrow of the Opportunists, the intentions of the Alliance were pacific, and that it was a good arrangement "as long as it remains a purely defensive alliance."[23] Jaurès, now imputing pacific intentions to the Triple Alliance, held that each alliance kept the other in check and curbed the chauvinistic and dynastic ambitions within each country, and that the two alliances were, by extending relations between them, "preparing and sketching a vaster alliance, the European alliance for labor and for peace."[24]

Subsequent events inspired Jaurès with a passionate hatred for Tsarism. In 1903, he attributed the Kishinev pogroms to "the systematic spirit of savage reaction that the Russian government has unchained in order to distract attention from its own despotism."[25] Viewing the Russo-Japanese War as the result of Russia's aggression in Manchuria and Korea and the government's desire to counteract the demands of the workers for reforms, he asserted that if France allowed her-

[22] *La Petite République,* Apr. 3, Sept. 1, Oct. 4, 1896, Nov. 13, Apr. 29, 1897. The Tsar, Jaurès declared, was brother to all the other emperors, and he "could not consent to a national reparation which would shake the dynasties of the Occident." The Russian Alliance meant, therefore, "the definitive mutilation of France, the eternal slavery of the conquered provinces, the consecration of the treaty of Frankfort . . ."—*La Petite République,* Oct. 11, 1896, Sept. 4, 1897.

[23] *La Petite République,* Sept. 18, 1902; *Œuvres,* Jan. 23, 1903, I, 398.

[24] *La Petite République,* Jan. 23, Sept. 18, 1902; *Œuvres,* Jan. 23, 1903, I, 398-99. Bismarck, Jaurès explained, had wanted to use the Triple Alliance for the maintenance of peace; and except for a short period when the German militarists and Crispi gave it an aggressive character, the Triple Alliance had used its influence to prevent war.

[25] *La Petite République,* June 6, 1903.

self to be drawn into Asiatic complications, this would be "one of the most monstrous scandals that history has known."[26] He sympathized with the Russian Revolution of 1905 and denounced the French for lending money to the Tsar.[27] Yet, Jaurès still maintained that France should hold fast to the Alliance because it was necessary for European equilibrium.[28]

Jaurès also welcomed the *Entente cordiale* with England, for he felt that the only two great democracies in Europe ought to stand together. But although the *Entente* appeared to him as "a new instrument, a new guarantee of peace and of civilization,"[29] he had occasion to learn that the *Entente* might be dangerous. As early as 1904, he realized that as France desired to recover Alsace-Lorraine and England feared Germany's economic competition, the *Entente* might be turned to aggressive use.[30] He denounced Delcassé and the English capitalists for trying to direct the *Entente* against Germany.[31] Yet in spite of these danger signals, Jaurès favored the Triple Entente, counseling that France remain allied with "sage and equitable England," and with "the wisest diplomats and the most liberal and most noble parties in Russia."[32]

Likewise, Jaurès welcomed the Franco-Italian rapprochement. This appealed to him because it brought the two governments together at the moment of France's attack on the Church.[33] He also regarded it as one of those developments which tended to attenuate "the exclusive and offensive character" of the two alliances; and he believed that as Italy formed a bond of cordiality between the two alliances, the

[26] *La Dépêche*, Feb. 12, 1904; *L'Humanité*, Oct. 8, 16, 17, 1904; *Œuvres*, Feb. 14, 1904, II, 63-75.

[27] *L'Humanité*, Jan. 7, June 25, 1906.

[28] *Ibid.*, Aug. 4, 1909.

[29] *Ibid.*, June 16, 1905; *La Petite République*, July 10, 1903.

[30] *Œuvres*, Nov. 10, 1904, II, 120.

[31] For example, *L'Humanité*, Apr. 6, June 7, 1905; *Pages choisies, op. cit.*, pp. 42-46.

[32] *L'Humanité*, Apr. 24, 1913. See Renaudel's statement in *Le Procès de l'assassin de Jaurès, Mars 24-29, 1919* (Paris, 1919), p. 96.

[33] *La Petite République*, Oct. 20, 1903.

rapprochement would hasten the transformation of the alliances into a single permanent league "from which every chance of war will be excluded."[34]

Jaurès, in spite of his desire for peace, sanctioned the aims which aggressive patriots hoped to gain by war with Germany. He fought for pacific settlement of all points of conflict between France and Germany—Alsace-Lorraine, colonies, the Near East; but at the same time, he insisted on the protection of France's "rights" and "interests."

Concerning the question of Alsace-Lorraine, Jaurès still expected "the coming of liberating democracy" to free "oppressed races and violated nationalities," and to bring France the "true revenge."[35] Moreover, he helped to keep alive French interest in Alsace-Lorraine by proposing, as a compromise of the question, that Germany grant autonomy to the two provinces.[36]

In 1903 Jaurès demanded that Germany abolish the status of Alsace-Lorraine as an "imperial province administered by the Emperor"; eliminate military service for its inhabitants; admit French culture into the schools and universities; and grant liberty of press, meeting, and association.[37] After 1909, Jaurès favored a more complete political autonomy, and in 1911 he warmly espoused the plan of the Alsatian Socialists to obtain for the two provinces "a constitution which would make them autonomous; representation in the *Bundesrat* and

[34] *Ibid.*, Apr. 11, 1901, Sept. 28, 1902, July 18, 1903.

[35] *L'Humanité*, Aug. 8, Oct. 18, 1905; *Discours parlementaires*, Introduction, p. 173.

[36] Jaurès now believed that when the inhabitants of Alsace-Lorraine "can freely express their sympathies for the France of the Revolution, when they will be sure of never having to carry arms against her, and when they can fully communicate to their children all the glories and all the genius of France, they will actually aid in the noble conciliation of the German genius and the French genius. This will be the true return to *la patrie*, the only return that will not cost humanity blood and tears, the only return that will not foment for still more centuries the spirit of combat and the infinite sequence of conflicting revenges."—*La Petite République*, Sept. 5, 1902; *Œuvres*, Jan. 23, 1903, I, 4ა8.

[37] *La Dépêche*, Aug. 28, 1903; *La Petite République*, Dec. 22, 1903.

self-administration with a republican form of assembly elected by universal suffrage, with functionaries chosen from among the Alsatians and Lorrainers themselves."[38] He held that these "guarantees" were the necessary preface to reconciliation between France and Germany, and that without them there would be in Europe "neither progress nor civilization."[39] It was only after 1910 that Jaurès changed his idea that a Franco-German rapprochement could come only after the granting of autonomy, and began to argue that autonomy could be obtained only by such a rapprochement itself.[40]

Jaurès also applied his policy of patriotism and peace to economic and colonial competition—a great source of French enmity toward Germany. Early in his career, Jaurès had favored colonial expansion. When he joined the socialist movement, he accepted the Marxist contention that imperialism grew out of the contradictions in capitalism which caused overproduction and underconsumption at home; but he held that intransigent opposition to imperialism was futile.[41] "In fact," he stated, "all the peoples have a colonial policy; and it is not our formulae of the future that will make them retrace their steps. The law of expansion and conquest to which all peoples yield seems as irresistible as a natural law; and even though we denounce eloquently all the villainies, all the corruptions, all the cruelties of the colonial movement, we shall not stop it; the human flood does not stop flowing because it has been filtered by us."[42] In view of Jaurès's extremely optimistic belief in the power of ideas to control economic and political movements, this was an unusual statement. A few years later Jaurès revealed that he really did not wish to check colonial developments.

In 1901, when Jaurès favored the promotion of France's

[38] L'Humanité, Nov. 11, 1909, Aug. 20, 1910, Jan. 31, 1911.
[39] Ibid., Feb. 28, Nov. 11, 1909.
[40] Ibid., Apr. 3, May 11, 1911, Mar. 12, 1913.
[41] La Petite République, May 17, 1896.
[42] Ibid.

influence in China, he remarked that "it is impossible to stop expansion, suddenly to halt the vital energies of the nation."[43] Two years later, he stated that he always seconded and always would second "the pacific and reasonable expansion of French interests and of French civilization."[44] In 1904, he argued, against Guesde, that English imperialism had benefited the natives and had increased the well-being of the English workers.[45] In fact, in his opinion even if England became socialist she would continue her colonial empire.

Jaurès never requested independence for a single French colony.[46] When he drew up a set of principles for a "practical attitude" toward imperialism, he not only omitted independence, but implied the retention of the colonies. His three principles were: first, the Socialists must, by following colonial developments carefully and by attacking the "excessive pretensions of each nation," guard against the possibility of war's arising from colonial competition; secondly, the Socialists must force the governments to give "a more and more international character to the principal economic forces that avidly arouse the peoples"; and thirdly, the Socialists must demand "the most humane treatment, the maximum of guarantees for the vanquished peoples or the subjected races of Asia, America, and Africa."[47]

Jaurès saw two dangers to the French colonial empire. The first was the yellow peril.[48] He warned England, France, and Holland, that only "a régime of guarantee, of equity, and of humanity" would keep the peoples of India, Indo-China, and

---

[43] *Ibid.*, Nov. 26, 1901.   [44] *Œuvres*, Nov. 23, 1903, II, 48.
[45] *Discours parlementaires*, pp. 126-30.
[46] Jaurès mentioned colonial emancipation only when discussing other peoples' imperialism. He called England's rule in India "murderous foreign exploitation"; he sympathized with Cuba; and he admired the "heroic combat for liberty" of the Philippines. See *La Petite République*, Aug. 12, 1897; *Action socialiste, op. cit.*, pp. 522-25; Preface to Henri Turot, *Aguinaldo et les Philippines* (Paris, 1899), pp. viii-ix.
[47] *La Petite République*, May 17, 1896.
[48] Jaurès had always feared that Japan, China, and India might join hands and rise against the Occident. See *ibid.*, Aug. 5, 1900.

the Dutch East Indies from seeking, "as a means of deliverance, the possible intervention of the large and organized peoples of the Far East."[49]

Then, too, the French colonies might desire to emancipate themselves. In proposing reforms for the natives of Tunis, he warned that in default of such reforms, "a storm will arise over all of African France, and terrible difficulties will accumulate for us."[50] He noted that economic unrest in Algeria —caused by the disappearance of small landholdings and by the competition of cheap French industrial products—was producing "a strong fanatical movement" against France; and he advised that reforms were necessary to show the natives how "noble and unselfish" the "genius of Europe" really is.[51]

While Jaurès strove to prevent colonial competition from engendering war and supported international management of still unoccupied regions, he intended to complement rather than abandon the pursuit of French rights and interests. Jaurès believed that his two principles would reconcile peace and patriotism in the field of commerce and colonies.

During the conflict between England and France over the Sudan in 1898, Jaurès insisted that France had the right to establish communications between the Congo Basin and the Nile Basin and the right of free navigation of the Nile.[52] He wanted France to defend "her dignity and her rights." He

[49] Œuvres, Nov. 10, 1904, II, 131-32.   [50] L'Humanité, Apr. 9, 1912.
[51] La Dépêche, May 1, 8, 1895. Jaurès, it is to be noted, insisted that France derive full benefit from her colonies. In 1896, when France had completed her conquest of Madagascar, he contended that she must exercise her sovereignty over the island and, in spite of the objections raised by the other powers, establish a tariff favorable to France. He stated: "We who are absolutely hostile to costly and dangerous colonial enterprises, nevertheless do not wish that France suffer any humiliation, any moral diminution. We will aid the government of our country, whatever it may be, to maintain resolutely the rights which so much French treasure and the loss of so many French lives have consecrated. This is an opportunity for France, who is at present, so the Moderates contend, the plaything of nations, to affirm energetically her rights and her strength."—Ibid., Apr. 1, 3, 1896.
[52] Ibid., Apr. 1, 1896, Apr. 29, 1897, Nov. 9, 1898; La Petite République, Apr. 3, 1896, Nov. 5, 1898.

praised the Opportunist government for using "firm language," and he denounced Russia for backing out of the "first situation in which she could help France." He inveighed against English chauvinism and the English capitalists who had "tried to obstruct our exploration, limit our influence, arrest our commerce everywhere"—in Egypt, Central Africa, and Madagascar.

Nevertheless, Jaurès was adamant against war. He decried the aggressive attitude of the French Nationalists; he called upon the proletariat to organize international meetings in order to force peaceful negotiations; and when the meeting at Fashoda of the French Captain, Marchand, and the English general, Kitchener, threatened a military outbreak, Jaurès demanded the withdrawal of the French.[53] To preserve French interests in that region and to prevent war he had already favored the application to the Nile of the international system used for the Danube and the Suez Canal; that is, a guarantee for all nations of free passage from the source of the Nile to the Sea.[54]

Between the Fashoda crisis and the series of Moroccan crises, the events in China gave Jaurès an opportunity to elaborate his view of joint international action. Jaurès favored the marketing of "French merchandise and French ideas" in China, and the establishment of schools and charitable organizations by the French government.[55] He demanded for France "the same guarantees, the same expansion, the same rights" that the others enjoyed. But he believed that France could obtain these ends without taking another slice of Chinese territory; and he feared that further territorial division of China would endanger the peace of Europe. He therefore suggested that the European nations should coöperate to establish "a régime of guarantees" in China; that is, to persuade China

[53] La Dépêche, Nov. 9, 1898; La Petite République, Nov. 5, 17, 1898, Jan. 26, Mar. 23, 1899.
[54] La Petite République, May 17, 1896, Aug. 12, 1897.
[55] Ibid., Nov. 26, 1901, Mar. 26, 1902; L'Humanité, Oct. 11, 1905.

"to concede loyally to all the peoples of Europe the same liberties and the same facilities for commerce, along with complete safeguards for the political and territorial integrity of China herself."

In 1903, a revolt in Morocco and a raid by Moroccan Berbers on French troops patrolling the Algerian frontier gave France an occasion for intervention. The reaction of Jaurès was that France had in Morocco rights and interests "of the highest order" which she must conserve.[56] He explained that because the Moslem world was a united whole and because developments in one Moslem region influenced the others, France had to exert "moral action" on the Moslem regions not directly under her control. Moreover, France had economic interests in Morocco and was forced to establish "an economic régime favorable to Algeria and to France." He proclaimed that this moral and economic action was necessary for the inhabitants of Morocco themselves; it would bring "guarantees of security, guarantees of well-being, means of development infinitely superior to those of this despoiling, anarchic, violent, evil Moroccan régime which, aided by the outbreaks of a morbid and bestial fanaticism, absorbs and devours all the resources of the country."

According to Jaurès, however, the interests of France could not be furthered by armed intervention and the establishment of a protectorate.[57] Such a policy, he warned, would alienate the Moroccan people. Furthermore, the difficulty of conquering Morocco—a mountainous country inhabited by nine million hardy, well-armed natives—would necessitate a large expeditionary force, costing thousands of French lives and adding millions to an already overburdened budget. By undertaking a military expedition, France would surrender her "rôle as mediator in maintaining the peace of the world." Hence, the proper

[56] Œuvres, Nov. 20, 1903, II, 42-43; La Petite République, Sept. 23, 1903.
[57] Œuvres, Nov. 20, 1903, II, pp. 43-47; La Petite République, Sept. 23, 1903; La Dépêche, Sept. 19, 1903.

method of furthering French interests was "to wait until the play of Moroccan affairs offers us an occasion favorable for pacific intervention." The present civil war would engender financial difficulties; and the Moroccan government would be glad to give France a favorable economic position in return for financial aid. If France gave the Moroccan government a share in the railroads she built and the mines she opened, the Moroccan people would be favorable to the extension of French influence. Jaurès was sure that the other interested countries, particularly England and Spain, would approve of this peaceful penetration and would give France the necessary permission.

In 1905, France sent a punitive expedition against raiders across the Algerian border, and shortly after, the visit of the Kaiser to Tangier threatened to precipitate a major crisis between France and Germany. Jaurès then added the danger of international war to his list of patriotic objections to French conquest of Morocco. He attacked the French government for having antagonized the German government, contending that the French militarists wanted an expedition and Delcassé wanted the prestige of having conquered Morocco single-handed; and, as a result, France neglected Germany's interests, defied her, and violated the Madrid convention of 1882.[58] Jaurès demanded that Delcassé give up his "shortsighted and vain policy"; and he insisted that instead of risking her security in "enterprises of hazard and barbarism," France should negotiate a settlement with Germany like that arranged with England. "Patriotism," he declared, "demands that diplomacy remove every equivocation and prevent, by frank explanations, all possible conflicts."

Jaurès, however, maintained that German diplomacy "is far from being above reproach."[59] In fact, "German militarism and absolutism have a large share of responsibility in this moral

[58] *L'Humanité*, Dec. 23, 1903, Apr. 1, 6, May 4, June 7, 1905; *Diplomatie et démocratie, op. cit.,* pp. 6-8.
[59] *L'Humanité*, Apr. 20, Dec. 23, 1905; *Diplomatie et démocratie,* p. 8.

crisis." Germany had aggravated the difficulties with "theatrical protestations"; she had forced France into a position of apparent submission to her; she had made bad use of the mistakes of French diplomacy; and she had tried to turn England against France. Indeed, Germany was now using against Delcassé the same policy "of brutality, of chiding, of menace," that she had used against France for thirty years. Therefore, Jaurès concluded, there must be no "parliamentary sanctions that are too unilateral"; and real opposition to war must be put forth by both countries.[60]

Jaurès believed that the best solution for the Moroccan problem could be reached by an accord between France and the other European nations.[61] He welcomed enthusiastically the Conference of Algeciras, which included France, England, Germany, Spain, and the United States. And he wanted the Conference to effect "an international organization of control and guarantee," and the economic "open-door."[62]

International control of the Moroccan police and finances, according to Jaurès, would serve French interests.[63] It would bring security for the Algerian frontier, protection of French residents and merchants in Morocco, a financial organization which would insure the payment of Morocco's debts, and a prosperity for Morocco that would also benefit Algeria. Moreover, international management would save France from alienating the natives by using force. Even a mandate for France, Jaurès maintained, would place the burdens of military expense and unpopularity on France, while the rest of the world would benefit from France's labor. The only exception to international management should be French ownership of the railroads that linked Morocco with Algeria, for upon these were dependent the latter's prosperity and security. In

---

[60] *L'Humanité*, Apr. 20, 1905.
[61] *Ibid.*, June 5, 1905.
[62] *Ibid.*, Apr. 10, Aug. 31, Sept. 2, 3, 1905.
[63] *Ibid.*, Apr. 10, Aug. 31, Sept. 2, 6, 1905, Jan. 4, 1906: *Journal officiel*, Dec. 16, 1906, pp. 4035-36.

short, Jaurès demanded that French interests be pursued without incurring the disadvantage of political conquest.

After Algeciras, three new Moroccan crises occurred. In 1906 France intervened during a civil war between the Sultan Abd-el-Aziz and Mulai-Hafid; in 1909 the French police arrested several deserters from the French Foreign Legion who had been sheltered by the German Consul at Casablanca, an action that evoked strong protest from Germany; and in 1911, when France again intervened in Morocco, this time capturing Fez, Germany sent a cruiser to Agadir to emphasize her claim to a share of the spoils. In these crises, Jaurès fought strenuously to preserve peace, pleading for the type of international coöperation exemplified by the Boxer expedition, and demanding that France cease provoking Germany with violations of the Pact of Algeciras.[64] When the danger of war became particularly acute in 1911, Jaurès was active in stimulating the French proletariat to join with the German proletariat in a great protest against war.[65]

But patriotic arguments played an important rôle in the demands of Jaurès for a peaceful solution of these crises. He opposed French intervention on the ground that Mulai-Hafid should be allowed to triumph because he would be able to create an orderly, independent Morocco in which France could continue her peaceful penetration.[66] He continually evoked the concept of France's mission and insisted that the Moroccan policy prevented her from fulfilling her rôle in serving peace and civilization.[67] In 1908, when the Young Turk Revolution broke out, Jaurès believed that the whole Moslem world was in ferment and that this situation gave France an opportunity to increase her influence among the Moslem peoples. But, he

[64] *L'Humanité*, Nov. 26, 1906, Apr. 1, 26, Sept. 4, 5, 7, 1907, Nov. 5, 6, 7, 1908.
[65] *Ibid.*, July 2, 3, 5, 7, 1911. Many large demonstrations were held throughout France, one of the largest of which occurred at Bustang, near the frontier, and was attended by many Germans.—Hubert-Rouger, *op. cit.*, 74-75.
[66] See *L'Humanité*, Aug. 26, 27, 1908, Mar. 10, 1911.
[67] For example, *Journal officiel*, Jan. 24, 1908, p. 99.

argued, if France continues her oppression of the Moroccans, her interests will be harmed by her loss of influence among the other Moslems, an influence that had come to her because she had been "a country of generosity and of right."[68]

France's security against an aggressive Germany was the outstanding consideration of Jaurès during these crises. He warned that the Pan-Germanists were always ready to conquer a bit of territory; that the German reactionaries sought to direct the German people against France in order that they might protect their political and social privileges from the Socialists and the democrats; that the English capitalists wished to embroil France in a war with Germany, hoping thereby to destroy the German naval and merchant fleets.[69] To provide these groups with the pretexts they sought, Jaurès proclaimed, was treason to France.

Thus, from 1903 to 1913, Jaurès fought the government's Moroccan policy because it threatened to create an international war and because (as he told the Chamber of Deputies) he was concerned for France, for her "material and moral interest."[70] Although resisting war, his concern for France brought dangerous denunciations of Germany. His views on Morocco were another lesson in patriotism as well as in peace.

Jaurès also formulated a patriotic policy for the Near East. From the time of the alliance of Francis I with the Turks in the sixteenth century, there had been strong political and trade connections between France and the Turkish dominions in the Balkans and Asia Minor, connections that had been strengthened by the influence of French Revolutionary ideology on the independence movements of the Balkan nations. As early as 1890 Jaurès declared: "Our influence in the Near East

[68] *L'Humanité*, Aug. 27, 30, 1908. When Jaurès spoke of French influence, he still thought of French interests. This is illustrated by his assertion that only a policy of justice and sympathy would "assure in the renewed world of Islam the highest ideas of France and the just diffusion of her interests."—*Ibid.*, Sept. 1, 1908.
[69] *Ibid.*, May 28, 30, July 17, 1908, May 2, 1911.
[70] *Journal officiel*, Jan. 28, Feb. 24, 1908, pp. 139-43, 417.

results from a long tradition of enlightened and tolerant protection toward the populations which, although different from us in race and religion, trust us. We will not desert this tradition."[71] France's trade relations with the Near East, he added, were an important factor in the growth of national prosperity, which in turn would permit France "to maintain, without strain, a large army, a large and powerful navy. . . ." This policy often brought Jaurès into collision with Russia; but it also resulted in severe condemnation of Austria-Hungary and Germany.

Jaurès desired France to intervene to protect the Armenians and the Macedonians; to realize the reforms promised by the Treaty of Berlin; to aid the Greeks against the Turks; and to establish Cretan autonomy.[72] He insisted that whereas Russia feared that the freedom of the Turkish national minorities would cause her own minorities to revolt, the problem of Alsace-Lorraine required that France "sustain everywhere the right of peoples to unite with whomever they choose."[73] Russia was the object of a large portion of Jaurès's criticism on the ground that she discouraged "the nationalist tendencies of the Balkan peoples"; but Germany, and in particular, William II, received severe condemnation. "This false great man," Jaurès said of William II, "is, for Germany, the meanest kind of a despot; his heart is a prison."[74] William wanted to suppress the Greeks because they represented the principle of liberty in the Near East, while the Sultan represented the principle of authority.[75] If France accepted "the subaltern rôle assigned to her by Prussian militarism," then she would sacrifice in these areas all her "traditions and interests."[76]

During the Balkan crises of 1908 and 1912-13, Jaurès's

[71] *La Dépêche*, Mar. 19, 1890.
[72] See *ibid.*, Mar. 10, Apr. 21, 1897, Feb. 19, 1903; *Action socialiste, op. cit.*, pp. 450-58.
[73] *La Dépêche*, Feb. 24, Mar. 10, Apr. 21, 29, 1897.
[74] *Ibid.*, Feb. 24, 1897.
[75] *Ibid.*, Mar. 10, 1897.   [76] *Ibid.*, Mar. 10, Apr. 29, 1897.

concern for France's interests as well as for peace led him to elevate the Austro-Hungarian Empire to the position of Europe's second most villainous state. Jaurès was extremely favorable to the Young Turk Revolution of 1908, an event that was generally regarded as advantageous for France and England rather than for Germany, because Germany had enjoyed the favor of the dethroned Abdul-Hamid. Jaurès approved the liberalism of the new government and its desire to free Turkey from European tutelage; and he proclaimed that it deserved all of France's sympathy.[77]

When Bulgaria declared her independence, Jaurès did not permit his friendship for the Young Turks to neutralize his partiality for independent nationalities. He approved Bulgaria's action, insisting,. at the same time, that France could really help the Turks by renouncing her Moroccan policy.[78] But when Austria-Hungary annexed Bosnia-Herzegovina, Jaurès was outraged. He likened the annexation to "the clumsy action of a flock of birds of prey which circles over the Turkish people."[79] When Austria and Russia threatened armed conflict Jaurès condemned both countries, holding that the crisis was due to "the base stroke of Baron von Aehrenthal and to the hypocritical protestations of Russian diplomacy."[80] He refused to sanction France's support of Russia; but, on the other hand, he demanded that Austria solve the problem by giving Bosnia-Herzegovina a democratic, constitutional régime.[81]

Jaurès's suspicion of Austria turned to hatred during the war of Serbia, Montenegro, Greece, and Bulgaria against Turkey in 1912; and the war of Serbia, Montenegro, Greece, Rumania, and Turkey against Bulgaria in 1913. Serbia demanded Albania, part of the territory taken from Turkey. While Russia approved, Austria, fearing an increase in Serbia's power, blocked Serbia's claims. An armed conflict seemed imminent.

[77] L'Humanité, July 15, Aug. 30, Oct. 6, 1908.
[78] Ibid., Oct. 6, 1908.
[79] Ibid., Oct. 11, 1908.   [80] Ibid., Jan. 1, Feb. 26, 1909.
[81] Ibid., Jan. 1, Feb. 26, 27, 28, Mar. 29, 1909.

Jaurès led the socialist çampaign for peace during this crisis. Even before the First Balkan War, he had foreseen the possibility of armed conflict between Russia and Austria over Albania, and had inveighed against the selfish land-grabbing policies of Austria, Russia, and France, holding that Turkey must be allowed to proceed with her reforms.[82] Then, when the outbreak of the war in the Balkans threatened to precipitate a general European conflict, he insisted that if this conflict ensued, both Austria and Russia would be equally guilty, for neither would be fighting for national honor or truly national interests.[83]

In order to forestall a conflict Jaurès proposed that an international socialist congress be summoned to voice the protest of the proletariat.[84] When such a congress was held at Basle, Jaurès took a leading part in this attempt to mobilize international proletarian solidarity against war.[85] After the Congress of Basle had disbanded, he strongly advocated the solution which it had proposed: an autonomous Albania within a democratic federation of the Balkan nations.[86]

But throughout the crisis, Jaurès exhibited extreme animosity toward the government of Austria-Hungary. To be sure, he criticized Russia, holding that Panslavism was partly to blame for the crisis; that Russia had agreed to the annexation of Bosnia-Herzegovina; and that she had organized the Balkan League in order to avenge herself on Austria.[87] But Jaurès's attack on Russia was offset by his attack on the ally of France's traditional enemy.

Jaurès repeatedly blamed the crisis not only on Russia but on "the Archduke of Austria and his clever cohort of Jesuits, fomenting, to the profit of the Hapsburg monarchy, a Slavic

[82] *Ibid.*, Aug. 7, Oct. 2, 3, 7, 8, 1912.
[83] *Ibid.*, Oct. 10, 14, 20, Nov. 10, Dec. 10, 12, 13, 1912.
[84] *Ibid.*, Oct. 7, 14, 1912.
[85] See Paul Louis, *Histoire du socialisme en France*, pp. 335-37; reports of the Congress of Basle in *L'Humanité*, Nov. 12, 1912.
[86] *L'Humanité*, Nov. 29, 1912.
[87] *Ibid.*, Nov. 10, 1912.

Catholicism."[88] "Austrian diplomacy," he said, "is responsible in large part for the troubles of the Balkans. The annexation of Bosnia-Herzegovina was effected in violation of international treaties; and, this annexation occurring on the day after the accession of the new Turkish régime, was an attack on civilization and peace. By stiffening Ottoman chauvinism Austria has wounded Serbian sentiment; she has intensified ill-feeling. She has awakened greed. By what right can she now unleash war in order to keep within the limits she fixes the movement she herself has caused?" Besides, because Austria gave her populations brutality when she should have given them justice, she was herself responsible for the nationalist agitation among the Serbs; and now she wanted to escape her just punishment by distracting the nationalist aspirations of her populations by a war. This idea of Austria's part in Balkan affairs remained with Jaurès and the French Socialists, ready to be used to condemn Austria's actions in 1914, and to condemn Germany for seeming to approve of them.

Thus, during the period from 1898 to 1914 Jaurès fought for peace, but he also preached a concrete form of patriotism based on the resolution to defend France against attack; to insure her security by means of a national militia and the Triple Entente; to restore the lost provinces; to further France's interests and prestige in China, Morocco, and the Near East. The party as a whole did not accept all the implications of Jaurès's policy; but from 1905 to 1914, the leaders of the party adopted the patriotic basis of that policy.

[88] *Ibid.*, Oct. 20, Nov. 10, Dec. 12, 13, 1912.

VIII

THE TRIUMPH OF REFORMISM

WHILE the conflict over policy was being waged between Hervé and Lafargue on the one hand, and the Reformists, led by Jaurès, on the other, the most vital question was: To which side would go the supporters of Guesde and Vaillant? The *Fédération du Nord* and the *Fédération de la Seine*, under the leadership of Guesde and Vaillant, respectively, were the most powerful socialist groups in France. During the Dreyfus Affair and the quarrel over ministerial participation, these groups represented the real bulwark of revolutionary socialism against reformism. But many of their followers became attracted by the promise of reforms—a promise enhanced by the stimulating effects of imperialist expansion on French industrial development; while others were won to the democratic method by the increasing successes of the Socialists at the polls.

After 1905 Vaillant became almost completely a Reformist. At the Congress of Nancy in 1907 and the Congress of Toulouse in 1908 Vaillant defended the electoral and parliamentary method as the adaptation of the class struggle to contemporary conditions.[1] In his opinion, universal suffrage permitted the attainment of a new social order by a gradual evolution.[2] Hence Vaillant supported national and municipal "public services"; an agricultural program based on reforms; and the pension bill to which Hervé and Lafargue were opposed.[3]

[1] *4ᵉ Congrès national . . . 1907*, pp. 505-6; *5ᵉ Congrès national . . . 1908*, pp. 155-64.

[2] Vaillant, *L'Évolution économique et la révolution sociale* (Paris, 1906), pp. 30.

[3] See *6ᵉ Congrès national . . . 1909*, pp. 226-29; *7ᵉ Congrès national . . . Nîmes, 1910*, pp. 257-67; *8ᵉ Congrès national . . . 1911*, pp. 336-37.

Vaillant's partiality for the Republic grew with his acceptance of reformism. In the decade after the Commune, the Blanquists had despised universal suffrage; but because of the persecution they had suffered under the Empire, they had believed that the Republic should be defended against every threat of the reaction.[4] In 1889, however, Vaillant, representing the *Comité révolutionnaire central*, signed the manifesto of the P.O.F. which condemned the Republic and republicans alike and asked the voters to repudiate both Ferry and Boulanger.[5]

With his turn to reformism Vaillant again expressed devotion to the Republic. At the Congress of Amsterdam Vaillant declared that "because the Republic is the necessary *milieu* for proletarian emancipation, they [Vaillant and his comrades] are ready to sacrifice their lives to save it."[6] This attitude toward the Republic was expressed in Vaillant's approval of electoral coalitions with the republican bourgeoisie. At the Congress of Châlons in 1905, Vaillant proposed a resolution that gave the federations the power to choose their own course on the second balloting.[7] This resolution, in opposition to the view that the federations should maintain socialist candidates on both ballotings in all cases, implied the freedom of the federations to support bourgeois republican candidates if the Socialists were running behind. At the Congress of Saint-Étienne in 1909, Vaillant proposed to give the National Council of the party more power in deciding policies on the second balloting, but the new motion provided for electoral coalitions of Socialists and Radicals to defeat the reaction.[8]

[4] See the articles of Blanqui and Vaillant asking the proletariat to defend the bourgeois Republic from the reaction, in *Ni Dieu, ni maître*, Nov. 20, 22, 1880.

[5] *Parti ouvrier français. Aux travailleurs*, Aug. 1889, pp. 3-5. See above, p. 17.

[6] *Discours de Jules Guesde, Auguste Bebel, Edouard Vaillant à Amsterdam*, p. 26.

[7] *2e Congrès national . . . Chalon 1905*, pp. 89-90.

[8] *6e Congrès national . . . 1909*, pp. 49-55. Vaillant's new motion provided that the socialist candidates should be withdrawn on the second balloting if they could not win by themselves, except when the National Coun-

In the period from 1905 to 1914 Guesde also favored the attainment of socialism by democratic means, and he took a position similar in many respects to that of Kautsky. On the one hand, he retained his old Marxian belief that there could be little change in the condition of the workers until they had conquered the state and socialized industry. Hence, he discounted or denied the efficacy of such reforms as old-age pensions, the repurchase of the West Railway, and the nationalization of mines.[9] Moreover, he retained his former idea that trade unions and coöperative societies are useful only to facilitate the conquest of the state—by recruiting members for the Socialist Party, by spreading propaganda, and by contributing money to the party.[10] Against Hervé, he argued for the suppression of revolutionary syndicalism, contending that it prevented the workers who opposed violent direct action from joining the unions.[11] He maintained, against both Jaurès and Hervé, that the trade unions and coöperatives must be brought under the wing of the Socialist Party.[12]

But when it came to the question of how the state was to be conquered, Guesde accepted both universal suffrage and insurrection. At Nancy in 1907 he stated that "we must be ready to seize political power, the essential instrument of our emancipation, by all methods, from the ballot to the general strike and insurrection."[13] But Guesde now seemed to place more

---

cil decided they must be maintained in order to defeat the candidates of the reaction. In other words, if the Socialist was leading, he would be maintained; if the Radical was leading, the Socialist would be withdrawn; and if a reactionary was winning and the Radical running third, the Socialist would be maintained. This meant an electoral coalition, for the Socialists would vote for a Radical in the lead or in second place to a reactionary, and the Radicals would vote for a Socialist in those positions.

[9] See *L'Humanité*, June 5, 1906; *8e Congrès national . . . 1911*, pp. 203, 217-18, 337-40; *9e Congrès national . . . 1912*, pp. 242-49

[10] See *3e Congrès national . . . 1906*, pp. 186-92; *7e Congrès national . . . Paris, 1910*, pp. 118-27.

[11] *4e Congrès national . . . 1907*, p. 493.

[12] *Ibid.*, p. 500; *7e Congrès national . . . Paris, 1910*, p. 125.

[13] *4e Congrès national . . . 1907*, p. 180.

reliance on the ballot. At the Congress of Limoges Guesde attacked Hervé for disparaging the electoral action that had brought 200,000 supporters to the Socialist Party.[14] At Nancy, he declared that the proletarians who "have spilled and still spill their blood" for "this electoral instrument" will not believe that it is of secondary importance; "it is not universal suffrage, it is not the ballot which can be held responsible for its sterility; it is the working class which must be accused, the working class, which, having in its hands such a weapon, has not known how to use it. The working class must be taught to use this weapon instead of rejecting, as some do today, the use of the weapon it possesses in favor of a weapon it does not possess."[15]

Guesde's desire to use universal suffrage was the decisive factor in his attitude toward the socialist electoral policy. In 1905, Guesde, siding with Jaurès and Vaillant against Lafargue and Hervé, favored socialist support of republican bourgeois candidates on the second balloting in order to defeat reactionary candidates; and he agreed that because the federations had always conducted their electoral policy on the second ballot "in a republican sense," they should be allowed to decide the attitude toward the bourgeois candidate in each particular case.[16] Likewise, at the Congress of Saint-Étienne in 1909, Guesde rejected Hervé's motion that the socialist candidate be maintained on both ballots, and he supported the existing resolution allowing the federations to choose their policies individually.[17] For Berth and Lagardelle this was the decisive proof that Guesde had become a Reformist.[18]

[14] *3e Congrès national . . . 1906*, p. 247.
[15] *4e Congrès national . . . 1907*, pp. 311-12.
[16] *2e Congrès national . . . Chalon, 1905*, pp. 103-4.
[17] *6e Congrès national . . . 1909*, pp. 500, 596-97.
[18] Lagardelle argued that this favoring of coalitions showed Guesde's desire to conquer the state by democratic means. A truly revolutionary attitude, he said, would be concerned only with propaganda and would insist on the maintenance of socialist candidates on both ballots.—Lagardelle, "Révolutionnairisme électoral," *Le Mouvement socialiste*, 1906, XVIII, 386-90.

Along with Guesde and Vaillant the vast majority of the Socialist Party turned to universal suffrage and the Republic and were willing to collaborate, in whole or in part, with the liberal bourgeoisie. Jaurès, Guesde, and Vaillant were followed by almost all of the younger leaders of the party, including Albert Milhaud, Albert Thomas, Marcel Sembat, Renaudel, Compère-Morel, Bracke, and Jean Longuet (grandson of Marx and nephew of Lafargue). Hervé had only a small following; those unionized workers who did not follow the advice of the Syndicalists to boycott the Socialist Party were followers of Guesde and Vaillant. As for Lafargue, he had never been a popular leader and had almost no following.[19]

The triumph of reformism was recorded in the resolutions of the party congresses. Sometimes the congresses attempted to arrange compromises in order to obtain a semblance of unanimity on general policy. For example, although the general resolution of the Congress of Toulouse in 1908 mentioned the necessity for direct action against the employers and affirmed the right of insurrection, it emphasized the importance of reforms and parliamentary action.[20] On the whole, however, the position of the Reformists dominated even those resolutions that were adopted unanimously. The resolution of the Congress of Saint-Étienne in 1909 on the necessity for a program of agricultural reforms was adopted unanimously— even though it omitted Hervé's view that the chief aim of socialist propaganda in the country should be to prepare the peasants to support a workers' insurrection.[21] This was also true of motions favoring "municipal services" and nationaliza-

[19] Charles Rappoport, another of the Guesdist group, was the only important member of the party who followed Lafargue in his adherence to the revolutionary method as it was understood by the Marxists in the eighteen-eighties. See Rappoport, *La Révolution sociale* (Paris, 1912), in *Encyclopédie socialiste*, edited by Compère-Morel, Vol. IV.

[20] *5e Congrès national . . . 1908*, pp. 484-85.

[21] *6e Congrès national . . . 1909*, pp. 588-90. For Hervé's views on an agricultural program, see *ibid.*, pp. 362-69.

tion of railways, both of which were passed without a vote by mandates.[22]

When the congresses voted a choice between two opposing motions, the reformist motion won. Jaurès's view that the Socialists should vote for the old-age pension project, then under discussion in Parliament, obtained a majority over a motion demanding the rejection of the law.[23] Similarly, at both the Congress of Limoges and the Congress of Nancy the view held by Jaurès that the trade unions could further the actual social transformation triumphed over Guesde's idea that trade unions were but primary schools for socialist propaganda.[24] Likewise, Jaurès's conception of coöperatives (that they would further the evolution towards a socialist order by introducing socialized property) prevailed over the conception of Guesde, who held that their value was limited to propaganda and financial support of the Socialist Party.[25]

The reformist views of the majority were most clearly expressed in the decisions concerning electoral tactics, for in 1910, 1911, and 1912, this problem of action on the second balloting was bound up with the whole question of revolution or reform. At Saint-Étienne in 1909 Hervé argued that because the attainment of socialism could come through insurrection only, electoral campaigns should aim at propaganda alone; and therefore socialist candidates should be maintained on the second ballot under all circumstances.[26] But the motion of Vaillant, proposing that if the socialist candidate could not be elected in a district, the republican candidate should be sup-

[22] *8ᵉ Congrès national . . . 1911*, pp. 442-43, 461.

[23] The motion was carried by a vote of 199 to 155, with 4 abstentions. *7ᵉ Congrès national . . . Nîmes, 1910*, pp. 435-38.

[24] At Limoges Jaurès's conception won by 148 to 130, with 9 abstentions; at Nancy his conception won by 164 to 141, with 1 abstention. *3ᵉ Congrès national . . . 1906*, pp. 135-36, 164-65, 201-3; *4ᵉ Congrès national . . . 1907*, pp. 344, 347, 524.

[25] Jaurès's conception won by 202 to 142. *7ᵉ Congrès national . . . Paris, 1910*, pp. 199-203.

[26] *6ᵉ Congrès national . . . 1909*, pp. 496-97.

ported against the reactionary, won by an overwhelming majority.[27]

At the Congress of Nîmes in 1910 the motion providing that the federations could use their own judgment in making alliances which would defend democratic institutions, extend political and syndical liberties, and work for secularization and social reforms, won by a large majority over motions prohibiting all alliances with the bourgeoisie.[28] At the Congress of Saint-Quentin in 1911, when the problem of tactics in the municipal elections arose, the federations were again empowered to support republican candidates on the second balloting.[29]

The final decision on the problem of patriotism in the unified Socialist Party followed the same course. With Jaurès went Vaillant and his followers. Vaillant, himself, as a member of the Blanquist group in the Commune, had the tradition of its republican patriotism behind him.[30] Even when he had been a revolutionary, the traditional association which caused him to value the Republic, also led him to retain the patriotism which had once been identified with devotion to the Republic.[31] There is some evidence, however, that the Blanquists, following the example of Blanqui himself, were gradually giving up their republican patriotism and assuming an attitude more in accordance with their revolutionary views.[32]

[27] Vaillant's motion won by 263 to 41. *Ibid.*, pp. 592-96.

[28] The motion favoring coalitions received 210 votes, and the motions opposing them received 23 and 18. *7e Congrès national . . . Nîmes, 1910,* pp. 490, 500-6.

[29] The motion for the maintenance of candidates on both ballotings was defeated by 372 votes to 21. The motion for the abstention of the Socialists on the second balloting if they could not win was defeated by 269 to 102. The resolution of the Congress of Châlons leaving the decision to the federations was passed without a vote by mandates. *8e Congrès national . . . 1911,* pp. 444, 453-56.

[30] See A. Zévaès, *La Question de l'Alsace-Lorraine et le socialisme* (Paris, 1917), pp. 6-8; *Auguste Blanqui* (Paris, 1920), pp. 161 ff.

[31] See *Ni Dieu, ni maître,* Jan. 2, 1881.

[32] In 1881, for example, Blanqui himself declared that a tricolor should not adorn a socialist meeting, because since the "Bloody Week," the tricolor had lost its meaning.—*Ibid.*, Jan. 2, 1881.

But with his return to reformism after 1905 Vaillant assumed a position quite similar to that of Jaurès. In fact, the motion of the Seine (the Limoges Resolution),[33] which Jaurès approved, was presented by him. "The nation," he said, "is a fact. It is the *milieu* in which the working class of a country evolves, and it is the cadre in which each working class becomes class conscious and begins to feel that it is bound to the working class of other countries, with the international working class, in the defense and struggle against internal and external rulers."[34] Hence, he argued, patriotism need not be separated from proletarian internationalism and peace. In fact, the opposition to war contained in the Limoges Resolution really served patriotism: it would prevent an invasion of the country; it strove to obtain militias which would provide superior defense for the nation; and it provided that the international proletariat would come to the aid of a country that was attacked.[35]

The decision of Guesde to defend the nation was even more important than that of Vaillant, for Guesde's followers were the best organized, most powerful group in the Socialist Party. If the Guesdists had accepted antipatriotism, the resulting "defeatism" would probably have had an important effect on the events of the War and the subsequent history of the labor movement in France and elsewhere. But the Guesdists cast their vote with the patriots.

Guesde opposed the revolutionary general strike at the outbreak of *any war whatsoever* on the ground that antipatriotism and antimilitarism interfered with the attainment of socialism.[36] The military general strike, according to Guesde, was an "anarchist dupery" and caused the workers to defer their conquest of the state until a war gave them an opportunity to revolt.

[33] See below, pp. 128-29.
[34] *3e Congrès national . . . 1906*, pp. 223; *L'Humanité*, June 16, 1905.
[35] *L'Humanité*, June 16, 1905; *3e Congrès national . . . 1906*, pp. 224-26; *4e Congrès national . . . 1907*, pp. 183-86, 191.
[36] *3e Congrès national . . . 1906*, pp. 239-47; *4e Congrès national . . . 1907*, pp. 181, 229-30, 307-12.

Besides, the antipatriotism implied in the general strike was an additional obstacle to the already difficult task of winning recruits to socialism. The Socialists should concentrate on spreading their propaganda by means of electoral action; and because the German Socialists would refuse the military general strike, antipatriotism would be a potent weapon against Socialists during electoral campaigns—especially in the frontier regions. Guesde maintained that wherever antipatriotism had been stressed socialist membership had fallen.[37]

Moreover, Guesde told the Congress of Nancy, the proposal for a military general strike would handicap the Socialists in those countries which banished and imprisoned them for advocating treasonable practices. Another argument used by Guesde was that if the military general strike was resorted to, it would disorganize the defense of a country with a strong socialist movement; and it would allow the crushing of this country by one with a small number of Socialists, thus inflicting a blow on the socialist movement as a whole. Also, in Guesde's opinion, the general strike at the outbreak of a war was doomed to failure, for then all considerations, even of the proletariat, would be subordinated to national defense; and, as had happened at the outbreak of war in 1870, the leaders of the insurrection would be arrested and shot as spies.[38]

But the crux of Guesde's argument against Hervé was that the workers must defend the nation in order to defend democracy. He remarked: "They say to the peasant, to the worker: 'You have no *patrie*.' . . . Since 1848, since universal suffrage has been put into his hand as a weapon, the proletarian has a *patrie*; and if he does not act with it, that is his own fault."[39]

[37] During one year, Guesde said, membership in the Socialist Party had dropped in the Department of the Yonne from 576 to 397; and in the Department of Seine-Inférieure, from 400 to 250. *4ᵉ Congrès national* . . . *1907*, p. 307.

[38] *3ᵉ Congrès national* . . . *1906*, pp. 240-41. The successful insurrection of September 4, 1870, Guesde added, took place, not at the outbreak of the war, but after a decisive defeat.—*Ibid.*, p. 257.

[39] *Ibid.*, pp. 243-44.

Hence, Guesde approved the first part of the Limoges Resolution because it clearly stated that as the proletariat could use universal suffrage to take over the wealth which is the *patrie*, the proletariat must defend the nation.[40]

Disagreeing with the idea of the general strike to prevent even an aggressive war, Guesde presented a motion which proposed a struggle against war that could be waged without electoral loss through antipatriotism and without sacrificing the defense of the nation. The heart of this motion (called the motion of the Nord) declared that war would disappear only with capitalism; that the only way the Socialists could fight war and militarism without weakening socialism was "by reduction of military service, pursued internationally; by the simultaneous refusal of all credits for army, navy, and colonies; and by the substitution of the general armament of the people for permanent armies. . . ."[41] This motion, in Guesde's opinion, would serve peace more than would antipatriotism; for the motion would aid socialist recruiting and would lessen the menace of standing armies.[42] At the same time, it would not prevent the Socialists from overthrowing capitalism at the conclusion of a war.[43]

Guesde was willing to take one step toward the prevention of an aggressive war. "In the presence of a threat of war of conquest or of adventure," he explained, "the representatives of the organized proletariat must hurriedly unite (as the last decision of the International Bureau anticipates) to take all possible measures to avoid the conflict."[44] But Guesde did not explain what these measures would or could be.

At the Congress of Limoges, three motions were presented by the committee on attitude toward war: Hervé's motion of the Yonne, advocating resistance to *all* wars by the revolutionary general strike; the motion of the Seine, presenting the views of

[40] *Ibid.*, p. 244; *4ᵉ Congrès national . . . 1907*, p. 311.
[41] *3ᵉ Congrès national . . . 1906*, pp. 244-45.
[42] *4ᵉ Congrès national . . . 1907*, pp. 305-6.
[43] *Ibid.*, p. 312.   [44] *Ibid.*

Jaurès and Vaillant that the nation should be defended if attacked, and that aggressive action should be resisted with all possible means, including the revolutionary general strike; and Guesde's motion of the Nord, rejecting the general strike at the beginning of *any* war.

The 285 votes represented in the Congress, of which 143 constituted an absolute majority, were divided among the three motions as follows: Yonne 31, Nord 98, and Seine 153.[45] That is, the motion of the Seine won an absolute majority; and it was henceforth known as the Limoges Resolution. The motion which favored insurrection at the outbreak of all wars received only about 12 percent of the total votes, and the remaining 88 percent went to the two motions that resolved to defend France if she were attacked.

At the Congress of Nancy in 1907 the motion of the Yonne was again rejected, by a vote of 251 to 41 with 12 abstentions.[46] The motion of Dordogne, which had replaced the motion of the Nord and which was approved by Guesde, was rejected by 175 to 123. The two parts of the Limoges Resolution were then voted upon separately. The first part, holding that the nation should be defended if attacked, received 251 affirmative votes, with 23 opposed and 30 abstaining; the second part, upholding the general strike in case of an aggressive war, received only 169 affirmative votes, with 100 votes (including those of the *Fédération du Nord*) opposed. The Resolution as a whole received 188 affirmative votes, with 16 opposing and 100 abstaining. In short, the vast majority wanted to defend France if attacked, and a smaller majority favored a general strike if France were the aggressor.

After the Congress of Nancy, the large majority which desired to defend France against attack was strengthened, while the small majority which approved a general strike to prevent aggression was weakened. One of the reasons for this change

[45] *3e Congrès national . . . 1906*, p. 263.
[46] *4e Congrès national . . . 1907*, pp. 315-21.

was that the Congress of Stuttgart in 1907, representing the international socialist movement, refused to accept the revolutionary general strike in an aggressive war.

At Stuttgart Jaurès pleaded with the Congress to accept the Limoges Resolution.[47] War, he said, could be prevented even under capitalism. And it was the duty of the Socialists to organize resistance to aggressive war along every possible line. But Jaurès was defeated, largely through the efforts of the German Socialists.

Rosa Luxemburg and the extreme left of the German Social-Democratic Party favored the revolutionary general strike in the event of any war.[48] The influence of Bebel, however, was predominant in the Party. Bebel argued that the proletariat had a fatherland; that Engels had corrected the mistake in the *Communist Manifesto*; that the Resolution of Limoges and Nancy would lead to the jailing of the German Socialists; and that it would encourage the German militarists to attack France with the expectation of having the French government weakened by a socialist revolt.[49]

Bebel proposed a counter motion; and a compromise was reached between his motion and the Limoges Resolution. The Stuttgart Resolution recommended that the Socialists work for the replacement of the standing army with militias; that they advocate arbitration; that they vote against military and naval budgets; that they organize popular demonstrations to prevent war; that if a war threatened, the International Bureau should decide on a course of action according to the circumstances; that if a war broke out, the Socialists should strive to end the domination of capitalism.[50] The failure of the motion to mention the general strike, even for the prevention of aggression,

[47] See proceedings of the Congress in *L'Humanité*, Aug. 21, 1907.
[48] *Ibid.*, Aug. 22, 1907.
[49] *Ibid.*, Aug. 20, 1907. For the attitude of the German Socialists toward patriotism, see C. J. H. Hayes, "Socialist Theory in Germany, 1863-1914," in C. A. Merriam and H. E. Barnes, *Political Theories: Modern Times* (New York, 1924), pp. 295-312.
[50] *L'Humanité*, Aug. 25, 1907.

was regarded as a severe blow to the movement for the general strike.

The force of this blow was recorded at the Congress of Paris in 1910. One motion declared that pacifist education, although admirable, was insufficient to obtain disarmament; that the Hague Court was "a farce, thought up by the bourgeoisie to dupe the proletariat once more"; and that, therefore, "only the revolutionary action of the working class can prevent an international conflict." A second motion limited itself to declaring that the international proletariat was the best instrument for preserving peace; and that the Socialists should strive to enlarge the field of arbitration and to substitute popular militias for the standing armies. The latter motion was carried by a vote of 292 to 34, with 9 abstentions and 19 absent.[51]

A second factor weakening the support of the general strike and insurrection as a weapon against war was the decline of revolutionary syndicalism and its antipatriotic doctrines. In the syndicalist movement there had existed a strong current of what was called "reformist syndicalism"—a syndicalism that was neither antipolitical, antidemocratic, nor antipatriotic. This current resulted, to a considerable extent, from the influence of the political Socialists (particularly the Guesdists) among the rank and file of the trade unionists affiliated with the C.G.T. It also resulted from the crushing defeat of the great railway strike in 1910. And the turning away from antipatriotism was stimulated by the increasing intensity of patriotic propaganda in the few years immediately preceding the World War.

The spokesman for reformist syndicalism was Auguste Keufer, a printer and secretary of the *Fédération du livre*, one of the strongest federations in France. Keufer, a Positivist, despised the Anarchists, condemned violent revolution as unsound, and proposed a gradual movement towards the new social order by means of the "reformist method."[52] The "reformist

---

[51] *7e Congrès national . . . Paris, 1910*, pp. 69-71.
[52] See "Le Congrès et l'opinion ouvrière," *Le Mouvement socialiste*, 1904,

method," he said, must stress *peaceful* trade-union action to gain concessions from the employers;[53] but it must also include political action—the use of democratic means to gain governmental reforms designed to increase the well-being and security of the workers.[54]

The reformist Syndicalists also rejected antipatriotism. Keufer's reply to the questionnaire of *Le Mouvement socialiste* was the only one which declared that the proletariat had a *patrie* and could be patriotic.[55] He stated: "I reply: 'Yes.' The worker has a *patrie* just as do the other citizens; and he can be a patriot. . . . The collective existence which permits the individual and the family to be born, to develop, to manifest their ideas, to satisfy their sentiments, to live freely, is *la patrie*. This same organism, of which the members speak the same language, follow the same customs, submit to the same obligations, in which families are bound together by common affections, protected by the same laws, united and guided by the same historical traditions, is, again, *la patrie;* and those who live in it can and must be patriots, for they are subjected to

---

XIV, 93-95; Keufer, "Les Deux Conceptions du syndicalisme," *Le Mouvement socialiste*, 1905, XV, 21-41.

[53] According to Keufer, "the energetic and pacific action of trade unions" must strive to obtain such reforms as the collective contract, aid the unemployed, and provide sickness and accident insurance. Keufer, rejecting the conception of strikes as skirmishes in the class struggle, recommended their use only as a last resort, to obtain "what the employers do not wish to grant by discussion and by demonstration of the legitimacy of the stated demands"; and they should be conducted without violence. Keufer, unlike the Revolutionary Syndicalists, favored the arbitration of labor disputes and suggested that the trade unionists should always maintain an active interest in the Councils of Labor. See "Les Deux Conceptions du syndicalisme," pp. 23-28, 33-35; A. Humbert, *Le Mouvement syndical* (Paris, 1912), p. 93.

[54] The effectiveness of governmental action, Keufer believed, was proved by the "frequent and happy modifications" of laws protecting women and children in industry; and by the admirable results of laws establishing compulsory education, providing accident insurance, suppressing the use of white phosphorus and white lead in industry, establishing mixed commissions for the arbitration of labor disputes, and so forth.—"Les Deux Conceptions du syndicalisme," pp. 30-32.

[55] "L'Enquête sur l'idée de patrie et la classe ouvrière," *Le Mouvement socialiste*, 1905, XVII, pp. 48-49. See above, p. 100.

its influences by the growing pressure of a long past." And, Keufer concluded, the attempt of mankind to obtain a happier life is impossible "without the indispensable aid of *patries*."

Keufer's replies to the other questions were conditioned by his acceptance of republican patriotism.[56] Political and geographic frontiers, he said, must be recognized until a pacific economic régime was established. Socialist internationalism was to be identified with the international organization of labor, but not with antipatriotism; and with antimilitarism only by its combat against "the spirit of conquest contained in militarism." Hence, Socialists could be patriots; for "love and defense of one's country" could be logically combined with "no less sincere internationalist sentiments." Keufer rejected the military general strike as impracticable, dangerous to those who attempted it, and "harmful to our country." The best means of preventing war was "to organize the international proletariat, to spread ideas of peace. . . ."

To ascertain the exact strength of the reformist Syndicalists is difficult because the vote of the congresses of the C.G.T. was by trade union rather than by proportional representation. For example, on the "Confederal Committee" in 1909, 27 federations representing 30,000 members had 27 votes, while 4 federations representing 130,000 members had 4 votes.[57] But in spite of this difficulty, it is possible to estimate roughly the relative strength of the two groups and the extent to which the trade-union members subscribed to antipatriotism.

As early as 1904, the reformist Syndicalists held that there were at least as many reformists as revolutionaries among the rank and file of the C.G.T.;[58] and there is some evidence to support their contention as far as the attitude toward patriotism is concerned. At the Congress of Amiens in 1906, the majority adopted an antipatriotic resolution presented by

[56] *Ibid.*, pp. 49-51.
[57] Saposs, *The Labor Movement in Post-War France*, p. 23.
[58] Keufer in "Le Congrès et l'opinion ouvrière," *op. cit.*, p. 96.

Yvetot. This resolution declared that because the army was used against the proletariat and because armed conflict duped the worker and sacrificed him to the profit of the capitalists, "the Congress affirms that antimilitarist and antipatriotic propaganda must always increase in intensity and in boldness."[59] Although the motion received a decisive majority (484 votes for it, 300 against, and 49 abstentions), almost all of the unions belonging to the large and powerful federations of the printers, the railway workers, the textile workers, and the tobacco workers, voted against it.[60] Thus, even in 1906, the actual number of patriotic workers in the C.G.T. may have been as great as, if not greater than, that of the antipatriots.

In 1908, an attempt was made by the reformist Syndicalists at the Congress of Marseilles to suppress the antipatriotic part of the Amiens Resolution and to stop the propaganda for a military general strike. Renard, the Guesdist, and Niel upheld the contention that antipatriotism was a political subject that tended to divide the workers.[61] Other speakers argued for continuing the spread of antipatriotic propaganda in the unions.[62] One of the most important parts of the discussion was the statement of Renard and Guérard that the reformist unions, such as those of the textile workers, were not mentioning antipatriotism and were increasing their membership more rapidly than the revolutionary unions.[63] The reformists, however, were again defeated. The resolution of the reformists advocated keeping antipatriotism out of the trade unions, and proposed that the Syndicalists arrange manifestations against war but take no action if the war should break out. This resolution was defeated by a modified antipatriotic motion which declared that the only frontiers to be recognized were those of class; that the

[59] *XVe Congrès national corporatif* . . . *1906*, p. 175.
[60] *Ibid.*, pp. 304-14.
[61] *XVIe Congrès national corporatif* . . . *1908*, pp. 186-92, 198-202.
[62] See addresses of Ebers, Thulier, Boudoux, Broutchoux, *ibid.*, pp. 176-82, 200-203.
[63] *Ibid.*, p. 209.

workers had no *patrie*; and that the workers must answer a declaration of war with a revolutionary general strike. The vote was 621 to 421 in favor of the latter motion, with 43 abstentions.[64]

After 1909, the reformists appeared definitely in the majority. In 1909, the reformist candidate for secretary of the "Confederal Committee" received the votes of 28 federations representing 168,000 members, to his opponent's 27 votes representing less than 100,000 members.[65] And in 1910 the C.G.T. came under the leadership of the moderates, Jouhaux and Merrheim.[66]

At the Congress of Marseilles in 1912, the wishes of the reformist majority obtained primary consideration.[67] This last congress before the World War condemned the Millerand-Berry Law which provided imprisonment for antimilitarist conscripts; but the only other antimilitarist work of the Congress consisted of a very brief resolution which affirmed the resolutions of the previous congresses on antimilitarism and recommended the continuation of antimilitarist propaganda.[68] No mention was made of antipatriotism; and the motion failed to state, as had been the custom since 1906, that the proletariat had no *patrie*. In short, as the year 1914 approached, the C.G.T., the organization which represented only the militant fraction of the proletariat (400,000 of the 1,064,000 members of trade unions),[69] was turning from antipatriotism.

During the last few years before the World War, anti-

[64] *Ibid.*, pp. 212-15.
[65] Humbert, *Le Mouvement syndical*, pp. 93-97.
[66] Saposs, *op. cit.*, pp. 429-30.
[67] The triumph of reformist syndicalism was not yet apparent in 1910. The motion which obtained the vote of the majority at the Congress of Toulouse favored the creation of a fund for the *Sou du soldat*—a special branch of the *Bourses du travail*—which attempted to draw the conscripts into the trade-union movement. The motion also contained a profession of antipatriotism. See *XVIIe Congrès national corporatif . . . 1910*, pp. 313, 333.
[68] *XVIIIe Congrès national corporatif . . . 1912*, pp. 191-93.
[69] These figures are for 1910.—Lorwin, *Syndicalism in France*, p. 194.

patriotism was also declining in the unified Socialist Party. Lafargue, having reached the age of seventy and feeling that his labors were no longer of value to the socialist movement, committed suicide in 1911. This meant not only a loss to the revolutionary, antipatriotic elements in the party, but also the disappearance of the last tie between Guesde and his revolutionary past. Then came another blow: the reconversion of Hervé in 1912.

Hervé attributed this third change to the fact that the settlement of the Moroccan dispute in 1911 had eliminated the danger of war and therefore the need for revolutionary action;[70] but the change was evidently due more to the recurrence of nationalist and monarchist agitation against the Republic during 1911 and the following years and to the decline of revolutionary syndicalism.[71] In March, 1911, months before the Moroccan settlement of November, 1911, Hervé expressed grave concern over the revival of monarchism and nationalist and clerical anti-Semitism; and by the end of the year he feared that this movement had attained the intensity it possessed during the Dreyfus Affair.[72]

To be sure, Hervé had ridiculed and condemned the Republic; but, in the old Blanquist manner, he hated the nationalist, clerical, and monarchist reaction even more than the bourgeois republicans and the Republic. Faced with the growing strength of the reaction, Hervé became more respectful of the Republic.

[70] 11° Congrès national . . . 1914, pp. 203-5.
[71] Although Hervé did consider that war would bring the opportunity for insurrection, it is difficult to believe that his complete disgust for universal suffrage and reforms was inspired by danger of war as much as by the influence of the Syndicalists. Besides, the danger of war was not eliminated by the Moroccan settlement, for it still existed in the Balkan Wars of 1912-13; and Hervé recognized this after he had turned reformist. Yet, while there was a lull in the danger of war from November, 1911, to the beginning of October, 1912, Hervé was still a revolutionist; and his decisive change to reformism took place after October, 1912—when the serious part of the Balkan crisis began. One may therefore conclude that war and peace were of less importance in Hervé's change than were developments within France.
[72] La Guerre sociale, Mar. 15-21, Apr. 5-11, June 28-July 4, 1911.

He explained that his attacks upon the republican government were cries of anguish because the Radicals were sabotaging "the republican faith in the soul of the people."[73] He declared that he had always been ready to defend the Republic against the reaction; and that, especially as the reactionary tendencies of the Radicals were disappearing, he would now defend the Republic "until death."[74] By 1914, Hervé had decided that the Republic had actually begun to draw the workers out of their enslavement; the return of Cæsarism with its ally, the Church, would plunge the workers back into subjection; and "in place of fighting to reconquer lost terrain, is it not better not to lose it?"[75]

Hervé now favored a return to the republican bloc—a coalition of Socialists and Radicals to fight the reaction.[76] The Radicals no longer appeared to him as traitors to the working class. He maintained that the true Radical Party was that of Brisson rather than that of Clemenceau; that the Radicals had in spite of their weaknesses accomplished much for the proletariat; and that their weaknesses could be eliminated by proportional representation—which would free the Radicals from dependence upon electoral coalitions with the reaction.[77] At the socialist Congress of Amiens in 1914 Hervé demanded coalitions with the Radicals both in the elections of 1914 and in Parliament.[78]

The change in Hervé's attitude toward the Republic and the republicans synchronized with a return to the idea of achieving socialism through democratic procedure and the attainment of reforms. This return was hastened by the impressive victory of the German Socialists in the elections of 1912, which, he confessed, made him feel that he had overlooked the real possi-

[73] *Ibid.*, Apr. 5-11, 1911.
[74] *Ibid.*, Apr. 19-25, 1911, July 31-August 6, 1912.
[75] *Ibid.*, Feb. 4-10, 1914.
[76] Hervé, *Mes Crimes*, pp. 19-22.
[77] *La Guerre sociale*, June 12-18, 1912, Feb. 4-10, 1914, Dec. 31, 1913-Jan. 6, 1914.
[78] *11e Congrès national . . . 1914*, pp. 204-11.

bilities of electoral action. He admitted that he had attacked German socialism because it was merely "a machine for voting and collecting dues"; but, he went on, he now believed that the four and a half million German Socialists constituted a powerful, disciplined, unified group; whereas the French Socialists, with all their revolutionary talk, were feeble, divided, demoralized, and disgusted.[79] In his opinion, the German victory, together with the receding danger of international conflict and the growing menace of Cæsarism, "invites and commands all revolutionaries who are not doctrinaires congealed in formulae, to modify their tactics . . ."[80]

In the period following the victory of the German Socialists, Hervé began gradually to sponsor reforms such as municipal housing; to argue with Guesde that the Socialists could "dismantle capitalism" by nationalizing banks, railways, and mines; and to praise the efficacy of the ballot.[81] By 1914 Hervé maintained that the concept of the class struggle was inaccurate; that the proletariat could rely upon the support of the petty bourgeoisie and the peasant proprietors; that the state was not an instrument of the capitalist class; and that "in proportion as universal suffrage is clarified and organized," the state will fall under the influence of the working class and the peasantry and "will be able to kill capital" as it had already killed the Church.[82]

Hervé now doffed antipatriotism and donned the republican patriotism of the period before 1905. He explained that his "flag on the dung-hill" speech was "fundamentally republican, violently anti-Bonapartist"; that he had used the nom-de-plume Sans-patrie because it was the title given to the republican opponents of the General Staff and the Church during the Dreyfus Affair, not because he wanted "to blaspheme against the

[79] *La Guerre sociale,* Jan. 7-13, 1912.
[80] *Mes Crimes,* p. 19.
[81] *La Guerre sociale,* Feb. 21-26, 1912, special number issued between those of Jan. 3-9 and Jan. 10-16, 1912, Feb. 18-24, 1914.
[82] *La Guerre sociale,* Feb. 18-24, 1914.

France of Jacques, of the Huguenots, of the Encyclopedists, of the Rights of Man, against all the glorious tradition of revolt, of free thought, of humanity, which France, together with the Italy of the Renaissance, with Germany of the Reformation, and with liberal England, represents in the history of progress and of civilization."[83] In fact, far from detesting France, it is "we, the so-called 'sans-patries' and 'antipatriots,' who love France with an ardent and clear-sighted love."[84] The Socialists were the true patriots because they wished to make the nation a mother to all without distinction; to lighten the economic burden of the standing army; to prevent the dissipation of the nation's resources in colonial wars; and to thwart the danger of a war in which 38 million Frenchmen would have to fight 70 million Germans.[85]

Hervé now adopted Jaurès's idea that socialist internationalism meant the federation rather than the disappearance of nations.[86] And because "the present nations carry the socialist nation of tomorrow within their loins," they must retain their present independence. "The imbecile and criminal idea that one can despise national independence," he said, "has never entered the mind of a single Socialist; still less has the monstrous idea of delivering his country to foreign domination."

Hervé resumed a patriotic stand on "the irritating and grievous question of Alsace-Lorraine."[87] In 1912, he declared that the Socialists could not "accept without protest the attack against human rights committed by Bismarck in 1871." He looked forward to the peaceful restoration of the provinces, either in exchange for Tonkin or Madagascar, or through the establishment of a republic in Germany. Two years later, Hervé was still more patriotic on the question of Alsace-Lorraine. When Déroulède (whom he had bitterly hated) died, Hervé eulogized him for having protested so vigorously

[83] Hervé, La Conquête de l'armée, pp. 137-38.
[84] Ibid., pp. 138-39.
[85] Ibid., pp. 139-41. See also La Guerre sociale, Feb. 4-10, 1914.
[86] La Conquête de l'armée, pp. 141-45.   [87] Ibid., pp. 148-49.

against "this odious mutilation."[88] He insisted that there could be no reduction in military expenses and no rapprochement with Germany until she had made moral reparation by giving Alsace-Lorraine autonomy.[89]

Hervé finally gave up resistance to war by means of the general strike and insurrection. In 1913, he took the position of the Limoges Resolution: to employ insurrection to stop offensive wars only.[90] Following Jaurès, he now considered that willingness to arbitrate constituted a genuine criterion to determine whether a nation was acting defensively or offensively. But in 1914, Hervé completely abandoned the insurrectionary general strike even in case of aggressive war. At the last party congress before the outbreak of the World War, held in the middle of July, 1914, Hervé rejected the Keir Hardie-Vaillant amendment to the Stuttgart Resolution, which proposed that an aggressive war be resisted not by the revolutionary general strike but by a strike in those industries which supplied arms, munitions, and transportation.[91] Hervé explained that he opposed the amendment because when he favored insurrection, there were insurrectionaries to be counted upon; but now the only way to prevent war was by "reformist action," and by effecting a Franco-German rapprochement through a solution of the problem of Alsace-Lorraine.[92]

Hervé's patriotism went beyond that of the majority of French Socialists. But by 1914, there was almost complete unanimity in the socialist movement on the resolution to defend France if she were the victim of aggression.

[88] La Guerre sociale, Feb. 4-10, 1914.
[89] Ibid.; 10e Congrès national . . . 1913, pp. 255-56.
[90] La Conquête de l'armée, pp. 145, 149-50; 10e Congrès national . . . 1913, p. 260.
[91] The congress proceedings in L'Humanité, July 16, 1914.
[92] Ibid.

IX

THE DÉNOUEMENT

THE French Socialists had decided at the Congress of Limoges that they would oppose aggressive action by the French government but would support the government in the defense of the country if France were attacked. In 1914, therefore, the Socialists were faced with the problem of deciding which nation was the aggressor. It was Jaurès to whom the Socialists turned for their policy.

The first five months of 1914 found Jaurès campaigning for patriotism and peace alike. He opposed the Three-Year Law on the ground that it was a menace to peace and to the defense of France; and at the Congress of Amiens, he proposed that opposition to the Law be made the condition of socialist support of the republicans on the second balloting during the parliamentary elections of 1914.[1] He demanded the solution of Balkan problems by "a sincere international entente with the object of assuring equal guarantees to all the religious and ethnic elements in the Balkan Peninsula."[2] At the same time, he insisted that although the Socialists would strive for peace, they would "not abandon without combat a single inch of France's territory, not a single paving stone of her streets, not a single fragment of her soil."[3]

In this period, also, Jaurès indicated that he bore no real enmity toward the Radical government under the leadership of his old comrade, Viviani. He declared that if the government put forth a strong program of reforms, the Socialists would support it.[4] In short, the stage was set for the Socialists to aid

---

[1] *11e Congrès national . . . Amiens, 1914*, pp. 366-67, 374-76, 424-26.
[2] *L'Humanité*, Aug. 27, May 25, 1914.
[3] *Ibid.*, Mar. 10, 1914.   [4] *Ibid.*, May 21, 1914.

the government in the defense of France—if her interests and security were considered by them to be endangered.

Jaurès, during the final crisis, believed that the interests and security of France were really threatened. From the day of the assassination of the Archduke Franz Ferdinand, Jaurès put the burden of responsibility for the crisis on Austria-Hungary and Germany. He regarded France and Russia as essentially pacific.

The animosity Jaurès had felt toward Austria-Hungary since 1908 was revealed when he attributed the assassination of Franz Ferdinand to the policies of the Archduke and of the Austrians generally. He neglected the provocation of the Serbs against Austria, and could not believe that the Serbian government had anything to do with the assassination.

Two days after the assassination of the Archduke, on June 28, 1914, Jaurès remarked that the Archduke had followed a policy based on "inconsistency and stupidity."[5] The Archduke, in his opinion, had excited the spirit of independence of the Serbo-Croats with promises of autonomy within the Austrian Empire, and then had tried to kill that spirit by attempting to force the Serbo-Croats into "the artificial framework of the Jesuitical domination of the Hapsburgs."

Moreover, according to Jaurès, the Serbs and Croats were necessarily exasperated by the "brutal annexation" of Bosnia-Herzegovina; by the "oppressive bureaucratic régime" inflicted on the annexed provinces; and by the arbitrary punishment of those who opposed Austrian policies.[6] Finally, the Archduke was responsible for the existing danger of war between Austria and Serbia. The Archduke had blamed Serbia for all the Austro-Serbian difficulties; this naturally led to the idea of finishing Serbia by a decisive blow; and although the Archduke had declared his peaceful intentions, "the contradiction of a confused and narrow policy" condemned him to war.

The assassination of the Archduke, Jaurès warned the

[5] *Ibid.*, June 30, 1914.   [6] *Ibid.*

Austrians, should indicate to them that they should not attempt to take revenge on the Serbs.[7] They should, on the contrary, practice a policy of equity and generosity toward the Bosnian and Croatian populations. Jaurès, at the same time, advised the Serbs and Croats to cease trying to establish an enlarged, independent Serbia, for such a state could only be erected with the aid of Russia and would certainly become a Russian vassal. But in spite of these last remarks, the assassination of the Archduke increased his bitter dislike of Austria and prepared him to condemn the severe Austrian ultimatum to Serbia on July 23.

Between June 30 and July 25, Jaurès sensed the tension that gripped Europe after the assassination of the Archduke. He made magnificent appeals for peace. War, he proclaimed, would mean "millions and millions of men threatening each other, destroying each other; the financial resources of the nations devoured day by day—in the service of death; economic life suspended, credit broken down, unemployment aggravated; the machine gun and typhus decimating both the vast armies and the civilian populations; misery destroying the ravaged peoples as well as the armies. What sorrow, what barbarism, what seeds of revolt! What a prodigious tension of nerves as a result of contradictory reports, as a result of the vicissitudes of victory and of disaster! Only death will be assured of a constant, monotonous triumph—over victors and vanquished alike!"[8] He warned both Russia and Austria that if they quarreled over the Balkans, a war would set loose forces that would tear them both apart.[9]

At the socialist Congress of Paris on July 16 and 17, Jaurès supported the Keir Hardie-Vaillant motion for a general strike in the war industries of the aggressor nation.[10] He explained, however, that the general strike did not mean giving up the resolution to defend France, which was menaced by the

[7] Ibid.   [8] Ibid., July 20, 1914.   [9] Ibid., July 24, 1914.
[10] Reports of the congress in L'Humanité, July 17, 18, 1914.

"brutality of Pan-Germanism." He insisted, moreover, that if war threatened, and the Socialists of both countries did not pledge themselves to use the general strike in order to restrain their nations from aggression, neither one ought to resort to the strike.

From the time Austria delivered her ultimatum to Serbia on July 23, Jaurès placed responsibility on her and on Germany. The Socialists could not then assay the share of France and Russia in the diplomatic responsibility for the crisis; and in the absence of information about the rôle of France and Russia, the determination of Jaurès and the other Socialists to protect France, together with their dislike of Austria-Hungary, their friendliness toward Serbia, their hatred of the German government, their acceptance of the Russian Alliance, contributed to their belief that Germany and Austria were aggressive, and that France and Russia were on the defensive.

After the Austrian ultimatum, Jaurès stamped Austria and Germany as the guilty nations. In the first place, Jaurès condemned Austria and attributed her ultimatum to sinister motives. On July 25, he wrote: "The note addressed to Serbia is frightfully severe. It seems devised either to humiliate the Serbian people or to crush them. The conditions which Austria wishes to impose on Serbia are such that one can ask whether the Austrian clerical and military reaction does not really want war and does not seek to render it inevitable. This would be the most monstrous of crimes."[11] Jaurès added that there still remained a chance for peace: if Serbia went "to the limit of concessions she can make," Austria could not attack her; and if Austria could prove that the murder of the Archduke was "known, encouraged, seconded" by Serbian "civil and military officials," then Serbia could not refuse "satisfactions and guarantees." But he feared that Austria wished to hasten an attack in order to avoid European intervention; and he asked why Austria had not submitted the *dossier* she had promised.

[11] *L'Humanité*, July 25, 1914.

On July 27, Jaurès decided that "it appeared from the first analysis of the Serbian reply that Serbia gave Austria important satisfactions and serious guarantees"; and that "war would be without excuse and without pretext."[12] Therefore, on July 29, after the Austrian declaration of war, Jaurès asserted that as Serbia had atoned for any "grave imprudences" by giving "ample satisfactions," the declaration of war was "unjustifiable."[13] He warned Austria that "imminent justice" would punish her for obliging "the whole world to witness an iniquitous abuse of force, or to seek, in the unleashing of a universal war, the most hazardous redress of an injustice."

In the meantime Jaurès had begun his attack on Germany. On July 26, 27, and 28, he wrote that he did not and could not believe Germany's statements that she did not know the text of the Austrian ultimatum before it was delivered and that she was trying to soften it.[14] Germany, he argued, could not have allowed Austria to take a step that would draw her into war without knowing what that step was. Moreover, if she did not know the contents of the ultimatum, she could not have decided "to go to the limit for Austria." "If this invasion [of Serbia] occurs," he exclaimed, "it will be necessary to judge severely, not only Austrian, but German diplomacy." As reports multiplied that Germany had only a summary of the ultimatum, Jaurès asked if Germany's lack of knowledge was due to "negligence, incapacity, or duplicity?" And he declared that peace or war depended on the answer to this question.[15]

In summarizing the indirect causes of the crisis on July 25, Jaurès had attributed it not only to the tyranny of Austria-Hungary over Bosnia-Herzegovina but also to France's example of aggressive action in Morocco and to Russia's agreement to let Austria have Bosnia-Herzegovina in return for the latter's support in opening the Straits to her warships.[16] But

[12] *Ibid.*, July 27, 1914.
[13] *Ibid.*, July 29, 1914.
[14] *Ibid.*, July 26, 27, 28, 1914.
[15] *Ibid.*, July 28, 1914.
[16] Address at Vaise, July 25, 1914, reprinted in *Pages choisies*, pp. 451-55.

this was the last time Jaurès mentioned the responsibility of France and Russia. He was unaware of France's part in stiffening Russia's arm, and he missed the significance of Russia's mobilization—the act which drew the German declaration of war.

On July 29, Jaurès spoke at the meeting of the International Socialist Bureau which had hastily assembled at Brussels for united action against the impending danger. Instead of warning the governments, Jaurès attacked the "beastliness of Austrian diplomacy" and chastized Germany.[17] He asked the proletariat to organize for peace, but he added: "The duty of the French Socialists is simple. We do not have to impose a policy of peace on our government. It practices one. I—who have never hesitated to take upon myself the hatred of our chauvinists for my obstinacy and who will never give up the idea of a Franco-German rapprochement—I have the right to say that at the present hour the French government wishes peace. The French government is the best ally for peace possessed by this admirable England that has taken the initiative in conciliation; and the French government gives Russia counsel of prudence and patience."

In L'Humanité of July 31, Jaurès had the first kindly word for Germany during a week of crisis; but, at the same time he approved Russia's mobilization and France's partial couverture, preparations comparable to partial mobilization. Jaurès wrote: "It is evident that if Germany had the intention of attacking us, she would have proceeded according to the famous sudden attack. She has, on the contrary, lost several days; and France, as well as Russia, has been able to profit by this delay; the one, Russia, by proceeding to partial mobilization, the other, France, by taking all possible precautions compatible with the maintenance of peace."[18]

[17] Ibid, July 30, 1914.
[18] Ibid., July 31, 1914. The complete mobilization of Russia's army was ordered about six o'clock on the evening of July 30 (four o'clock in Paris). The article which appeared in L'Humanité on July 31 was probably written

Jaurès's approval of France's action lessened the effectiveness of his struggle for peace or for a localization of the conflict. On July 25, 27, and 28, and at the International Socialist Bureau at Brussels on July 29, Jaurès urged the workers to protest against war and to support all attempts at mediation.[19] But in all his appeals for peace he never mentioned a general strike; for he believed that the French government had no aggressive intentions and no responsibility for the crisis.

On the morning of July 31, Jaurès was still striving for peace. He led a delegation of socialist deputies to ask the Premier to use a firm tone with Russia; and he begged the Premier not to abandon himself to a belief that war was inevitable.[20] Moreover, according to Renaudel, who was with Jaurès on July 31, he was contemplating an appeal to President Wilson, asking him to do what he could for peace.[21] But his close friend, Commandant Henri Gérard, declared that on the 31st, Jaurès had remarked to him: "I must telegraph to Wilson that the cause of France is just." Then Jaurès had added: "Let us hope that England marches; let us hope that England understands!"[22] That evening, Jaurès was shot in the back. He died immediately.

The assassination of Jaurès was an ironic tragedy. The assassin, Raoul Villain, was a neurotic young man who had been excited by nationalist invectives against Jaurès. He had been particularly inflamed by the charge of the Nationalists that Jaurès, in opposing the Three-Year Law, was a traitor to

---

on the evening of July 30, and so Jaurès may not have had accurate information concerning the fact that complete, not partial, mobilization had been ordered.

[19] *Pages choisies,* July 25, 1914, p. 455; *L'Humanité,* July 27, 28, 30, 1914.

[20] See Longuet's statement in Pignatel, *Jaurès par ses contemporaines* (Paris, 1925), pp. 148-49.

[21] Renaudel's statement in *Le Procès de l'assassin de Jaurès, Mars 24-29, 1919* (Paris, 1919), p. 100. In 1917, the French Socialists said Jaurès had contemplated asking Wilson to arbitrate. See "Réponse au questionnaire en vue de la conférence de Stockholm," reprinted in *Le Parti socialiste, la guerre, et la paix* (Paris, 1918), p. 15.

[22] *Le Procès de l'assassin de Jaurès* . . . , p. 179.

France.[23] But after the War, the patriotism of Jaurès was given the highest recognition by republican France. The remains of Jaurès were removed to the Panthéon—the Jacobin temple to *la patrie*—where they lie near the other great republican patriots buried there.

For four days the French Socialists mourned for the loss of Jaurès; and then they marched, firmly convinced that Jaurès would have bid them march. On August 1, Hervé wrote: "Listen! He speaks to you. Do you hear him? . . . he says: 'My friends, my children, *la patrie* is in danger! They have assassinated me! In wishing to avenge me, do not assassinate *la patrie!*'"[24]

From the beginning of the crisis, the leaders of the party had agreed with Jaurès in his analysis of events. Official manifestoes signed by Guesde, Hervé, Vaillant, and others had asked the French government to support England's attempt at mediation and to try to restrain Russia; the manifestoes declared that France must not be dragged into a conflict over Serbia; and they affirmed "all our doubts as to the obligations of the secret treaties which we have never known and which our Parliament has never ratified."[25] But the manifestoes blamed the crisis on the "abominable" attack of Austria on Serbia and on "perfidious and provocative" German diplomacy.[26] One manifesto, that of July 29, attacked "most aggressive and imperialist Germany, which seems to have chosen its hour for an enterprise of violence without precedent, and which will one day

[23] *Ibid.*, pp. 8, 25. For the other reasons why Villain singled out Jaurès for attack, see *ibid.*, pp. 8-25. For the extent to which the Nationalists were inflamed against Jaurès, and the extent to which Villain was steeped in nationalist ideas, see *ibid.*, pp. 252-67.

[24] *La Guerre sociale*, Aug. 1914.

[25] See manifestoes of the Administrative Committee and of the Socialist Group in Parliament, reprinted in *L'Humanité*, July 28, 29, 1914; the manifesto of the *Féderation de la Seine*, Aug. 2, 1914, reprinted in *Le Parti socialiste, la guerre, et la paix*, pp. 108-9.

[26] *L'Humanité*, July 28, 1914; *Le Parti socialiste, la guerre, et la paix*, pp. 108-9.

see returning against itself the abuse which it makes of brutal force."[27] The manifestoes exonerated France of any guilt, that of July 28 declaring that "the French government has shown in the present crisis a very clear and a very sincere desire to destroy or lessen the dangers of a conflict."[28]

At the meeting of the International Socialist Bureau on July 29 and July 30 the French Socialists failed to propose the general strike. Moreover, at the Brussels meeting, the German Socialists asked the French if they would act with them in signifying their disapproval of the war by rejecting war credits; but the French Socialists replied that if France were attacked they would vote the credits, and the only condition they would impose would be "that the French government must give evidence of its peaceful intentions."[29] Consequently, the Bureau limited itself to issuing a manifesto advising the proletariat to intensify its demonstrations against war and to ask the French and German governments to restrain Russia and Austria.[30]

On August 2, after the death of Jaurès, the French Socialists signified their future course. A manifesto of the *Fédération de la Seine* stated that "to an aggression against republican and pacific France, to an aggression menacing civilization and humanity, we shall reply with all our might and with all our energies."[31] After the official declarations of war, the French Socialists, contending that France and Belgium were "fighting for their existence against the brutal aggression of German imperialism," threw almost their entire weight into the conflict against Germany.[32] The triumph of patriotism came on August

[27] *L'Humanité,* July 29, 1914.   [28] *Ibid.,* July 28, 1914.
[29] See "Réponse au questionnaire . . . ," *op. cit.,* p. 21.
[30] See *L'Humanité,* July 30, 31, 1914.
[31] Manifesto of the *Fédération de la Seine,* reprinted in *Le Parti socialiste, la guerre, et la paix,* pp. 108-9.
[32] Joint manifesto of the French and Belgian Socialists, reprinted in *Le Parti socialiste, la guerre, et la paix,* p. 113. The manifesto stated that as Serbia's reply to the Austrian note was "pacific and conciliatory, it can no longer be doubted that Imperial Germany inspired and wanted the war." The French government, on the other hand, "sincerely wanted peace"; and it tried to restrain Russia as the French Socialists had demanded. More-

28, 1914, when Guesde and Sembat entered the ministry. A manifesto of the Administrative Committee of the party explained that this action was necessary because, as Jaurès had envisaged, the first reverses must be followed by a supreme effort; and the French Socialists were willing to make this effort, for "we are certain that we are fighting, not only for the existence of *la patrie*, but for liberty, for the Republic, for civilization."[33] Thus, in the name of liberty, the Republic, *la patrie*, the French Socialists closely bound themselves to the French bourgeoisie in the conflict with the Germans.

Subsequently, a very small minority of the French Socialists, heeding the call of the Bolsheviks, finally arrived at a denunciation of the War;[34] but the majority continued their patriotic support of the government. They contended that they were fighting for the rights of nationalities, including the return of Alsace-Lorraine, and for a new world in which international coöperation would replace national rivalries.[35] Alsace-Lorraine was won. But the war and the years that followed brought the French Socialists very little closer to their goal of international coöperation. Disillusioned, Sembat, socialist member of the war ministry, admitted that the dearly-bought victory of Versailles had been, after all, a "defeated victory" for French socialism.

---

over, after mobilization, the German troops crossed the frontier, while the French troops remained eight kilometers behind the line. Finally, the manifesto concluded, Germany invaded Belgium and Luxemburg without just cause.

[33] *Ibid.*, p. 112.

[34] Louis, *Histoire du socialisme en France de la Révolution à nos jours,* pp. 357 ff.

[35] See "Réponse au questionnaire . . . ," pp. 24-27.

LIST OF WORKS CITED

GENERAL WORKS

Assanis, L., *La Société française à travers les siècles*, Paris, 1913.
Bernstein, Samuel, *The Beginnings of Marxian Socialism in France*, New York, 1933.
Charnay, M., *Les Allemanistes*, Paris, 1911.
Cornilleau, R., *Types et silhouettes*, Paris, 1919.
Da Costa, Charles, *Les Blanquistes*, Paris, 1912.
Desanges, Paul, and Mériga, Luc, *Vie de Jaurès*, Paris, 1924.
Dunning, William Archibald, *Political Theories from Rousseau to Spencer*, New York, 1926.
Estey, J. A., *Revolutionary Syndicalism*, London, 1913.
Fournière, E., *La Crise socialiste*, Paris, 1908.
France, Ministre du Commerce, *Rapport général sur l'industrie française*, Paris, 1919.
Hayes, Carlton J. H., *Essays on Nationalism*, New York, 1926.
—— *France, a Nation of Patriots*, in *Social and Economic Studies of Post-War France*, ed. by Carlton J. H. Hayes, Vol. V, New York, 1930.
—— *Historical Development of Modern Nationalism*, New York, 1931.
Hubert-Rouger, *La France socialiste*, in *Encyclopédie socialiste*, ed. by Compère-Morel, Vol. III, Paris, 1912.
Humbert, A., *Le Mouvement syndical*, Paris, 1912.
—— *Les Possibilistes*, Paris, 1911.
Hyndman, William, *The Record of an Adventurous Life*, New York, 1911.
Josephson, Matthew, *Zola and His Times*, New York, 1928.
Kritsky, N., *L'Évolution du syndicalisme en France*, Paris, 1908.
Lavy, A., *L'Œuvre de Millerand*, Paris, 1902.
Lévy-Bruhl, L., *Jean Jaurès: esquisse biographique*, Paris, 1924.
Lorwin, L. L., *Syndicalism in France*, second edition, New York, 1914.

Louis, Paul, *Histoire du mouvement syndical en France, 1789-1906*, Paris, 1907.

—— *Histoire du socialisme en France de la Révolution à nos jours*, Paris, 1925.

Mason, E. S., *The Paris Commune, an Episode in the History of the Socialist Movement*, New York, 1930.

Moon, Parker Thomas, *The Labor Problem and the Social Catholic Movement in France*, New York, 1921.

Orry, A., *Les Socialistes indépendants*, Paris, 1911.

Perrin, P. C. M. J., *Les Idées sociales de Georges Sorel; thèse pour le doctorat*, Algiers, 1925.

Pignatel, F., and others, *Jaurès par ses contemporaines*, Paris, 1925.

Rappoport, Charles, *Jean Jaurès*, Paris, 1915.

Renan, Ernest, *Discours et conférences*, Paris, 1887.

Saposs, David J., *The Labor Movement in Post-War France*, in *Social and Economic Studies of Post-War France*, Vol. IV, ed. by Carlton J. H. Hayes, New York, 1931.

Seignobos, Charles, *L'Évolution de la 3e République*, in *Histoire de France contemporaine*, ed. by Ernest Lavisse, Vol. VIII, Paris, 1921.

—— *Histoire sincère de la nation française*, Paris, 1933.

Seilhac, Léon de, *L'Utopie socialiste*, Paris, 1908.

Théry, E., *La Fortune public de la France*, Paris, 1911.

Thomas, Albert, *Histoire anecdotique du travail*, Paris, n. d.

Valatx, L., *Monographie sur le mouvement de la population dans le Département du Tarn de 1801 à 1911; thèse pour le doctorat*, Albi, 1917.

Weill, Georges, *Histoire du mouvement socialiste en France*, Paris, 1924.

Zévaès, Alexandre, *Auguste Blanqui*, Paris, 1920.

—— *La Question de l'Alsace-Lorraine et le socialisme*, Paris, 1917.

—— *Le Socialisme en France depuis 1871*, Paris, 1908.

PRIMARY MATERIAL: BOOKS AND PAMPHLETS

Allemane, Jean, *Le Socialisme en France*, Paris, 1900.

—— *Nôtre Programme*, Paris, 1902.

Aux travailleurs; Conseil national du P.O.F. (Collection of manifestoes, 1889-1899), Paris, 1902.

Baudin, Millerand, and others, *Les Forces productives de la France,* Paris, 1909.

Bernstein, Eduard, *Socialisme théorique et démocratie pratique,* Paris, 1900.

—— *Evolutionary Socialism.* Trans. by E. C. Harvey, New York, 1911.

Berth, Edouard, *Les Derniers Aspects du socialisme,* Paris, 1908, 1923.

Delesalle, Paul, *L'Action syndicale et les anarchistes,* Paris, 1900.

—— *Les Deux Methodes du syndicalisme,* Paris, n. d.

Griffuelhes, Victor, and Niel, Louis, *Les Objectives de nos luttes de classe,* Paris, 1909.

Guesde, Jules, *Essai du catéchisme sociuliste,* Brussels, 1878.

—— *La Loi des salaires et ses conséquences,* Paris, 1881.

—— *Services publics et socialisme,* Paris, 1883.

—— *Çà et là* (a collection of editorials, 1876-1887), Paris, 1914.

—— *Socialisme au jour le jour* (a collection of editorials, 1884-86), Paris, 1899.

—— *Quatre Ans de lutte de classe* (a collection of parliamentary debates, 1893-98), Paris, 1901.

—— *État, politique et morale de classe* (a collection of editorials, 1881-86), Paris, 1901.

—— *Collectivisme et révolution,* Paris, 1906.

—— *En garde!* (a collection of editorials, 1889-92), Paris, 1911.

Guesde, Jules, and Lafargue, Paul, *Le Pourquoi et comment du socialisme,* Lille, 1883.

—— *Programme du Parti ouvrier,* Paris, 1883.

Guesde, Jules, and Jaurès, Jean. *Les Deux Méthodes,* Lille, 1900.

Guesde, Jules, Auguste Bebel, Edouard Vaillant, *Discours de Jules Guesde, Auguste Bebel, Edouard Vaillant à Amsterdam,* Paris, 1904.

Hervé, Gustave, *Leur Patrie,* Paris, 1905.

—— *Histoire de France pour les grands,* Paris, 1910.

—— *L'Internationalisme,* Paris, 1910.

192   LIST OF WORKS CITED

Hervé, Gustave, *Mes Crimes*, Paris, 1912.

—— *La Conquête de l'armée*, Paris, 1913.

Jaurès, Jean, *Alliance française: association nationale pour la propagation de la langue française dans les colonies et à l'étranger; conférence de Jean Jaurès*, Albi, approximately 1886.

—— *Discours à la distribution solennelle des prix, 31 juillet, 1888*, Albi, 1888.

—— *La Réalité du monde sensible; thèse pour le doctorat*, Paris, 1891.

—— *Les Preuves, Affaire Dreyfus*, Paris, 1898.

—— *Action socialiste* (collection of articles and speeches, 1886-97), Paris, 1899.

—— Preface to Henri Turot, *Aguinaldo et les Philippines*, Paris, 1899.

—— *La Constituante, 1789-1791*, in *Histoire socialiste*, ed. by Jean Jaurès, Vol. I, Paris, 1901.

—— *La Législative, 1791-1792*, in *Histoire socialiste*, Vol. II, Paris, 1901.

—— *La Convention, 1792-1795*, in *Histoire Socialiste*, Vols. III and IV, Paris, 1902.

—— *La Guerre franco-allemande, 1870-1871*, in *Histoire socialiste*, Vol. XI, Paris, 1908.

—— *Études socialistes* (collection of editorials, 1901-2), Paris, 1902.

—— *Discours parlementaires* (collection of parliamentary debates, 1886-94), Paris, 1904.

—— *Diplomatie et démocratie*, Paris, 1906.

—— *Discours à la jeunesse*, Paris, 1905.

—— *Conférence à Nîmes*, Nimes, 1910.

—— *L'Armée nouvelle*, Paris, new edition of 1915.

—— *Pages choisies*, edited by Paul Desanges and Luc Mériga, Paris, 1922.

—— *Œuvres de Jean Jaurès*, edited by Max Bonnafous, Vols. I-VI, Paris, 1931-34.

Jaurès, Jean, and Guesde, Jules, *Les Deux Méthodes*, Lille, 1900.

Jaurès, Jean, and Lafargue, Paul, *Idéalisme et matérialisme dans la conception de l'histoire; Conférence, 1894*, Lille, 1904.

Jaurès, Jean, and others, *L'Action du Parti socialiste*, Paris, 1902.
Kautsky, Karl, *Le Marxisme et son critique Bernstein*, Paris, 1900.
—— *Le Programme socialiste*, Paris, 1900.
Lafargue, Paul, *Le Communisme et l'évolution économique*, Paris, 1892.
—— *Evolution of Property*, London, 1894.
—— *Programme agricole du Parti ouvrier français*, Lille, 1894.
—— *Le Socialisme et le conquête des pouvoirs publics*, Lille, 1899.
—— *Le Socialisme et les intellectuels*, Paris, 1900.
—— *Le Patriotisme de la bourgeoisie*, Paris, 1906.
—— *Social and Philosophical Studies*. Trans. by C. II. Kerr, Chicago, 1906.
—— *Le Déterminisme économique. La Méthode historique de Karl Marx*, Paris, 1907.
—— *Right to Be Lazy and Other Studies*. Trans. by C. H. Kerr, Chicago, 1907.
Lafargue, Paul, and Jaurès, Jean, *Idéalisme et matérialisme dans la conception de l'histoire; conférence, 1894*, Lille, 1904.
Luxemburg, Rosa, *Réforme ou révolution*, Paris, 1932.
Malon, Benoît, *Le Socialisme intégral*, Paris, 1891.
—— *Précis de socialisme*, Paris, 1892.
Marx, Karl, and Engels, Friedrich, *Manifesto of the Communist Party*. Authorized English translation, London, n. d.
Millerand, Alexandre, *Le Socialisme réformiste français* (collection of articles and speeches, 1893-1902), Paris, 1903.
Parti socialiste, la guerre, et la paix, Le, Paris, 1918.
Pelletier, Madeleine, *Idéologie d'hier: Dieu, la morale, la patrie*, Paris, 1910.
Pelloutier, Ferdinand, *Le Congrès général du Parti socialiste français*, Paris, 1900.
—— *Histoire des Bourses du travail*, Paris, 1902.
Pouget, Émile, *Le Syndicat*, Paris, 1907.
—— *Les Bases du syndicalisme*, Paris, n. d.
—— *Le Parti du travail*, Paris, n. d.
Procès de l'assassin de Jaurès, mars 24-29, 1919, Paris, 1919.

194   LIST OF WORKS CITED

Rappoport, Charles, *La Révolution sociale*, in *Encyclopédie socialiste*, Vol. IV, ed. by Compère-Morel, Paris, 1912.
Renard, Georges, *Le Socialisme intégral et Marxisme*, Paris, 1896.
——— *Le Régime socialiste*, Paris, 1898.
Sarraute, Joseph, *Socialisme d'opposition, socialisme de gouvernement, et lutte de classe*, Paris, 1901.
Sembat, Marcel, *Defeated Victory*. Trans. by Flory Henri-Turot, London, 1926.
Sorel, Georges, *L'Avenir socialiste des syndicats*, Paris, 1901.
——— *Introduction à l'économie moderne*, Paris, 1906.
——— *La Décomposition du Marxisme*, Paris, 1908.
——— *Les Illusions du progrès*, Paris, 1911.
——— *Réflexions sur la violence*, Paris, 1909. First published in *Le Mouvement socialiste*, 1906, Vol. XVIII.
Sorgue, *L'Unité révolutionnaire*, Paris, 1901.
Vaillant, Edouard, *Suppression de l'armée permanente et des Conseils de guerre*, Paris, 1924.
——— *L'Évolution économique et la révolution sociale*, Paris, 1906.
Vaillant, Edouard, Jules Guesde, and Auguste Bebel, *Discours de Jules Guesde, Auguste Bebel, Edouard Vaillant à Amsterdam*, Paris, 1904.
Yvetot, Georges, *Le Nouveau Manuel du soldat*, Paris, 1908.
——— *A. B. C. syndicaliste*, Paris, 1911.
——— *Syndicat et syndicalisme*, Paris, n. d.

REPORTS OF CONGRESSES

Compte rendu sténographique non-officiel de la version française du cinquième Congrès socialiste international tenu à Paris du 23 au 27 septembre 1900, Paris, 1900.
Congrès général des organisations socialistes françaises, Paris, 1899. Compte rendu sténographique officiel; Deuxième Congrès général . . . Paris, 1900; Troisième Congrès général . . . Lyon, 1901; Quatrième Congrès général . . . Tours, 1902.
2ᵉ Congrès national du Parti socialiste . . . Chalon, 1905; 3ᵉ Congrès national . . . Limoges, 1906; 4ᵉ Congrès national . . . Nancy, 1907; 5ᵉ Congrès national . . . Toulouse, 1908; 6ᵉ

Congrès national . . . Saint-Étienne, 1909; 7ᵉ Congrès national . . . Nîmes, 1910; 7ᵉ Congrès national . . . Paris, 1910; 8ᵉ Congrès national . . . Saint-Quentin, 1911; 9ᵉ Congrès national . . . Lyon, 1912; 10ᵉ Congrès national . . . Brest, 1913; 11ᵉ Congrès national . . . Amiens, 1914.

XIIᵉ Congrès national corporatif . . . Paris, 1900; XIIIᵉ Congrès national corporatif . . . Montpellier, 1902; XIVᵉ Congrès national corporatif . . . Bourges, 1904; XVᵉ Congrès national corporatif . . . Amiens, 1906; XVIᵉ Congrès national corporatif . . . Marseille, 1908; XVIIᵉ Congrès national corporatif . . . Toulouse, 1910; XVIIIᵉ Congrès national corporatif . . . Havre, 1912.

PERIODICALS

Action directe, L', syndicalist, biweekly.

Dépêche de Toulouse, La, (La Dépêche), liberal republican, daily.

Guerre sociale, La, socialist, daily and weekly.

Humanité, L', socialist, daily.

Journal officiel.

Mouvement socialiste, Le, socialist, biweekly, monthly, bimonthly.

Ni Dieu, ni maître, socialist, daily.

Petite République, La, socialist to 1905, daily.

Revue historique, scientifique et littéraire du Département du Tarn, quarterly.

Revue socialiste, La, socialist, monthly.

Socialiste, Le, monthly.

INDEX